tugl.

The Classic Line

A STUDY IN EPIC POETRY

THE
Classic Line

A STUDY IN EPIC POETRY

BY Albert Cook

1966

Indiana University Press

BLOOMINGTON AND LONDON

To My Students

Contents

Preface

The epic has figured so large for so long in received culture and in the minds of great poets, that anyone concerned with the nature of poetry ought surely to include it in his thinking. Yet epic poetry has lost the critical preeminence it held from antiquity down to the times of Schlegel and Goethe, or Sainte-Beuve and Arnold. Critics who approach the epic no longer seem inspired by the theoretical challenge that draws the least of their number alert when lyric poetry is in question. Emil Staiger, for all his informed sensitivity and force, for all his breadth, can see fit to confine his discussion of epic in the excellent *Grundbegriffe der Poetik*[1] to a single example, the *Iliad*.

Yet most of our assumptions about poetry rest on our experience of lyric poetry and are consequently limited by its peculiarities. The lyric constitutes only part of poetry, and a theory of poetry based on just that highly attractive part cannot satisfy fully, even for that part. The modern critic who reads mostly lyric poetry, if he theorizes on the basis of lyric alone, will find himself involved in all the dangers of an exclusive preoccupation with the familiar. We give great attention to figures and tropes because the lyric poet tends to embroider his statements, as he does his rhythms. The successful epic poet, however, packs senses into his verse while keeping his statements remarkably direct and his rhythms normative. And epic poems, in their considerable differences from each other, are alike in not relying heavily on the ornaments that our own lyric poetry has accustomed us to expect of all poetry. Each epic poem is built on a "classic line" whose effects do not essentially rely on figurative language. These effects, to be ascertained, require prolonged critical attention.

In taking a long theoretical look at the style and thought of some notable epic poems, I have tried here not so much to define the nature of epic poetry generically as to ascertain the critical conditions under which each epic poem I discuss has managed to succeed as a poem. In this way questions about poetics, kept always in view, might be approached from a fresh direction.

I am grateful to many for help with this book, in particular to the Fulbright Commission for Germany, which gave me a grant during 1956-57 so I might work out this project; to the classical seminar at the University of Munich, which granted me office privileges and the use of their facilities at a crowded time for themselves; and to my students in Cleveland, who entertained dialogue with me on these questions, especially Charles Boer, Charles Doria, John Clarke, and Jean Calhoun. Among those whose readings have helped improve the manuscript are Josephine Miles, Frederick Locke, John Finley, and John Moore, whose astute and careful critique of a part of the chapter on the *Iliad* enabled me to make certain distinctions more precisely. A part of that chapter has appeared in *The Niagara Frontier Review,* which I thank, along with *The University of Toronto Quarterly,* published by the University of Toronto Press, where some of the material from the Milton chapter was published in an earlier form.

To my secretary, Mrs. Virginia White, I am grateful for her remarkably accurate preparation of copy and for other work in connection with the book. And I should like to thank Miriam Farley and Dorothy Wikelund for keen editorial assistance. Special acknowledgment goes to my wife Carol for making the Index, and for much else.

Introduction

Poe,[1] if wrong, was on the right track, as usual, when he argued that no long poem could be sustained. He was saying something perceptive about epic—though in unwarrantedly negative terms. No long poem can be sustained, if by sustained we mean built into the heightened moment of the lyric poem. If we seek heightened moments in epic, we will reduce the epic poem to a series of purple passages, as Poe wrongly did. And to do this is to misread even the passages we regard as purple passages.

To be sure, if we read for purple passages, we do not write about them. Trained to keep our eyes on the structural whole, we would not honor such a critical weighting of purple passages as Arnold's[2] interesting principle of touchstones. Yet the plot of an epic stands out as odd as a skeleton if its flesh of poetic statement and blood of rhythm escape the critic who would, in effect, discuss the *Iliad* and the *Odyssey* as though they were novels.

Confronted with the epic, we content ourselves with the loose and unexamined, if valid, distinction between "primary" and "secondary" epic, or with the anthropological (and not, without considerable adjustment, literary) stratification into "oral" and "written," cheerfully begging the question about the distinct possibility that all epics may have been written down. In these terms, what are we to say of the Christian author of *Beowulf,* who perhaps had read the *Aeneid* and surely brushed Latin culture?

And in order to explain the immense superiority of the *Iliad* to *Beowulf,* of both to many another "primary" saga, we must have recourse to the principle of complexity alone (as though they were novels, but without making as rigorous demands of their complexity as we would make of a novel's) or to the principle of economy of construction alone (a principle practiced superbly by many a contemporary hack writer. We would be resting on the untenable assumption that merit for Homer resides in his having, like a scientist, "discovered" narrative economy).

If we describe Homer's literary technique wholly in terms of its adherence—which I believe Parry[3] proved—to the sort of oral conventions practiced by the Yugoslav bards, then how are we to account, in terms of his poetic practice, for Homer's excellence? We agree with antiquity in esteeming Homer's poems above almost any others. On the other hand, the Yugoslav bards,[4] as they come through in translation, strike my considered judgment as not much better than "primary" hacks, exhibiting in their narratives—of diction and rhythm I cannot judge—all the common vices of triviality, superficiality, and gratuitous excitement. That Homer apparently worked in a similar tradition tells us much about the history of literary transmission but almost nothing about Homer himself; that is, about the essential attributes which distinguish Homer's poetry.

We have put ourselves off by perpetuating, without refining it, this offshoot of Schiller's distinction between *naive* and *sentimentalische Dichtung,*[5] the same as the one between "primitive" and "civilized" that Cassirer[6] found a bar to unbiased philosophic inquiry into different stages and types of thought.

We seem, in fact, to imply by setting "oral" against "written," "primary" against "secondary," a distinction between conscious and unconscious. Vergil would then, on this showing, be conscious of his art, Homer unconscious. To put it this way may bring to mind certain features of each poet. Yet we cannot proceed on such an assumption without the risk of patronizing Homer on the one hand or limiting Vergil on the other, exalting the "primary" as inimitable on that ground alone and treating as effete the "secondary" (the very term is pejorative! Was not Homer, a receiver of tradition, as "secondary" as Vergil?).

Now poetry is a human act of saying that harnesses the mysterious and aboriginal responses of rhythmic pattern and recurrence. It is, in a common attribution, *immediate,* and being immediate it will not unfold very significantly when held under the categories "conscious-unconscious," even when those categories are judiciously applied. Put differently, the poem may be asked with any rigor to be "conscious" only of its own area of immediate statement, of which it is *ipso facto* conscious through its success at identifying words with rhythms. It is even *ipso facto* unconscious through its very immediacy. It is what it says and how it sounds. If consciousness is made to intrude, and leaves its traces in the form of altered words and tampered rhythms, then it folds back and leaves something else in the poem "unconscious." The fully reasoned control of the poem would turn it into a monstrous philosophic machine—which could be a form of highly civilized poetry (and toward this Valéry seems to have aspired). The "secondary" Milton remains unconscious of the primitive sources of the Jungian imagery Maud Bodkin[7] finds in him, not only as unconscious as the equally "secondary" Vergil was of the golden bough's echoes, but also to the degree that the "primary" author of *Sir Gawain and the Green Knight* did not know about his Oedipal archetypes. If Vergil manipulates the machinery of Alexandrian rhetoric, which Homer could have known nothing of, he probably follows by instinct alone the laws of the Vergilian caesurae which later grammarians formulated for him.

We must, in short, come to the poems, the epics themselves, and listen to their evocations of human destiny, watch their delineations of the human image. If we come with a terminology devised for lyric, we must only be disappointed; we will look, to adopt Staiger's brilliant but too summary definitions, for a Memory (*Erinnerung*) that lyric evokes, when epic gives us only presentation (*Vorstellung*).

Of terminologies, consider so simple a one as Josephine Miles' in *The Poem*.[8] In her terms, a speaking voice opts for a rhetorical and syntactical framework, *structure;* the poem refers to items in the outside world, *substance;* it has rhythmic patterns, *sound*. Take the permutations, the varying emphases, of *structure, substance,* and *sound;* with them well-nigh any lyric poem can be described, and revealingly analyzed. Not so an epic, of which the *structure* is always too large to be calibrated with this verbal instrument and the voice too impersonal. The *substance* receives too quirky a presentation in an epic, now as flatly detailed as the catalogue of the ships or the awaking of Satan in Hell, now as foreshortened as Helen on the Wall or Adam Eating. And the *sound,* if confronted in these terms, would give so monotonous a response as to seem least important of all, an attribution we would resist with all the power of this or that mighty line resounding in our ears.

In order to use this, or any other "lyric" set of terms, on the *Iliad* or *Paradise Lost,* we would be obliged, in effect, to break the poem up for its purple passages; or we would have to assign some special rhetorical purpose to an unusual foreshortening or a strikingly long catalogue of substantial details. We might then (falsely) handle Helen on the Wall or Satan Descending as admirable lyrics. But epic poems are not reducible to lyric fragments or novelistic stories; they have their own laws.

It is the purpose of this book to weigh something of those laws and, in weighing them, to speak in general about poetry.

In the ballad a hero characteristically braves and incurs death under conditions that arouse the deep epic responses and fit into the exemplary epic molds. Ballad style, too, displays a directness of statement and an absence of small artful variation that differs markedly from what, through immersion in lyric, we are accustomed to expect from shorter poems. The ballad subject and the ballad style serve as a convenient introduction to three medieval epics about folk heroes, *Beowulf, Roland,* the *Cid.*

Much about the *Iliad* recommends that one take it, as Staiger does, for the model epic. I have presented a full-dress discussion of the *Iliad,* because much that one says about it may apply in great measure to the *Odyssey* as well, and in some measure to other epic poems.

Consequently the third chapter, on the *Odyssey,* is confined to just two features of the poem, Homer's choice of a manageable subject for it, and his means of including various kinds of experience within its single compass.

My procedure from Homer on has been chronological, not because the points I wished to make were mainly historical, but because each of Homer's successors existed within a strong tradition, and each faced similarly the problem of choosing and adapting from that tradition materials and means consonant with his own poetic purpose. A chronological presentation has the advantage of allowing the critic to take some cumulative effects in the tradition for granted.

In the period of well over six hundred years between Homer and Vergil a great deal happened to the technique of verse. A style was developed, which I have called the refined style. This "classical" style was accommodated to epic usage by Vergil; Dante and Milton also utilized some features of it, not to speak of the countless other poets who, in striving for what we call classicism, were trying, I believe, to build certain features of the refined style into their verse. It had been perfected by the Alexandrians; though in very special ways, and not by them alone. Hence we are in a sense speaking too restrictedly when we characterize the stylistic concerns of Propertius and Catullus, or Vergil, as Alexandrianism. They share the refined style with the Alexandrians, and with earlier Greek poets too.

This style, while used in various genres, is crucial to the verse of epic poetry from Vergil on, and I have devoted a separate chapter to it.

In my last three chapters, on Vergil, Dante, and Milton, I have dwelt on each poet's shorter efforts of apprenticeship in gradually realizing how he would go about forging the refined style into an epic instrument. I have given a prolonged consideration to style throughout, to diction and syntax and rhythm. It is here, as these features harmonize into the particular line each epic poet has found for himself, that one can feel the very quick of an epic perception; that the verse base of the line is wrought to a finality appropriately called classic.

The Classic Line

A STUDY IN EPIC POETRY

Part One

CHAPTER ONE

Folk Destinies

THE total purpose that an epic hero mobilizes puts him at the center of his society, whether Adam's archetypal society of two, Dante's idealized society of the immortal, Beowulf's society of warriors threatened by the supernatural, Aeneas' fated society of the future, or the society where Achilles, in the very throes of "alienation," finds his total being.

In this full commitment of action he embodies the risk of death. And the sense of that risk communicated by the poem, charges the hero's actions with a sense of mortality, of a mortality that is common since his actions are also presented as exemplary. In fact, he is so totally involved in mortality that he can seldom stand aside from himself to contemplate his own death more than in a brief summary or valedictory, whether he dies almost at once like Roland or succumbs, heavy with age, like Beowulf. Nothing in the vast intellectual scheme of the *Divine Comedy* allows for even so simple a meditation on death as "Timor Mortis Conturbat Me" or Claudio's speech to the Duke in *Measure for Measure*.

In epic, the hero's conduct is at once evoked and governed by the ideals to which the poem gives formal substance. In societies that are close to a tribal organization, these ideals are bound up in a code. The poem creates a tension between the code and its mortal limits: Achilles is an ideal hero, but flouted; he is justly angry, but unjustly

3

persists in anger. Beowulf can cope with the supernatural for a long, long time; but silently he is aging.

Now ballads characteristically call into play a code that at the same time may be overcome by conditions of mortality. Ballads in short compass exhibit some of the essential features of the epic. Like epic, the ballad refers to the communal life amid which it is originally performed. Like epic, it characteristically tells a story, of the human spirit persisting through and beyond mortality, in the face of an overwhelming environment, in response to a communal code. (To call this persistence "tragic" would import the coordinates of an alien imaginative type.)

Furthermore, both ballads and epic poems were recited to the accompaniment of music. Punctuating the sameness of a bard's voice as it moved through line after standard epic line, the harp or the lyre played, a distant and surely irregular echo of the regular verse. If the accompanying music is itself regular, a song of some pattern instead of a chant, and if the song's patterns are made to coincide with those of a simple stanza—then we have a ballad.

In "The Three Ravens,"[1] for example, the syllables as they are sung proceed deliberately through their notes, except for a quickening in part of the refrain. "Derry-derry down down" is accelerated, as though under the pressure of forces unknown enough to result only in nonsense syllables but recurrent enough to form a refrain.

The Knight of the ballad has died under the code. Above him hang the three ravens, almost like plenipotentiaries of the overwhelming environment of mortal life. The first stanza insists on their fixity as they sit over the envisioned *fait accompli,* perched in archetypal number and color:

> There were three rauens sat on a tree,
>   Downe a downe, hay downe, hay downe
> There were three rauens sat on a tree,
>   With a downe
> There were three rauens sat on a tree,
> They were as blacke as they might be.
>   With a downe derrie, derrie, derrie, downe, downe

The one of them said to his mate,
'Where shall we our breakefast take?'

'Downe in yonder greene field,
There lies a knight slain vnder his shield.

'His hounds they lie downe at his feete,
So well they can their master keepe.

'His haukes they flie so eagerly,
There's no fowle dare him come nie.'

Downe there comes a fallow doe,
As great with yong as she might goe.

She lift vp his bloudy hed,
And kist his wounds that were so red.

She got him vp vpon her backe,
And carried him to earthen lake.

She buried him before the prime,
She was dead herselfe ere euen-song time.

God send euery gentleman,
Such haukes, such hounds, and such a leman.

Later versions, as Bronson[2] notes, concentrate on the meal of the ravens. This one (the earliest known, from Ravenscroft's *Melismata,* 1611), has the very creatures the knight owns for being a combatant, the hawk and the hounds, check the ravens on the ground and in the air. The code is evoked in the word "slain," which vaguely but persistently implies honorable conditions and a courtly situation. You are not "slain" if stabbed in the back, or trampled by a horse.

Because it is wedded to music, and because it has so high a proportion of refrain, this ballad cannot be treated as a lyric poem in words. It is quite simple, and to read "ironic shock" into it, as Brooks and Warren do,[3] argues for a complexity of language not to be found in the ballad tradition at all. If we look at the language of this ballad, after we have noted a few genuinely lyric touches like the charged metaphor of the doe, the adjectives "fallow" and "earthen," perhaps the hidden metaphor in "prime" and "even-song" (day equals year, time itself is a pilgrimage and so gets canonical hours), we are left with statements baldly designative. Fields are always green, wounds always red. And each statement, through the tripartite refrain—which Bronson speaks of as one of the oldest types—is given a magical repetition.

We think of poetry—of lyric poetry—as involved in tropes, playing constantly over and under the bare "prosy" statement; surely not so direct as this ballad is. It is precisely in such a concentrated verbal flash and interplay as are scarcely to be found in this or other ballads, that Coleridge[4] finds "the specific symptoms of poetic power":

> In the two following lines for instance, there is nothing objectionable, nothing which would preclude them from forming, in their proper place, part of a descriptive poem:

> > Behold yon row of pines, that shorn and bow'd
> > Bend from the sea-blast, seen at twilight eve.

> But with a small alteration of rhythm, the same words would be equally in their place in a book of topography, or in a descriptive tour. The same image will rise into semblance of poetry if thus conveyed:

> > Yon row of bleak and visionary pines,
> > By twilight glimpse discerned, mark! how they flee
> > From the fierce sea-blast, all their tresses wild
> > Streaming before them.

The second passage, Coleridge asserts, would illustrate how Shakespeare "gives a dignity and a passion to the objects he presents." But our ballad would seem to fail this canon; it more resembles the first passage than it does the second, nor can we conceive of a ballad so full of tropes as the second passage.

This ballad proceeds by the straight declarative statement, and yet does manage to convey "dignity" and "passion." A magic almost incantatory, as of wonder at the mere fact of the finished life, comes into play through the repetitions. The first line repeats three times before it is capped with the identical rhythms of the rhyming line. In between the two lines comes nonsense, which carries the tune, and itself insists, by syllable-jumbling contrast, on the factualness of the language. The voice prepares through the nonsense for its next designation, and when the voice breaks into sense, it becomes more regular and deliberate, slower in the musical time as in the spoken cadence.

The words are sung, not chanted. Song keeps the cadences of the spoken statement from achieving any of the fine rhythmic discriminations inside the cadence which we get in the varying emphases of the dramatic lyric. In a ballad, cadences must be rendered as in equal emphasis, not only (as they are) in the style of the zither-playing Appalachian mountain singers, but in any conceivable ballad style. The song, like the language, strikes at a dead center of presenting in the identities of rhyme a total situation, one summed up and appraised at the end of this particular ballad.

The song alone does not set the mood: as Bronson abundantly demonstrates, the same song used once for "sad" words may be used again for "happy" ones. And the same ballad may be sung to different tunes of varying other uses. Still, the mood of the ballad rises from both together, and this neutrality-in-isolation of the music, as well as its simplicity, keeps the mood of the words clear and simple.

Where a lyric poem confects some special set of evocations around our common mortality, a ballad plays more directly to the heart of it. The "feeling" of a lyric poem is unique unto itself, but the feeling of one ballad is nearly identical with that of another. The code remains the same, the details differ. So the rhythm of a ballad does not vary on a fine scale, syllable by weighed syllable, as in lyric. The syllables progress loosely, and the spoken rhythm corresponds simply to the life-feeling it expresses.

Far more modulated than any ballad could be are the rhythms of lyric poems in what Coleridge[5] calls the neutral style (as close as lyric poems can come to the "natural" declarativeness of the ballad):

> Sweet day, so cool, so calm, so bright,
> The bridall of the earth and skie,
> The dew shall weep thy fall to-night;
> For thou must die.   (HERBERT)

Scarcely a phrase here but changes the rhythm; no line reproduces the caesura pattern of another. The syllables are all weighed, and all function artfully. In "The Three Ravens," on the other hand, caesurae are sung as nearly identical. Because they follow the song; but the song is part of the poem.

So broad are a ballad's rhythmic effects that when the ballad departs from rhyme, it does so indifferently, content with whatever echo seems to rise from the statement. Assonance in ballad is an accident allowed by the wide circle of possible echo, and not an artful variation.

Yet the rhythm of the ballad "sounds as a trumpet" (the phrase is Sidney's). How far is the regularity of a ballad from that of other direct verses!

> I put my hat upon my head
> And walk'd into the Strand;
> And there I met another man,
> Whose hat was in his hand.

No trumpets here. We join Coleridge in his contempt for such lines. But the crowding syllables in the first and third lines of the more common ballad stanza—indifferent to subtle variation—carry the pressure of the voice as it makes its calm, declarative way to the end of a death according to the code. The trumpets are heard, for instance, in "Johnnie of Cockerslee":

> Johnnie rose up in a May morning,
> Call'd for water to wash his hands;

'Gar loose to me the gude gray dogs,
That are bound wi' iron bands.'

.   .   .   .

'What news, what news, ye gray-headed carle?
What news? come tell to me.'—
'I bring nae news,' said the gray-headed carle,
'But what these eyes did see.'

The voice catches at the excitement in the second of these stanzas;
but here the second and the fourth lines, the rhyming ones, preserve
their metric near-identity, letting the first and the third lines do
the main work of carrying the extra caesurae and the extra syllables.
To say of this poetry that it counts accents only, and to compare it
to Coleridge's *Christabel,* to *The Rime of the Ancient Mariner,* or
to Hopkins' lyrics, would be to overlook its rough and comparatively
artless modulation. Here the heedlessness to accent of the voice
speaking prose has been half harnessed to an unvarying stanza
pattern.

Both the patterned stanzas of some ballads and the chants of others
serve to suggest rhythmically the feeling of mortality that is also
expressed in the tale. The voice presses against the stanza, so evoc-
atively that one is tempted to compare it with the way life in the
poem is shown to press up to the death that embodies, and also
entombs, its honor in the code:

Now Johnnie's gude bend-bow is broke,
And his gude gray dogs are slain;
And his body lies dead in Durrisdeer,
And his hunting it is done.

This poet does not build the private speech into a contribution to
the named language coming after him, as Shakespeare and Dante
do. He uses the common words, at a dead center of style, and also of
the feeling which he evokes in his listeners. The feeling is as much
alike in ballad after ballad as the rhythm of one ballad resembles

another, though of course all are not wholly alike. The four-line stanza of the normal ballad with its alternate, pulsing lines, seems to grow excited at the presence of death, while in its more objective and more regular couplets "The Three Ravens" gives the impression of succumbing numbly to the idea of death.

The language of a ballad does not construct its own overtones of connotation; it borrows them, and borrows them wholly, out of the common folk imagination. For example, its numbers are archetypal: the three ravens, or the seven foresters whom, all but one, Johnnie has slain:

> Johnnie has set his back to an aik,
> His foot against a stane,
> And he has slain the Seven Foresters,
> He has slain them a' but ane.

The very name of the tree that Johnnie leans on arouses a sense of participation in epochs as it echoes back into prehistory; it was worshipped by the druids. The vegetation, and the hard ground of the stone which primitive man shapes into idols—this pair, tree and stone, recur in the folk imagination as far back as Homer (ἀπὸ δρυὸς οὐδ ἀπὸ πέτρης).

The words—"oak" and "stone"—trumpet a feeling of mortality that the singer and his listeners evoke among themselves. And each singer may alter the simplicity of the ballad as it passes through his hands without changing it much, though its quality can be heightened and purified (or lowered and corrupted). For each ballad strikes to a common center; each is an incantation of declarative statements that stave off mortality by giving in to mortality as the one end, cause, ground, limit and glory of honor. The ballad gives us no constellated lyric universe, but, in its simplest form, the unitary tale, indifferent to this detail or that. Detail, of course, it must have; now and then, magical detail. To that rhythm, always the same, like his own heartbeat, the hero is sent out into the world and its mysteries; the world brings its mysteries in on the hero, through the pattern of battle or lawlessness which he cannot master, and yet does master.

The tale of a ballad often includes one or more sudden twists as the death approaches; the unexpected death of the leman, Johnnie's failure to kill the seventh forester, his success at getting a message home to his mother via the winging bird. Or Lord Randall's curse on his sweetheart, Robin Hood's dying refusal to grant Little John the last boon of burning the murderess's hall, the arrow shot to his grave. Or Little Musgrave's fatal falling off to sleep, Lord Barnard's sudden regret. These moments of sudden intensity catch the heroic temper as rising above the events to which, at the same time, the hero is going under.

Epic is like ballad in its assumption of a total code taken along with all its possible contradictions (a Christian knight may still hate a pagan in an un-Christian way), in its dependence on the tale for the skeleton of its argument, in its simple declarative base. But ballad, like lyric—and like elegy or pastoral or other shorter poems—differs from epic in the essential relation of words to poetic rhythms. We are accustomed in poems to a direct, in artful poems to a precise, correspondence of the rhythms with the statements. But any epic has a line even simpler than the ballad stanza, though it perforce presents—if its wider scope be more than mere linear extension—a more complex feeling of mortality. In an epic, consequently, the simple line does not echo directly, as the simple ballad stanza does, the life feeling of the poem. In epic, then, the relation between statement and rhythm is one of contrast or counterpoint, and the pull of a more or less complex life view in the poem's total statement (therefore in each part) is felt against, not at first just with, each simple unit of the mighty traditional line. This gives the rhythm in an epic a function quite different from that of the rhythm in shorter poems, and this difference is important—as important as rhythm must be in a poem.

2

Beowulf performs his deeds of prowess while abiding by a code as simple as that of the hero of a ballad. For him, though, the fulfillment of mortality approaches in a longer span, half a century and more. The supernatural has come to haunt the near wilderness, and its terror is embodied in his antagonists: Grendel, the Dam, the dragon. A deliberation to stave off terror broods in the hero's intimate purpose. He must feel terror when the sum of what is known consists in the necessity of facing the unknown with his whole being: of undergoing the perennial risk, within the perennial condition, of mortality. Everything around him urges him to brood on this terror if he is going to stave off terror for his followers about "the might of the unknown" (eofoð uncuþes, *Beowulf* 961).

A sense of the hero's deliberation broods in the very rhythms, with their slow progressive movement from half-line to half-line, and their heavy beats. In *Beowulf* the voice pauses in the middle of every line, pauses so strongly that the unit of the half-line constitutes the nucleus of the rhythm. Too slow to sing, though the harp may have been strummed along with it, this nucleus, with two strong beats, suspends the totality of possible statement while the utterance is being made.

The double accent in each half-line bears down hard. And the suspension after the mid-line pause—surely longer than the conventional caesura of, say, the alexandrine, and so practically equal in length to the end-line pause—holds the voice up in a suspense heavy with mystery.

Within the half-line itself, the double accent alone, simple and heavy, determines the count. Eduard Sievers[6] classifies these into five types (three of equal, two of unequal feet), and further into subtypes. And Pope[7] hypothesizes a rest of the voice and stroke of the harp, along with a musical lengthening of certain syllables, to clear up certain difficulties found in "hypermetric lines" and other clausulae. But these variations, however faithfully described, strike the ear with the roughness of the ballad stanza, not with the fineness of Vergil's hexameters, which the precision of Pope's and Sievers' Alexandrian classifications would suggest. The heavy double accent is heard; then comes the pause; then two more accents. Beyond

that, the ear picks up in a strong line only a couple of unaccented syllables, in a weak line many such syllables struggling against the pivotal accents. If we try to calibrate the metrical effects along the lines of modern critical analysis, we cannot, I believe, find such a tonal correspondence for the types as Klaeber[8] offers us for Sievers'.*
The extra accents are not tightly built as in most lyrics, but loosely, as in a ballad.

Carried over from half-line to half-line is the link of the alliteration, in vowel or consonant, sometimes stronger within the half-line, sometimes stronger in the carry-over. The alliteration, bound in its rule firmly to the accented syllables, strikes down hard with a consonant, or opens out fully with a vowel. Something known is offered in the word's sound from the very beginning: that is, before we hear the word, we know that it is to follow the pattern (where with rhyme, we hear the word first, then, when it is rounded out, perceive the conjunction with the other rhyming word). In the constant expectedness of the alliterative rhythm, we have a rhythmic parallel to the warrior's sense of steadfastness amid the overwhelming confrontations of this supernatural-riddled universe. Each word bears its accent, and heralds in alliteration its known link with its far fellow across the gulf of the middle pause.

The poem, in its short half-line bursts, anchors on the heavy syllables and binds with alliteration. The bands of words are kept as small by the half-line as the bands of warriors by the economy of the wilderness. And the knot of the half-line is suspended. What

---

* "One would like, indeed, to associate type A with steady progress or quiet strength, to call B the rousing, exclamatory type, to consider type C the symbol of eagerness checked or excitement held in suspense; D 1-3, and D4, though heavier and less nervous, would seem to have an effect similar to C and B respectively; E with its ponderous opening and short, emphatic close is likely to suggest solemnity and force. However this may be, we can hardly fail to perceive the skill in the selection of successive types in syntactical units, like B+A/A: 80-81^a, C+A/A: 96-97^a, 99-100^a, B/A+E: 109^b-110, C+A/A+C/A: 2291-93^a, or in the case of longer periods, C+A/D$_4$+A/A//+C/A(//)+C/A //+B: 1368-72, and with totally different effect, A$_3$+A/D$_{4x}$+A/A$_3$+A/C +A/A$_3$+A/A//+B/C+A: 1728-34. A nice gradation is attained by the sequence of types, 49^b—50^a: *him waes geomōr sefa,/murnende mōd*."

comes next may be apposition, vocative, main clause, qualifying phrase; we never know, and cannot predict from what has come before in the sentence.

Within the half-line, we are given something closed off and therefore limited: something known. Beyond the half-line lies the unknown, the more so that the ear rests on no strongly directive pattern of syntax.

This short rhythmic pattern is suspended in the "variation" of the syntax. And the long pattern too, of the overall narrative, constantly both recapitulates and digresses, suspending the straight progress of the narrative. The "variation" of the style, reinforced by the short bursts of the metre, keeps everything equally suspended. So in the world the poem tells about, allegiances are absolute, but everyone is mortal, and fate can come on as swiftly as the second half of the line, as simply as an alliteration, as heavily as an accent.

Heroes live typical lives, doughty on all sides (*gehwaer dohte*) as Unferth admits Beowulf to be; all dimly sense mortality. Scyld Scefing, at the beginning of the poem, is lonely like Beowulf. He is an orphan, while Beowulf serves not his father but an uncle. Scyld is buried as honorably by his mourning people as Beowulf himself finally is.

All men are alike under the code, and so the hero is only a superlative of every man's positive. Correspondingly, every phrase in the poem is a simple summation, an expression of the known. Each half-line, in coming after the prolonged pause of caesura or end line, and in being about equal in short length to any other, has an epigraphic ring to it, as though suggesting the whole of the hero's life while communicating a given part:

> Oft Scyld Scēfing   sceaþena þrēatum,
> monegum mǣgþum   meodosetla oftēah,
> egsode eorl[as],   syðð̄an ǣrest wearð
> fēasceaft funden;   hē þæs frōfre gebād,
> wēox under wolcnum   weorðmyndum þāh,

oð þæt him æghwylc   ymbsittendra
ofer hronrāde   hȳran scolde,
gomban gyldan;   þæt wæs gōd cyning!

Oft Scyld Scefing	from hordes of enemies
From many tribes	their mead-stools tore.
Affrighted the earls	since first he was
Found unwealthy.	Help therefore he bade,
Waxed under the skies	in worship throve,
Until that each one	of those dwelling about
Over the whale road	must hearken to him,
Tribute must give him.	That was a good king!

(BASED ON MONCRIEFF[9])   (4-11)

We begin in mid-career with name and repetition: "oft" and "Scyld
Scefing," the hero as one who can repeat his acts (the way Beowulf
does throughout his life). The poet takes him at an archetypical
point, as confronting troops of enemies "or call them a number of
tribes." So the poem, in its variation, seems to say. "He affrighted
the earls"; and suddenly it switches from the height of his power,
when he may deprive others of the props of their joy, the mead-
stools, back to the time when he was himself devoid of riches,
fēasceaft. Each attribute is temporary for the moment of presentation
because it comes in syntactic sequence; but because of the half-line
suspension it also has the ring of permanence: once a conqueror
always a conqueror; once an orphan always an orphan awaiting
solace (*frōfre*). To say that Scyld grew under the heavens equals
all the preceding attributions. Or that he throve in worship—this
does too. We have not stages, but aspects, taken of childhood or
maturity, of aloneness or leadership, of struggle or power. The
subjects hearken or they give tribute: we heard before that they
were sociable to him (*frōfre*), that they regarded him highly
(*weorðmyndum*). These disparities fit together, as a structural an-
thropologist might analyze them. The career may be summed up in
an adjective, "he was a good king."

In prose all this would seem repetitious. In the half-lines, it

strikes a total poetic pose, and the strong emphasis of the accents
makes the reading voice seem to strive to crowd the whole sense of
the king's life, verbal and emotional, into the one half-line attribution.

The importance of each unit, the weight it bears, makes it summary, and keeps the narrative progress from seeming slow. We are
given variations on the theme of heroism to such a degree that the
theme becomes the variations; such is mortal life as the poem presents it, whole at every point.

Flashes more than descriptive, then, are transmitted in the description of Scyld's funeral:

> Him ðā Scyld gewāt   tō gescæphwīle
> felahrōr fēran   on Frēan wǣre;
> hī hyne þā ætbǣron   tō brimes faroðe,
> swǣse gesīþas,   swā hē selfa bæd,
> þenden wordum wēold   wine Scyldinga —
> lēof landfruma   lange āhte.
> Þǣr æt hȳðe stōd   hringedstefna
> īsig ond ūtfūs,   æþelinges fær;
> ālēdon þā   lēofne þēoden,
> bēaga bryttan   on bearm scipes,
> mǣrne be mǣste.   Þǣr wæs mādma fela
> of feorwegum   frætwa gelǣded;
> ne hȳrde ic cȳmlīcor   cēol gegyrwan
> hildewǣpnum   ond heaðowǣdum,
> billum ond byrnum;   him on bearme læg
> mādma mænigo,   þā him mid scoldon
> on flōdes ǣht   feor gewītan.
> Nalæs hī hine lǣssan   lācum tēodan,
> þēodgestrēonum,   þon þā dydon,
> þē hine æt frumsceafte   forð onsendon
> ǣnne ofer ȳðe   umborwesende.

> Turned aside then Scyld   in the time shaped for him,
> Full-ripe, to fare   in the Lord's keeping.
> They bare him then out   to the brink of ocean,
> His sweet companions,   so himself had bidden,

While his words had weight,

A beloved land-chief
There in the roads
Icy, out faring,
Laid they down then
Bestower of bracelets
Their man by the mast.
Fretted gold ferried
Nor heard I of a keel
With brave weapons
With bills and byrnies;
Many treasures
In the flood's keeping
Nothing less
Of their possessions
Who at his first faring
Alone over ocean,

welcome friend of
  Scyldings;
long had he reigned.
ring-stemmed she stood,
an atheling's craft:
the beloved prince,
in the breast of the ship,
There was a mass of wealth,
from far away.
more comely garnished
and battle-weeds,
on his breast lay
that must with him
fare afar.
of gifts they allowed him,
than had those
forth had sent him
an infant indeed.

(26-46)

Alone he came, and alone he went, *aenne ofer ȳðe, umborwes-ende*. The hero comes out of the unknown and disappears into the unknown. A sense of the unknown lies heavy upon the poetry that speaks of him. Yet outwardly he is surrounded by the known. In the clearing of the wilderness he is followed by a visible cluster of warriors. He owns tangible treasure, which he takes along when he dies.

The hero's code concentrates not on feeding the body, cultivating the land, and so on, or even on natural warfare; but rather on the ideal of facing the unknown unflinchingly. Yet, while his code is to brave the unknown, his success is measured by this tangible treasure. To fulfill the code in this poem is to give rings. To give rings is to be beloved, and to be in the Lord's care, two conditions which in turn get the treasure that the hero is then obliged to give. Going through this process brings him to the height of his vigor (*felahrōr*) as well as to his fated time (*gesceaphwīl*). The height of life is the point of death. Since any element of the hero's involvement shares the unitary wholeness of the code, the elements are exchange-able (goodness for fullness of life, fullness for rings, rings for goodness, and so on). A oneness prevails between the mortal spirit of the hero and the life of his sharing *comitatus*.

Everything possesses a share in the glitter of shield, hilt, and ornament; and a ship, the very funeral ship, has a ringed prow (*hringedstefna*). The ship, still, is icy (*īsig*), and eager to embark (*ūtfūs*). The ice is too literal to serve as a metaphor for death; it has merely a tonal portent, a portent like that perpetually carried in the heaviness and abruptness of the rhythm. The treasure is aboard; once the hero passes the bound of death, the hands put him in the flood's keeping (*on flōdes aēht*). He departs far (*feor gewī-tan*) to a destination that is not specified—though this is to some extent a Christian poem—but only located in the unknown beyond him.

Beowulf, unlike Achilles or Aeneas or Adam or the Cid, has no singular destiny, other than to help clans by going out against super-natural creatures. Here all leaders are like one another, threatened by feuds and monsters. So Scyld, Hrothgar's ancestor, may be like Hrothgar, and Beowulf like both; the poem dwells, without having to draw the resemblance, on his aloneness, akin to Scyld's; on his followers' comparable devotion, as manifested in the last rites. It stresses, again, by silent analogy, Hrothgar's similar susceptibility to feuds, his similar prosperity in middle life.

Joy comes to the band through the hero; or sorrow, depending on whether the hero, and therefore his band, copes or does not cope with life. A ballad (*gyd*) can concentrate on the sorrow (*geomor*) Grendel brings, as the poem says. Similarly, Hesiod[10] says that when a man is full of sorrow, he will be cheered if he listens to heroic poems—themselves sorrowful; and the recommendation is for a psychic homeopathy that St. Augustine later scorns.

The hero in ballad or epic always copes with his struggles to the last; therefore he can be fully depressed only when he is to die. Still, the sight of the dragon, the incursion of Grendel at night, the approach to the Dam's fearful forest that even stags shun—all these keep the spirit of the hero in a perpetual balance between hopeful joy at prosperity and the all-embracing fear of his own mortality, between the known and the unknown.

By perhaps another homeopathy, it is the unknown that must fight the unknown. If lucky, a chief can handle his own feuds, but it takes the stranger Beowulf to conquer the night-ravaging descendant of Cain. He is also brought to the poem as someone unknown, since it begins with the Scyld dynasty and Heorot. His name drops out of the poem once Hrothgar has been introduced, and he is not identified on arrival. Beowulf does not name himself until he has been challenged on shore, much later arriving at court to say "I am Beowulf." He lands at a cliff by the sea, a cliff not unlike the one beneath which he loses his life after conquering the dragon (and above which, facing the sea, his barrow will stand).

The Danes, relying on what they know of strange ships, give Beowulf's small band the reception of feuding marauders. Acquiescing on faith at the presented hope (the officer makes a small speech declaring that one must know when to trust), the Danes bring him to the court where he names himself for the first time. So far so good: but the fear all feel has only been driven deeper. Unferth, the orator, with a "personal" motive for guilt (he has killed a brother), with jealousy at Beowulf's prowess, voices everyone's fear by challenging Beowulf about a swimming contest that rumor says he once lost to Breca on a stormy ocean. Beowulf says Unferth is drunk, but not that he is wrong. He claims he saved Breca's life and conquered sea monsters (not unlike those who will swim after him in the Dam's bottomless mere). And Unferth is silenced.

Now this is not really a personal feud between Beowulf and Unferth. All members of the band respond alike to a leader. When this response is not met, they abandon an unresponding king like Heremod, who gives no rings; they expel the unaccording warrior.

And so Hrothgar neither rebukes Unferth nor apologizes for him to Beowulf; he merely expresses a reassurance that Unferth, the tribe's orator, has evoked by working out the fear that is its opposite.

After the expulsion of Grendel, when Beowulf has proved himself, Unferth again voices the underlying sentiments of the whole band, this time a strengthened and hopeful confidence: it is the now sober Unferth who hands Beowulf the heirloom sword Hrunting to use in the combat with Grendel's mother. "Personal" motive, again, can scarcely exist here except incidentally, and so the poet need make no comment about Unferth's "overcoming of jealousy." Where there is no inner life—except the root fear of mortality—there can be no inner struggle. Unferth feels as the tribe feels, and is more articulate about it: their orator. On the first occasion his personal history happens to give him a motive for challenging Beowulf and thereby articulating the group's apprehension before a stranger. But the second time the group fear has been allayed by the heroic action against the monster. Unferth is attuned to the group, and so he has no jealousy to swallow in offering Beowulf Hrunting. To see inconsistency between his initial jealousy and his subsequent generosity would be as false as to construct a complex characterization for him. He merely voices what he responds to, the group feeling of fear or hope, as the unknown is either bested or terrifyingly unexpelled. In sharing with his fellows an unwillingness to enter the combat, he "forfeited his reputation for heroic deeds" (dōme forlēas/ellenmaērthum, 1470-1).

The group feeling locks its members into its known quantum, somewhat as the half-line locks the words.*

Beyond lies the unknown; Hrunting, which has never failed in combat with mortals, fails against the Dam. In her strange underwater dwelling itself, must Beowulf find the weapon against her,

* Such correspondences between style and society, to hold at all, must hold for both style and society. Or to put it differently, the poet who wrote *Beowulf* has succeded precisely in carrying off a correspondence that other Anglo-Saxon poets had not, a success we may confidently call imitative or sympathetic form, *pace* Yvor Winters.

and it is the giant's sword, glimpsed on her wall, with which he kills her for good and all. He has been underwater so long that the Danes, assuming he has died, calmly leave the bank; but his followers, with more to lose, remain standing about sick at heart:

Ðā cōm nōn dæges.   Næs ofgēafon
hwate Scyldingas;   gewāt him hām þonon
goldwine gumena.   Gistas sētan
mōdes sēoce   ond on mere staredon;
wīston ond ne wēndon,   þæt hīe heora winedrihten
selfne gesāwon. —

Then came nones of the day;   from the ness departed
The haughty Scyldings.   Went homewards from
thence
The Gold-Friend of men.   The guests were sitting
Sick in mind,   and staring on the mere;
They feared and they felt not   that their friend and Lord
Himself they might see.   (1600-05)

This narration is too heavy with feeling for descriptive elaboration, as the arrival of Grendel is told in bursts of terror to which details of appearance and action are incidental.

Beowulf had earlier boasted, after Grendel and after hearing the prophetically analogous song of Sigemund's combat with the dragon, of his own coping with the unknown:

'Wē þæt ellenweorc   ēstum miclum,
feohtan fremedon,   frēcne genēðdon
eafoð uncūþes.

We this courage-work   with great good will,
Fought and performed,   fiercely dared we
The might of the unknown.   (958-61)

And now Beowulf emerges from the mere, exulting. Having conquered, he goes home shortly, inherits a kingdom like Hrothgar's, and rules it, the poem tells us succinctly, for fifty years.

This epic expends little poetry on the natural combat of feuds and wars. These it keeps steadily in the background, and we learn, in the firm subordination of digression, about the perilous balance of loyalties among the Frisians and the Swedes. In Beowulf's world, too, it is part of the Geats' background that to the south over water lie the friendly Danes, to the north over land the hostile Swedes.

In his fealty to the code, Beowulf resembles his fellows. As a hero he transcends them, and so touches their mortality, through his three supernatural combats. The first is like the second in certain ways: Grendel is the son of his Dam. Beowulf uses a weapon (first an arm, second a sword) against both. Both are night creatures that venture out to attack man, Grendel for jealousy of the joy in Heorot, his Dam for revenge. Beowulf conquers the first in a single night, the darkness and the short time as though symbolizing the ignorance, yet inevitability, of the young hero establishing himself. A man arrives at once; *on n'arrive pas deux fois*. Having proved himself, Beowulf need not wait for his next exploit. He ventures forth, swims to the very bottom of the mere, and, on the very next livelong day, by a light that the poetry dwells on, kills the monster and brings back treasure.

Through the whole middle of his life he awaits the next encounter, for fifty years. The third exploit, again, resembles the second (not the first). This time, too, he has a sword, but he cannot make it work; his main weapon is a shield. The dragon, like Grendel's Dam, has treasure, also underground, also near an expanse of water. He must likewise be sought out. The friend, not the hero, finishes him off; and the hero, as he foreknew, must die. The friend says he has died for his people. In the episode of the Dam we heard much about the time of day and about the light; with the Dragon we hear nothing. There is neither day nor night in the poetry, but a stark absoluteness of time, suggesting finality.

The structure of the poem, from one small digressive section to another, and also in the overall relation of the three combats, hangs on analogy, not on cause, as befits a poem imbued with the unknown. Points of analogy invite interpretation, as though they were metaphors of the hero's life course: youth, middle prosperity, old age. And so they are, in terms of our later formulating time. To call them metaphors, though, is to bring into prominence for analysis and categorization what in the poem remains unnamed because unknown. The poem, of course, draws for its strength—as perhaps all narrative poems in any historical epoch do—on myth, on those circumstances or episodes so rooted in the human condition that they may be found all over the world: the bottomless pool, the mysterious underground light, the night ravager, the dragon sitting on the immemorial hoard, the hero dying as he conquers, the long almost fatal swim, the band of twelve followers among whom one singles himself out, the miraculous stranger, and so on. To diagrammatize the myth anthropologically says anthropological things about the poem: Beowulf as the bee-wolf or bear, Scyld Scefing as the Lord of Sheafs, a Harvest King. A Freudian reading, too, returns Freudian readings to the critical context: the sword as the penis of the hero, the mere of Grendel's mother as the amniotic fluid, a return to the womb, taking vengeance for the wounding of the id (Grendel?). So a Jungian reading: flood and fire, horse and cliff, ship and barrow.* Even a religious reading may sum up the bearing of the hero to God, but it alters the poem's main emphasis. For the poem accepts Christianity, the way it accepts paganism, as an element in the total life feeling of the group. The clan stands doughtily under a known code against a mortality unknown in its coming.

The strength of this myth lies in the hero's being pitted against the unknown. If we translate it into something known, we approach Milton, who relates Adam elaborately to the Christian truth. To present a diagrammatic analysis of the Beowulf myth as though that were the burden of the poem would be like offering a currency

---

* Likewise, to diagrammatize the myth into the tables of "mythèmes" offered by Claude Lévi-Strauss,[11] might provide a schematic equivalent for the poem, but would by definition leave the poem's particularity unexamined.

valuation of the rings the king gives: all their poetry lies in their glitter, not in their exchange value, for they are never exchanged. This poem never deals with economics, the struggle for survival, that wresting of a living from the wilderness which surely must have occupied the main effort of those small Germanic bands; economics fades in *Beowulf* to a place smaller by far than farming and hunting occupy in the *Iliad* and the *Odyssey*.

From beginning to end the hero encounters the unknown, resolving his life as he spends it. The group huddles around the known; and in establishing that for them, the hero loses his life, incurring catastrophe: the Geats know that the Swedes will resume a feud at Beowulf's death; just as Beowulf, in a narrative curiously complicated as to past or future time, either senses or prophesies that at this departure from the Danes they will have to put up with feuds once again. The narrative proceeds from joy to sorrow, victory to defeat, portent to calm to portent, in its strong suspended language. And at the same time it carries an undercurrent of resolution. The poem opens strong, *Hwaet,* and speaks of bygone lifetimes, *gēardagum,* summing up the lonely victory of the remote Scyld. At the end, it quietly resolves Beowulf's death, in a tone prepared for by nothing but the total settling of the life, into a kind of relief and gentleness:

> cwǣdon þæt hē wǣre   wyruldcyning[a]
> manna mildust   ond mon(ðw)ǣrust,
> lēodum līðost   ond lofgeornost.

> They say that he was   a World King,
> Of men the mildest   and to men kindest,
> To his people most pleasant and for praise most eager.
>
>   (3180-2)

Of these attributions, only the last two sum up any of the poem's action: the rest voice only an undercurrent, the unknown and

unexpected fulfillment, transmuting grimness into gentleness. So
the whole course of the hero's life hangs together, though each
episode presents something new that holds only the obscurest links
with the others. All men must die, but how they know not. All must
wholly cope, but wholly they cannot. The hero raises this need to
the pitch of feeling; all gratefully do him homage. Only thus, not in
his temper or in the acts put in the poem, can he be summed up as

> manna mildust ond mon (ðw) ǣrust,
> lēodum līðost ond lofgeornost.

Eager for praise, yes; because otherwise he would be alone, and by
that single fact unheroic in a world which dramatizes no heroism
of aloneness but only the unique act of living out the height of the
common life by mastering the aloneness for everyone.

Only in this sense, too, can they call him a World-King. He has
lived out the sum, but not the paradigm, of submission to life's
needs, and so is a king, a magic winner if not a ruler, of the earth.

Beowulf is not himself mild, but sad and submissive, as he orders
his tomb, placing it "symbolically" on the site of his last combat,
where it can overlook that place and sign of the unknown, onto
which Scyld's corpse was launched: the sea—

> 'Ic ðāra frætwa Frēan ealles ðanc,
> Wuldurcyninge wordum secge,
> ēcum Dryhtne, þē ic hēr on starie,
> þæs ðe ic mōste mīnum lēodum
> ǣr swyltdæge swylc gestrȳnan.
> Nū ic on māðma hord mīne bebohte
> frōde feorhlege, fremmað gēna
> lēoda þearfe; ne mæg ic hēr leng wesan.
> Hātað heaðomǣre hlǣw gewyrcean
> beorhtne æfter bǣle æt brimes nosan;
> sē scel tō gemyndum mīnum lēodum
> hēah hlīfian on Hronesnæsse,
> þæt hit sǣlīðend syððan hātan
> Bīowulfes biorh, ðā ðe brentingas
> ofer flōda genipu feorran drīfað.'

I for these riches
to the Ruler of All my
thanks,
To the Worshipful King
in words will say,
To the Lord Eternal,
whereon I here do look
For that I might
for mine own people
Ere my death day
conquer such things.
Now I for the precious hoard
have paid with my
Old life laid down,
look thou still
To the people's need;
may I be here no longer.
Bid the battle-famed ones
build me a barrow
Bright with the bale-fire
on the brink of the cliff;
It shall for a memory
to my people
Be walled up high
on the whale's headland,
So that seafarers
in future say
Beowulf's Barrow
who with their brave ships
Over mists of the flood
from afar shall drive.

(2794-2809)

Treasure, the people, the lord: on these Beowulf dwells, returning in suspended phrase after suspended phrase, the repetition hinting at the unifying link among them. To your people you give treasure if you are right with the Lord. You get treasure by the favor of the Lord and gain people. People who have a treasure-giving leader are blessed by the Lord.

To get treasure the leader is facing, squarely and alone, the Dragon that sits on the treasure and threatens the people and opposes the Lord. But the dragon also lies beyond all three in his own darkness. In the last line, the mists remain over the flood through which ships will drive from afar.

Beowulf sums up before facing the Dragon, in this passage, and not afterwards in a dying speech, as we might expect: his death lies beyond, in the action of the poem. The code has no real words for the meaning of death, only heavy rhythms and resonant myths. Hence the hero's words do not elaborate on the Dragon, but are confined to the code of what is known about treasure, people, and Lord. The other, the unknown, resides in overtones. Light and dark come in here, as often at high moments in the poem. But with no elaboration. Unmentioned is the loneliness of the cliff, the flash of treasure and funeral fire. This speech closes on the barrow, a memorial for his people, like the poem itself, which comes to a quieting close on the memorial eulogy, and on the powerful visual note of cliffs coming suddenly into a sailor's view out of a sea fog.

The variation of style in *Beowulf* does not work so as to embroider statements into turns of phrase. The variation is from half-line to half-line, and the syntax, so loose as to be strictly neither hypotactic nor paratactic, does not permit of complicated poetic association and heavy inter-echo across the half-lines. Within the half-line, the state-ment is always simple, the long pause keeping the half-line the predominant unit of syntax. Each prominent half-line bears in its few words a heavy utterance of the hero's destiny. We move along through the story, but slowly enough to have its truth borne in on our minds. Truth (*sōðe*) indeed, is the very word the poet uses to speak of poetry:

> guma gilphlæden, gidda gemyndig,
> sē ðe ealfela ealdgesegena
> worn gemunde, word ōþer fand
> sōðe gebunden; secg eft ongan
> sīð Bēowulfes snyttrum styrian,
> ond on spēd wrecan spel gerāde,
> wordum wrixlan;

> A man boast-laden of ballads mindful
> Who a large number of the old sagas
> A quantity remembered, a new word found
> Bound with truth; tcok up the tale
> Of Beowulf's voyage, wisely stirred it,
> Successfully uttered the skillful tale
> Changed it with words; (868-74)

This picture, of the bard improvising on old sagas, accords with Parry's description of oral practice in ancient Greece and modern Yugoslavia. The special features of this particular statement are involved in the necessity it implies of driving (*wrecan*) the words, an expression which we may only anachronistically call a verbal metaphor. The words are in the mind, and the poet stirs them (*styrian*) with wisdom (*snyttrum*). So managed, they will be "successful," "bound with truth." In this pre-philosophical age, we may not press for truth to be defined, and yet the ring of the word "soothsayer" in our later ears may also lead us to give this Anglo-Saxon word too much of a magical connotation.

At the same time, it is the new word of variation, the "other word" (*word ōþer*), found by the poet, that is bound with truth, and so we cannot say that "bound with truth" means true to the facts of the story. It is the *variation* that makes for success, the skillful or wise stirring, and not the knowledge of the facts in the poet's head. He keeps changing his words (*wrixlan*), and presumably each change will be bound with truth. For it is the new word that is bound with truth (*word ōþer . . . sōðē gebunden*), not the whole story: the poet sees the story progressing by the bound, heavily uttered ("driven") units, each of which must ring with the depth of the truth of human destiny.

3

That rarest of writers, the fully successful epic poet, manages to get all of his poem's sense into a simple line and a single rhythm. The lyric poet's fine stylistic adjustments and delicate rhythmic variations, when adopted for a longer poem, close an imaginative structure into mere didacticism (*Works and Days*), or mere narrative sophistication (*Troilus and Cressida*), or prettily proliferated allegory (*The Faerie Queene*) or even an heroic code too simply aristocratic (*Orlando Furioso*). All such poems, for all their beauty and scope, lack the achieved depth and unity of *Beowulf;* they lack, in Arnold's vocabulary, "high seriousness." In devising his phrase, Arnold was trying to put in terms of tone what could be better put in terms of style, rhythm, and meaning: in terms of form and content. Tone is a vague criterion, because one's own predilections may lead him to restrict it unjustifiably, and it would seem that Arnold expected always a certain solemnity to accompany "high serious-ness." It usually does, in fact, but not in the case of the *Odyssey,* which carries off with a faint smile matter weighty enough to have inspired in the poet the kind of solemnity to which Arnold re-sponded with such sensitive discrimination.

Hovering near an epic seriousness is a poem which has the subject of a ballad and the length of a lay or a short epic, *Sir Gawain and the Greene Knight.* This poem stands reasonably close to *Beowulf* in convention and style, and yet its poet, aiming for the delightful grace notes of lyric, has produced a work of a quite different, and lesser, kind.

The legend of this later alliterative poem seems as promising as that of *Beowulf,* with its accessible world of the grail, its chapel in the forest, its journey to the wilds by the sea, its tie with the course of the year and with the love-test, its Oedipal echoes. The poet, embroidering the story, constantly charms, and he succeeds in sug-gesting mystery, as well as a sweep of time, by taking at the start a backward look all the way, not to *Beowulf*'s gulf of the past, *gēardagum,* but to something specific if ancient: Troy. But he simply does not catch anything like the penetrating starkness of *Beowulf*'s opening lines, and he ends with nothing comparable to the great tonal resolutions of *Beowulf.* Instead, he capitulates by rounding out with Troy again, and he closes with the pious moral we should have expected the poem to bear without the need of summing up.

The rhythm of the poem ambles along by fits and starts, pausing for a summary in the alternately rhyming short lines of the "bob-and-wheel" interruption, a grace note unthinkable in the single-minded surge of an epic. These intermezzi reveal how close to the spirit of the simplest lyric the poem is moving all along, when it can consonantly allow such abrupt modulation:

> Wroþe wynde of þe welkyn wrasteleʒ with þe sunne,
> Þe leueʒ lancen fro þe lynde and lyʒten on þe grounde,
> And al grayes þe gres þat grene watʒ ere;
> Þenne al rypeʒ and roteʒ þat ros vpon fyrst,

And þus ȝirneȝ þe ȝere in ȝisterdayeȝ mony,
And wynter wyndeȝ aȝayn, as þe worlde askeȝ,
        no fage,
Til Meȝelmas mone
Watȝ cumen wyth wynter wage;
Þen þenkkeȝ Gawan ful sone
Of his anious uyage.

With the sun the wild wind of the welkin is wrestling,
The leaves from the limbs drop and light on the ground,
And the grass all greys that was green before;
Then all ripes and rots that formerly flourished,
And thus the year passes in many yesterdays
And winter, in truth, as the way of the world is,
        Winds again,
Till the Michaelmas moon
Comes with the winter's pledge;
Then Gawain thinks full soon
Of his troublesome voyage.

(525-35, BASED ON BANKS)[12]

We get the sense of the wind in the movement of the lines, the
sense of the year's changes rustling in the uneven progression. These
alliterative lines are headlong. Then we stop on "no fage" and prepare for the noisome voyage, which is on Gawain's mind as singly in
all the variations of the year as these few accents and rhymes ring
regular against the tripping irregularities of the alliteration.

No life view rises from these effects. Unexpressed in the poetry
is that sense of destiny that this myth might have afforded. A lyric
delight, a lyric surprise, a lyric desolation later in the poem, a lyric
terror and a lyric apprehension. The poem handles all these, and
knits them into its tapestry. But terror and delight do not hold
together in a single, all-embracing view, "bound with truth." The
life feeling of this charming poem manages to sparkle always with
something of anxiety, always with something of delight. And yet,
once the Green Knight looses the riddle, we return to the surface
world we had never really left, and destiny has been no more than a

lyric glimpse, a test of an episodic inconsequentiality, as the rhythms and fanciful tropes of the poem had been telling us all along.

Rhyme in a narrative poem, as Milton sensed, is enough of a "bondage" to have prevented everyone but Dante from rising to an epic fullness. Auerbach,[13] when he compares the "parataxis" of the *Chanson de Roland* and its free assonance to the movement of the *Chanson d'Alexis* fails to note the crucial distinction that the rhymed poem is built to a much smaller lyric order on a much more merely rhetorical frame:

> *Quant sa raison li at tote mostrede,*
> *donc li comandet les renges de sa spede,*
> *ed un anel dont il l'out esposede.*
> *donc en ist for de la chambre son pedre;*
> *en mie nuit s'en fuit de la contrede.*

> When he had showed her all his reason,
> he consigns to her the thong of his sword
> and a ring with which he had married her.
> Then he went out of the chamber of his father's house;
> in the middle of the night he fled from the country.

The stanza here is small and regular, whereas the *laisses* of the *Chanson de Roland* are longer, and of such varied length that they cannot be felt as a structural element in the rhythm, only as a rather larger break than the uniform end-line provides. In the *Chanson d'Alexis* we do have what may be called, with Auerbach, a parataxis. The simple narrative of the last line in the stanza quoted can be felt as a variation from the rhetorical frame of the others, which the rhymes or near rhymes emphasize the more by interlacing, and by such turns of syntax as the precisely placed repetition of *"donc."* Five lines are the unit here, not one; within that unit, the last line, for all its epigrammatic force, does not rise to the isolated majesty of the *Roland* line.

This stanza constitutes part of a small inter-echoing lyric unit.

The rhymes heighten the lyric identities, too: *mostrede* (show), *spede* (sword), *esposede* (marry) and *contrede* (country) form among themselves a sound-enforced elaboration of equivalence and contrast. The *sword* is part of the *showing* that *marrying* opens into. To have *married* is to *show*, and to *show* is to give up the *sword;* to *show* the *sword* is to give up *marriage.* All this involves leaving the *country*, a word more remotely related, and so we skip a word, one that rhymes faultily with *mostrede, pedre.* "The father's house," too, has a special relation of its own with *mostrede.*

The five-line stanza makes of this one syntactic, as well as one rhythmical unit. To have so small a pattern so fully elaborated obviates the simplicity of the epic fullness here, as also in the gorgeous, and lyrically limited, stanzas of Tasso, Ariosto, and Spenser.

4

In the *Chanson de Roland* itself, the hero, again, moves through his code to an epic confrontation of the mystery of death. The honor of staying with the rear guard loses Roland his life; the blast of the horn across the high mountains and shadowy valleys sounds too weak and too late.

The mystery remains, voiced but not mastered by the poem. In the *Iliad*, and in *Beowulf*, the poem controls the unknown that it presents, through its fable and through the verse. When Charlemagne weeps before his massed Army at a high point of *Roland*, we are given nothing to explain, or even to focus, his tears. We know why Achilles weeps, why the followers of Beowulf hang deeply dejected about the mere. But not, in the poem, why the Emperor weeps.

For one thing the fable remains too stiff for us to organize it totally, as though the poet, aware of his tremendous subject, were afraid of letting it get out of hand. He stays on the whole too close to his armies. And then he gives his uncertainty away by presenting the irrelevant trial of Ganelon in the last section of the poem. We are accustomed to such irrelevancies in the digressive heroic poems of the French medieval tradition and of many others. But a genuine epic poem sets itself higher goals, and such a poem disappoints us when it falters before attaining them.

In a sense the poet takes his world too much for granted, as the poet of the *Cid* also does: his hatred of the pagans works too automatically to function consonantly in the poem (leaving questions of morality and consistent Christianity entirely aside).

Consequently, perhaps, there is something stark and laconic in the style of *Roland,* a stiffness inseparable, in the poem we have, from its own special epic grandeur.*

The scale of an epic expands squarely out of the ultimates it projects and voices, the ultimates of death, of total response to a code. The starker the ultimates are felt to be, the more the world the poet presents can be taken objectively for granted: and this direct assumption may have the effect of increasing the stark objectivity of his language. In *Beowulf* the unknown excites the language and works up the rhythms. In the *Chanson de Roland,* the ultimates stand starkly present in the patness of the rhythms. And the language of the poem moves ahead in the plain armor of statements so bald as to seem less touched by rhetoric than almost any prose. So bald, indeed, that Auerbach's ascription to it of "paratactic" seems either inadequate or exaggerated:

> *Paien s'adubent des osbercs sarazineis,*
> *Tuit li plusur en sunt dublez en treis.*
> *Lacent lor elmes mult bons, sarraguzeis,*
> *Ceignent espees de l'acer vianeis;*
> *Escuz unt genz, espiez valentineis,*
> *E gunfanuns blancs e blois e vermeilz.*
> *Laissent les muls e tuz les palefreiz,*
> *Es destrers muntent, si chevalchent estreiz.*
> *Clers fut li jurz e bels fut li soleilz:*
> *N'unt garnement que tut ne reflambeit.*

* Matthew Arnold[14] tries to dismiss *Roland* from the company of high poems by contrasting its special stiffness against Homer's easy flow.

> Ready they make hauberks Sarrazinese,
> That folded are, the greater part, in three;
> And they lace on good helms Sarragucese;
> Gird on their swords of tried steel Viennese;
> Fine shields they have, and spears Valentinese,
> And white, blue, red, their ensigns take the breeze,
> They've left their mules behind, and their palfreys,
> Their chargers mount, and canter knee by knee.
> Fair shines the sun, the day is bright and clear,
> Light burns again from all their polished gear.
>
> (MONCRIEFF 994-1003)

Parataxis implies a kind of connection. Here each line rings clear, as end-stopped as the half-line of *Beowulf,* and far more isolated, because no syntactic suspension is allowed. The ear almost never waits over the end of the line to pick up a missing connection.

Straight on come the pagans, in their enumerated equipment. "Ranked" (*estreiz*) is the final descriptive word. Roland and Oliver, at the head of the rear guard, pause to await them. The understood anxiety and firmness of the pair seem compressed into the next line, a sudden and simple ascription of clarity to the day and beauty to the sun. The poem, with its characteristic abruptness often introduces at a pitch of suspense, such sudden lines about landscape or light or terrain:

> *Clers fut li jurz e bels fut li soleilz:*

So clear was the day, and so beautiful the sun, that there was no piece of armor that did not reflect it:

> *N'unt garnement que tut ne reflambeit.*

It was reflected into the eyes of Roland and Oliver, of course. But their apprehension is left to the imagination, not stated. Nor is it exactly "represented," as in a modern work. Such lines come too rarely for that. They are locked in their apprehension as friend and foe alike are locked in their armor, and as each statement is locked in the inexorable and nearly invariable decasyllables, with their uniform pause on the fourth syllable.

After so long a list of armor, the clearness of the day and the beauty of the sun interrupt, and the very interruption catches up the mind to expectancy. Far later, as the pagan troops arrive over water at Saragossa, we will hear a distant echo of this line:

Clers est li jurz e li soleilz luisant

Clear is the day and shining is the sun

Across the ranked, stiff, unsuspended lines of the poem such distant and disjunct statements echo like the horn of Roland across the mountains into the ear of Charlemagne.

This sharp directness of statement does afford an immediate narrative gain in the disproportionately long battle scenes. The pitilessness of enumerated wounds is thereby highlighted, the bluntness of troop movement or blow. But what, within the poem, do the wounds mean? The wounding in Homer is central but not disproportionately described; his poetry leads us to a meaning, but this poetry does not.

It moves, rather, so starkly, so concealing in its mystery that while an epic feeling is evoked, we cannot explain the central action in ways that will assign a reason within the code to every actor.

Roland is clear, but his clarity lies in the verse and in the fable, and not in the kind of statement we have for Achilles or even the kind of implication we have for Beowulf. And no natural explanation will tell us why Ganelon in his first speech to the pagan king Marsile (467-500) acts like a good emissary of Charlemagne, when he is shortly to propose the traitorous and fraudulent plot that results in Roncevaux. To presume for Ganelon here a subtle Machiavellian manoeuvre, even if such a boastful initial speech made any Machiavellian sense, would attribute to Ganelon a subtlety of character no more exampled for him—or in this verse—than for Unferth in *Beo-wulf*. But *Roland* does not, as *Beowulf* does, supply us with a frame-work where we can furnish other, tribal, reasons.

Why, too, when Ganelon proposes Roland for the rear guard, does Roland thank Ganelon and boast of prowess in the first answering strophe, then curse Ganelon in the second? Gaston Paris and other editors would reject one strophe or the other, and Bédier[16] provides an elaborately motivated policy on Roland's part quite inconsonant with the outspokenness of the speeches, the brief directness of the lines. Auerbach accepts this interpretation. He maintains, uncon-vincingly, that the friendliness of the first speech is needed for the enmity of the second. But he cannot explain why Charlemagne would stand powerless by and weep:

> *Li empereres en tint sun chef enbrunc,*
> *Si duist sa barbe e detoerst sun gernun,*
> *Ne poet muer que des oilz ne plurt.*

> The Emperor keeps his head bowed,
> Strokes his beard and twists his moustache,
> He cannot keep his eyes from weeping.   (771-4)

Now we can imagine the silent tears to be Charlemagne's response to that sense of destiny which all are powerless to control, just as he is powerless "to keep his eyes from weeping." The rhythms of the poem, in the inexorable progression of the decasyllables, have been carrying that sense of relentless destiny. But the language does not explain, suggest, or even simply name, the reason for Charlemagne's tears. We might expect an act from the commander here, standing as he does between two strong, conflicting subordinates. Still, for him to stand there powerless and weep would be inconsistent only if the poem offered us some criterion for consistency of motive. And it does not.

Why, too, does Roland refuse to sound the horn three times at Oliver's urging, and then himself plead to do so once Oliver dis-suades him? The right moment must come, we may say: the horn, in its tragic force, must express the death of one, the dying of the other, for them to concur on blowing it. On the level of natural motive, though, we have a mystery. And it will not do to say with Auerbach that "this function of the repetition is to make the scene more intense; as in the *Chanson de Roland* generally, both the urgent-intense and the manifold-simultaneous are represented by the repetition and addition of many, and frequently artfully varied, individual occurrences."[17] Urgent-intense, yes; but there is nothing of the manifold-simultaneous in this poem, and nothing of artful variation. The march of the lines is too straight to permit of either. Nor does that march of lines sum up the code of the poem: it reverberates both the simple code and something, but not enough, of the mortality beyond the code. It captures the mystery of the weeping, of the horn, of the lone lines about clear days and shining suns or high mountains and shadowy valleys, of the abrupt destinies of Roland and Oliver.

The known is present: the armies have a route and a purpose, a hierarchy of familiar officers. And so is the mystery of the unknown, as it breaks out in Ganelon's actual treachery or Roland's isolation. All this does not give us a measure for the relations in the poem between the known and the unknown. We cannot concur with Auerbach that "for the men who figure in it nothing of fundamental significance is problematic. All the categories of this life and the next are unambiguous, immutable, fixed in rigid formulations."[18] Yes, but who is to tell when the categories will be invoked? That is a mystery so puzzling in the poem that even its blunt grandeur of stiff movement cannot quite contain it. For it is the verse, as always, that carries the apprehension of mortality.

The *Chanson de Roland* has no stanzas, only *laisses* of widely varying length. With the *laisse,* the lines are linked by a terminal assonance that continues for a widely varying number of lines. The assonance serves to make one line a muted echo of one or several others without tying the individual lines to the patterned movement of couplet or triplet.

Rhyme chimes exactly: every ending is tonic. In assonance the difference of consonants muffles the repetition of sound, in a varied approximation to rhyme, letting each line stand alone by the difference, but proclaiming its kinship at the end in the repetition. Moreover, the open part of a syllable in assonance, the vowel, is always the same. The closed part, the final consonant, alone differs. While the syllable is open, rhyme is always possible, until the closing phonemic group. As the mouth of the reciter closes on silence, his closing utterance imparts a solitariness to the line by identifying assonance and not rhyme. He does not quite make it for the identity of rhyme, as Roland does not quite make it back to *Terre Major*.

The missing echo rings with disappointment in the closing of the line's last syllable. End-blunted, the lines in their stark progress bear an elegiac overtone. Something is missing, and each time there is the gap of another statement, barely linked in cadence to its predecessors. Roland stands up in battle but is killed; he is able to blow but not speak the sorrow of his death across the mountains. The whole army, at a mere foreboding of tragedy, can weep. When they do, Charlemagne himself is again unable to restrain his tears:

> *Carles li magnes ne poet muer n'en plurt.*

But as they weep, they are ranked. The poet, rising to no full verbal definition of the mortal condition, does manage to keep the stolidity in the same frame as the "tenderness" (*pitet*) through the assonances, and through a careful, end-stopped, isolation of statement.

The army weeps as it moves, and moves as it weeps:

> *Halt sunt li pui e li val tenebrus,*
> *Les roches bises, les destreiz merveillus.*
> *Le jur passerent Franceis a grant dulur.*
> *De. XV. liues en ot hom la rimur.*
> *Puis que il venent a la Tere Majur,*
> *Virent Guascuigne, la tere lur seignur;*
> *Dunc lur remembret des fius e des honurs,*
> *E des pulcele e des gentilz oixurs:*
> *Cel nen i ad ki de pitet ne plurt.*

Sur tuz les altres est Carles anguissus:
As porz d'Espaigne ad lesset sun nevold.
Pitet l'en prent, ne poet muer n'en plurt.

High are the peaks, the valleys shadowful,
Swarthy the rocks, the narrows wonderful.
Franks passed that day very sorrowful,
Fifteen leagues round the rumour of them grew.
When they were come, and Terra Major knew,
Saw Gascony their land and their seigneur's,
Remembering their fiefs and their honours,
Their little maids, their gentle wives and true;
There was not one that shed not tears for rue.
Beyond the rest Charles was of anguish full,
In Spanish Pass he'd left his dear nephew;
Pity him seized; he could but weep for rue.   (814-25)

In each of the first three lines here, the fullness of the six syllables
after the caesura allows for an adjective of greater emotive resonance
than those of each first half line. We have *tenebrus* for *halt, mer-*
veillus for *bises, grant dulur* for *Jur.* The longer expressions, evocative against the designativeness of the shorter ones, stand also as a
kind of opposite to them: a high mountain is not tenebrous, the
gray is not marvelous, day and great sorrow seem not to go together.

In the designations, uniformly declarative, everything appears in
a uniform light. Therefore, by syntactic echo, the statement about
the high mountains and shadowy valleys, for all its nearly Vergilian
impressionism, borrows from its stiff form some of the directness
of the line that says for fifteen leagues their march could be heard
(so clearly do these mountains echo!). And the matter-of-factness
of this, in its turn, picks up reverberation both from the impressionistic Vergilian line and from the line about their remembering their
fiefs and their honors:

Dunc lur remembret des fius e des honurs,

This line possesses qualities of both the emotive and the descriptive
line: the tonal range is always the same. We do not rise to impression

or fall to fact; impression and fact coexist in every ten-syllable, assonantal line.

Standing out most signally from the progression of the story are the striking, echoing lines like the first in the passage above. Often such lines begin the *laisse,* as this one does. Taken singly, this line would be a statement of purely impressionistic tone describing the landscape or the light of day. What is more, the inversion of the sentence, its formulaic character, and its very isolation both in the end-stopped convention and even more in the disjunction from the flow of the story—all these imply something more than descriptive impression:

> *Halt sunt li pui e li val tenebrus.*

Standing alone, such lines have the character of sibylline or oracular utterance, like the sub-Biblical, sub-sibylline imagery of Charlemagne's dream (725-30). We might speak of them as metaphors, if the poem offered any other supporting metaphorical structures. They would set the scene, if the scene were otherwise touched in. But, in its very isolation, we cannot imagine this line to carry on through the scene as a visible background to the action. We do not think of high mountains and shadowy valleys by the time we have crossed them, and speak in another end-stopped line of Charlemagne's weeping.

Such lines sum up the natural world. Nature, turned to abruptly at the outset of a moment of tension, seems to share the mystery of the battle itself.

In this particular passage,

> *Puis que il venent a la Tere Majur,*

the distant muting of something like a refrain can be heard; the sound across the poem makes the arrival at "Major Land" more final than it would otherwise seem without the fulfilling, near-refrain (*Tere Major* comes last here, but usually first):

> *Tere Major remeindreit en repos.* (600)
>
> *Tere Major vos metrum en present.* (952)

Tere Major, ço dit, metrat a hunte, (1532)

Tere Major, Mahumet te maldie! (1659)

Tere Major mult est loinz ça devant. (1784)

Sometimes the echoing line recurs soon enough to have a capitulative force, as in the two lines about Charlemagne's weeping. One *laisse* begins:

Oliver sent que a mort est ferut. (1952),

The very next alters only the final word and the simple verb:

Oliver sent qu'il est a mort nasfret. (1965)

The landscape words, of day or sun and mountain and valley, recur across a longer distance, and vary more, than either of these:

Halt sunt li pui e tenebrus e grant,
Li val parfunt e les ewes curant.

High are the mountains, and shadowy, and great,
The valleys deep and the waters running.   (1830-31)

The mysterious formula, varied, enters to aid the sound of the horn:

Halt sunt li pui e la voiz est mult lunge, (1755)

High are the mountains, the (horn's) call very long.

And again, much later, at the death of Roland:

Halt sunt li pui e mult halt les arbres. (2271)

High are the mountains, very high the trees.

Still later, the near-refrain lends its force to the march of the emperor rejoining his troops:

Passent cez puis e cez roches plus haltes,
Cez vals parfuns, ces destreiz anguisables,

> They pass these mountains, these rocks very high,
> These deep valleys, these anguish-filled defiles.   (3125-6)

These lines recur too far apart and vary too much to be called a refrain. They stand to refrain as assonance does to rhyme. At the high moment, often at the beginning, sometimes in the middle, they clarion out an echo that the ear, picking it up, recognizes as something from a context like though far.

The music of the *Chanson de Roland* remains stiff, the characters hidden, the incident disjunct. The miracles do not body forth the Unknown, as in *Beowulf*. The standing still of the sun for Charlemagne imitates *Judges* gratuitously. And to have Europe shaken and darkened at the wounding of Roland, while it conforms to a folk motif about heroes, scarcely carries more epic force here than, we may conjecture, do such effects of nature in the Russian *byliny* cited by Bowra.[19] To have an epic requires more than a reciter, a standard line, a folk assumption, and a swashbuckling story. The poet must rise to epic breadth of verse, and compose out of an epic center of fable, as the poet of Roland comes close to doing.

5

A classic line, a hero to project a sense of mortality—these alone, properly handled, will suffice for an epic poem. The *Chanson de Roland,* for all its uncertainties, manages to convey its sense of the mystery in our common human destiny. And so does a poem whose episodes have an even more random cast about them, the *Cid,* the last half of which is dominated by the ununified, gratuitous episodes of wedding and trial.

Like *Roland,* this poem brings no code explicitly into prominence for the hero, and no sense even of an ideal to match Roncevaux. Instead of a conscious motive, we are given only the self-sufficiency of the hero and a loose adherence to Spain. All the sense of mortality comes through in the verse, and in the being of the Cid.

The hatred of pagans here does not have even a real state of war to justify it. Jews and Moors are simply beyond the pale, and any fraud toward them is justified. Count Ramon's fear of fraud from the Cid is senseless, "for never has he committed an act of perfidy," —to a fellow Christian, it goes without saying. The poem, beginning with fraud to Jews, abounds in fraud against Moors.

Death is not an obstacle to the Cid: his death is mentioned offhand at the end of the poem, without cause or sequence. Rather, the unknown resides in his personal destiny; his risk of success stands as a sort of figure for his mortality. It is poverty that serves to measure his solitude. All he has, the verse says, is lance and sword. If these do not win out for him, he cannot survive on the lean land.

He moves across the land, not young, but middle-aged, the father of marriageable daughters. He is so alone, so impoverished, so out of favor with the king—the poem itself does not explain why, even though history does—that the heavy gates of his own town will not open to his knock.

The self of the hero substantiates his life in winning property through prowess. The poetry, as in *Roland,* builds up his actions without offering terms to explain them. Through the years he conquers the land gradually, small town by small town, till all of a sudden Valencia is his. The king's favor is rewon through gifts. The followers are kept by gifts spoken of as free; they are not expected gifts, like the rings an earl bestows on his thanes in *Beowulf.*

Material goods, mysterious in origin, are to be won by sleights of diplomacy or risks of battle and not by hard effort at the lean land. Count Ramon, defeated, goes on a hunger strike, challenging the very assumption that all men want to survive. The Cid is strangely moved at this gesture, and he offers him a freedom he had not hinted at before, if only the count will eat. The faithless princes of Carrion are neither killed, like traitors in *Roland,* nor exiled as they would be in *Beowulf,* but stripped of their property. The Cid even refrains at a certain point from killing the Moors; probably because, as the King says when he begins to pardon the Cid, "We will gain more by this than by further punishment."

The poem, in the face of its own evidence about hardship, bravely reasserts that the Cid was born at a good hour, girded on his sword at a good hour. He is always "My Cid." Praise abandons him no more than the rhythm fails to catapult him strongly over the line's medial pause: there is always more to come, and the formula of his lucky birth, repeated enough, will turn out to be true; just as King Alfonso, served long enough, will relent and at last bestow the formulaic praise on his banished vassal:

> *Saludadme a mio Çid,   el que en buena çinxo espada;*
>
> Greet my Cid for me   he who in a good hour girded his
> sword   (1961)

In the *Cid* an assonantal line balances evenly before and after the caesura. Three beats to each half-line buoy up the narrative to a pitch of high-sounding verse. We do not have the formal tightness of the regular alexandrine, for these lines are nearly as free as *Beowulf* in allowing extra unaccented syllables. And the movement, like the free geographical swerving of the *Cid* himself, has some of the impetuosity of the ballad. But the line must make an effort to buoy itself up, for the caesura outlasts the mild one of *Roland;* it is almost as stiff a unit as the half-line divider of *Beowulf.*

But the long line remains the principal and dominant rhythmic unit. The half-line will not hold up at all independently, the way it does in *Beowulf.* Assonance is even less regular than in *Roland,* and this uncertainty of ear, combined with the unevenness of the lines, keeps the powerful movement rushing.

Nor is the syntax suspended to allow for short word-groupings, as in *Beowulf.* The line succeeds in leaping the silence of its middle pause, as surely as the Cid overcomes his isolation; and the narrative moves as economically, but as surprisingly, as does its hero:

Dios nos valió   *e vençiemos la lid.*
A la tornada,   *si nos fallarédes aqui;*
si non, do sopieredes que somos,   *indos conseguir.*
Por lanças é por espadas   *avemos de guarir,*
si non, en esta tierra angosta   *non podriemos bivir.*

God availed for us   and we have won the fight.
At the return indeed   you will meet us here.
If not, where you find we are   follow us there.
With lances and with swords   we have to help ourselves.
In this lean land otherwise   we cannot live.

(831-34)

Each half-line is lean, possessing none of the epigrammatic fullness of the *Beowulf* half-line. The syntax demands continuation, and after the voice has held itself back, it comes through richly, carrying a reminder of deprivation in the distance of the echo from assonance to assonance.

The statements in ballad and in epic are generally direct, with a ring of factualness and objectivity to them. In *Roland* they are exceptionally so, and also in the *Cid,* even though it lacks the metric regularity of *Roland.* The verse is not marshalled line by line, and still the effect is cumulative: the Cid is a lone warrior, whose disjunct exploits eventually add up (silently) to a success signalled by his great prosperity.

From this directness, the solitude of the Cid finds no outlet in the poetry. The action alone carries him along. He can only boast in the teeth of probability (though not of fate, for he was "born in a happy hour"). Not only his poverty but his own inner life gives his boast the lie: he weeps in the first line of the poem as we have it. The directness, the near literalness, of his absolute disgrace, etches in the solitude of the hero at the very outset; and for this he finds not words but tears.

As mortality appears under the figure of deprivation and disgrace (the poem begins with these; it does not need the intimations of mortality found in *Roland* or *Beowulf*), so the condition of the hero appears in the opaque, unsymbolic explicitness of the detail, calling, like all such poetry, on the motif: the locked door, the nine-year-old girl, the weeping hero. It also depends, Salinas[20] tells us, on the facts about Burgos. The Cid's destiny resides, unexpressed, in the real detail of an actual outer world, the way his mortality resides in the property he gathers.

The facts are richest at the beginning, when he is poorest:

> *De los sos ojos*   *tan fuertemientre llorando,*
> *tornava la cabeça*   *i estávalos catando.*
> *Vio puertas abiertas*   *e uços sin cañados,*
> *alcándaras vázias*   *sin pielles e sin mantos,*
> *e sin falcones*   *e sin adtores mudados.*
> *Sospiró mio Çid,*   *ca mucho avié grandes cuidados.*
> *Fabló mio Çid*   *bien e tan mesurado:*
> *"Grado a ti, señor*
>   *padre,*   *que estás en alto!*
> *"Esto me an buolto*   *mios enemigos malos."*
> *Allí pienssan de*
>   *aguijar,*   *allí sueltan las riendas.*
> *A la exida de Bivar,*   *ovieron la corneja diestra,*
> *e entrando a Burgos*   *oviéronla siniestra.*
> *Meçió mio Çid los*
>   *ombros*   *y engrameó la tiesta.*

> With his eyes   so strenuously weeping
> He turned his head   and was looking at them.
> He saw the doors open   the back gates without
>   hinges,
> The perches vacant   without skins and without
>   mantles
> And without falcons   and without hawks hooded.
> My Cid sighed,   for much he had great cares.

My Cid spoke well	and so measuredly:
"Thanks to you Lord	Father who are on high
"This is how they have served me	my evil enemies."
Then they thought to lead	then they let out their bridles
At the exit of Vivar	they had the crow on the right
And entering Burgos	they had it on the left.
My Cid shrugged his shoulders	and lifted his head. (1-13)

The people stand at their windows weeping for him, but none dares receive him. He rides by in silence. The King has "before night" sent his mandate that anyone who speaks to him will lose his property, his eyes, and his head. The nine-year-old girl, who does not open the door, herself knows of the prohibition. But she voices the blessing of all, and the Cid is no more held back by the ban—though he must invest some of his life in succeeding to remove it—than the metre allows the syntax to contain, the way *Beowulf* does, a separable unit within the half-line preceding the great caesura.

Here the Cid weeps directly; the poetic impact of the empty perches and the other redolent details is likewise direct. Sighing for a reason the obviousness of which does not prevent the poem from mentioning it, he speaks as measuredly as the poem does, and utters the obvious. The centrality of his experience, the unexplained mystery of his destitution, carry his solitude without symbol or even action, and there is nothing in his recovery to counterbalance this solitude or qualify it other than in the action.

In its literalness, the poem's language, to use the terms of Salinas, *reproduces* reality, even in the literal look of Burgos, or the real mileage between minor towns, barely and simply, without amplification. "In the objective neatness of the perception . . ." says Salinas, "life is reproduced as it is seen."[21]

In this epic, in *Roland,* in *Beowulf,* in the resonant ballad, a literalness of words need not throw rhetorical shadows or build dialectical castles. Given the theme, the words, carried in their appropriate rhythm, bear directly through a classic summation of a total condition. They are classic in the root sense, *normative*.

The words are *there*, if the life is there, the whole life of the hero. It can somehow be partial, or dimly focussed, and still come through. The action catches the feeling if it only tries to centralize itself through the feeling; the Cid, inarticulate, random, and materialistic, is nevertheless a whole and epic man, as every simple line asserts without turning one way or another to ask the hidden reason why.

CHAPTER TWO

The Signal Fires

THE *Cid, Roland, Beowulf,* as the names imply, center on the actions of a single hero. Heroic poems and ballads typically do so. The hero, in his adequacy before the known terms of his own world, attains a victory of the spirit before the unknown. The poem, in a sense, defines his adequacy. But by virtue of his central position in the poem, the solitary hero is conceived as someone who, in turn, completely fills out the world of the poem.

Now the term "epic" is popularly used to designate works quite different from those centering on a single hero. In loose common usage, the word "epic" suggests, in fact, just the opposite, a treatment not of one person but of vast numbers, diverse characters included in a panoramic sweep of various actions.

There is an epic poem which answers this description, the *Iliad.* Much of what has already been said of epic poems holds generically, and is then true of the *Iliad.* Its language is direct in a reader's immediate perception, and it remains so under stylistic analysis; it does, finally, offer a code. And at the same time it does have one predominant hero; the poem is quite explicit on this point, indicating the hero's anger as its subject in the very first line:

Sing, O goddess, the wrath of Achilles, son of Peleus

The *Iliad* is, of course, a larger poem than any so far discussed. And it measures the hero against a coordinated and panoramic world. For this reason, and for others, it has been taken as the epic *par excellence,* and also as a normative poem for the entire genre. It might then profitably be discussed, as I shall discuss it, at greater length than even its high intrinsic interest would proportionately recommend.

The *Iliad* is dominated, as Simone Weil[1] stresses, by force, by power. All the characters are subjected to it equally, and this central fact puts Achilles and Agamemnon, Hector and Priam, in a different perspective from Beowulf and the Cid. Beowulf has power, the Cid needs power. Each acts freely for it, alone and self-sufficient. In the *Iliad* no character, as Achilles learns, can be sufficient unto himself. The mortal condition involves a person in subjection to various networks of power.

Between the Trojans and the Achaeans the question of power has deadlocked them into a long-standing war. While among the horse-taming, long-gowned Trojans power is muted into near-harmony, the Achaeans do not have agreement about power. Instead, characteristically for them, a quarrel flares up about balance of power. This quarrel between warlike Achilles and ruling Agamemnon, drawing everyone in, serves as the poem's central action.

The two kinds of struggle for power, war and internal competition, themselves conflict, and tragically: Achilles' anger hurts the Achaeans' fighting strength. Through this conflict the poem brings the heroes to test their sense of immediate and ultimate purpose.

It is understood from the outset that power prevails. And it is war, not agriculture, that creates property-gathering power. Deprived of power, a person can fall out of the active ranks entirely and become property himself, a slave, with the brutal consequences Simone Weil spells out. Agamemnon, in his characteristic imprudence, flaunts these consequences before the priest Chryses:

> The girl I will not give back; sooner will old age come upon her in my own house, in Argos, far from her own land, going up and down by the loom and being in my bed as my companion.[2]
>
> (I, 29-31)

Chryses, racked with fatherly grief, still finds it in him to utter, as he offers Agamemnon ransom, a gratuitous speech of horripilating abasement: he hopes the gods may grant the plunder of Priam's city.

Chryses "felt terror" (*edeisen*) and went away alone along the shore, as the despoiled Achilles is shortly to do. Then he prays to invoke his own kind of power, the favor of Apollo. Power checks power, Apollo's pestilence strikes the Achaeans. When Agamemnon asks his own priest why, Calchas, a politician himself, is diplomatic enough to couch his answer in a way that defers to the ruler's power.

Power in battle is force, to use Simone Weil's word. In social structure it is rulership. In the world of things it is property. In the world of people it is freedom of movement. But the power (for which the poem has no single special word) is always one and the same, and the characters appear always in its hard epic light. Their complications arise from what power exacts. Calchas does not dare to address the powerful Agamemnon right away. In asking for Achilles' powerful protection, Calchas utters a maxim of diplomatic psychology which we might call remarkable if we were willing to blind ourselves enough to imply a condescension towards Homer:

> For a king when he is angry with a man beneath him is too
> strong,
> and suppose even for the day itself he swallow down his
> anger,
> he still keeps a grudge that remains until its fulfillment
> (I, 80-82)

These are the facts of power, and the poem keeps them always in view, never deviating to pay them special notice. It offers, consequently, an organization at once more complicated and more objectified than that of a drama, which brings special emphases of relationship to bear on its characters. Here all realize and react to the world of power in its many forms and manifestations. Calchas' opposition to Agamemnon is dwarfed by everyone's subjection to power (which Calchas fears to interpret). He calls, then, on Achilles, whose power is characteristically flattered at Calchas' request, as

Calchas characteristically intends. So Achilles oversteps himself in promising protection to Calchas.

Calchas, hearing the promise, "felt a heartening" (*etharse*). He tells the truth, leaning heavily on the word "priest"—his one open power gambit. Agamemnon, again, characteristically flaunts his power to curse Calchas, and flounders for a redress of his own power by taking Briseis in exchange for Chryseis. Then Achilles steps forth to initiate their quarrel. His speech uses, as it must, the vocabulary of property and power:

> Son of Atreus, most lordly (*kúdiste*), most loving of
> property (*philokteanotate*),   (I, 122)

In his advocacy, Achilles then presents a sound but imprudent principle: no scrap of property remains undivided among the powerful; if Agamemnon wishes more property before Troy is sacked, logic compels that he unjustly take it from someone else, though Achilles raises this last point with the greatest delicacy of deference:

> it is unbecoming for the people to call back things once given.
> (I, 126)

Agamemnon, though overwrought, never wholly forgets the prowess of the man he is addressing. His own speech, like Achilles', follows contours nervously determined by the central fact of the other's power. He proposes to take Achilles' prize—and then quickly brings in alternatives: he will take Ajax's or Odysseus's. Then he waves away the whole proposal uneasily by referring it to a later deliberation, using a plural verb so as to imply the advice of other powerful leaders. The verb itself (*meta-phrazo*) also implies some alteration of the conditions he has just stated. While he shows his power in the attempt to break the discussion off abruptly, he effectually readmits his guilt by naming the sacrifice Calchas had proposed. And he offers a final pride-swallowing reparation: Achilles alone is marvelous enough (*ekpaglotat'*) to have formal charge of Chryseis on her way back.

But the deadlock over power exceeds the capability of the heroes to cope with it. The quarrel is pitched further, and the great breach becomes an accomplished fact.

2

In the *Iliad,* for all its epic singleness of view, there exists at the same time a complexity of motive and complication of types undreamed of in *Beowulf* or the *Cid.* The singleness, and the complexity, are produced in the action, and yet there must be a principle in the action that relates each separate act to a central view, that provides each act at the same time with its own structure. Otherwise we would have no way of distinguishing the action of the *Iliad* from that in any haphazard metrical chronicle.

This principle is to be found in the perpetual contrast between people, and between events. The contrast, once presented, remains a steady ground for each confrontation; the poet is not obliged to deviate from the necessarily direct style of his verse in order to designate some special contrast.*

From the beginning, with powerless Chryses against powerful Agamemnon (priest against ruler), we are given contrast; and contrast holds all the way to the final encounter: Priam kissing the hands of man-slaying Achilles. At the very center of the poem stands a contrast—godlike, brilliant Achilles against wide-ruling Agamemnon. The warlike, bronze-greaved Achaeans are set against the long-gowned, horse-taming Trojans. Agamemnon and Nestor, Odysseus and Thersites, Menelaus and Alexander, Menelaus and Pandarus, Diomede and Glaucus, Hector and Andromache: the confrontations of the poem perpetually contrast them, bringing one situation into play against another, and another. When Helen from the wall points out the Grecian heroes to Priam, she may be called daughter-in-law against father-in-law; and at the same time she is

---

* I have discussed the contrasts of the *Iliad* to make another point in the final chapter of *The Dark Voyage and the Golden Mean* (Cambridge, 1949).

beautiful young woman against old man, stranger against native, victimizer against victim, guilty against the guiltless.

The designations of the scene permit all these interpretations; they are in the poem, not just in our sophisticated intelligences, which could not find them so omnipresently in the *Nibelungenlied* or the *Pharsalia*. Contrasts may be seen to reside in the smallest actions of the poem. When, for example, Agamemnon finally selects Odysseus for the sacrificial embassy to Chryses after choosing Achilles and suggesting Ajax, we immediately have the contrasts Agamemnon-Odysseus, Achilles-Odysseus, Odysseus-Ajax, Achilles-Ajax.

Always contrast, and always the single view. By virtue of Homer's single view, the contrasts can be multiplied indefinitely. We can extend them at will to ones not given in any action of the poem: Andromache-Helen, Priam-Nestor, Diomede-Sarpedon, Patroklos-Alexander. Or we need not confine ourselves to a given pair—Helen-Achilles, Priam-Agamemnon, Diomede-Ajax, Diomede-Alexander.

This omnipresence of contrast keeps a perpetual relation in view between one hero's destiny and another's, between the two warring peoples, and even between the actuality of imperfection on one hand—angry Achilles, overweening Agamemnon, the encompassing horror of war—and the implied possibility of perfection on the other—the pious warrior (we have Hector to contrast with Achilles), the just ruler (Priam implicitly shames Agamemnon), what is right and proper for man but never fully realized, the world of peace (glimpsed in the similes and in the Trojan scene).

Now these epic contrasts in the *Iliad* may be called ironic only loosely. Irony, by its very structure of saying or showing one thing and meaning another, refers to a rational norm, and it is usually comic. (The phrase "tragic irony" envisages tone and not schema.) The father of Jane Austen's Emma is slow-witted by contrast with her, and she is herself imperceptive till she realizes an always possible Austenian lovingkindness. No character of Stendhal's can do more

THE SIGNAL FIRES 55

than submit to irony, but the world is conceived as incongruous
(against an implied impossible ideal of congruity where love would
not be limited, and at the same time not be terrestrial love). Homer's
world is not incongruous: war, mortality, remain supreme congruities. And to exempt one's self like Achilles from these social
conditions, even if one is a prime fighter of divine origin, entails
isolating paradox. In irony, the ironic action counters the implied
norm: quick-wittedness is right for Emma, and her father's slow-
wittedness wrong. Cruelty is wrong to Stendhal, but one is incongruously forced to encounter it, even to use it. Laforgue's wistfulness
evokes a norm of sane potency for which he finds himself excru-
ciatingly inadequate.

In the *Iliad,* the contrasts do not counter a norm; and so are not
ironic. Taken together, they are themselves the norm, the very condition that totally defines man, the points that specify one man's
situation. For Menelaus to lose Helen goes with his nature, as for
Alexander to withdraw from battle. Helen, at the very moment she
wishes to repudiate Alexander, is driven into his arms by Aphrodite.
The contrast points to no incongruity; it opens up a complexity of
total contrast between eroticism and battle, where battle itself dis-
gusts the appetite it whets. Aphrodite enters the battle herself not
long afterward. Athene finds this inappropriate: the intellect makes
distinctions and finds love incongruous in war. But Aphrodite,
wounded as she is, faces her sister *philommeides,* laughter-loving.
We are not meant to read only irony into Aphrodite's smile: "I
the goddess of love remain serene even when I bleed" (we think
irresistibly of the goddess' smile on certain archaic statues). "You,
the Intellect, cannot possibly understand why I have fought." "Yes,
it is inappropriate for me to be wounded; you are right; I am the
smiling goddess of love and hereafter I will keep out of War's way."
The epithet does mean all this, but it also points a contrast that
lies beyond all these, to a central situation in which contrast is
itself the norm (and does not counter a norm, as in the irony of

drama, fiction and lyric poetry). Aphrodite, an immortal, carries on her total existence in this situation just as mortals do. The contrast keeps in the same epic perspective both the individual characteristics and the always present central condition, the epic whole that is more than its contrasting parts.

Moreover, the contrast implied by the irony in a novel always fixes on a single incident: Mr. Woodhouse is stupid specifically about the marriage of his daughter's friend, then about some other specific occasion. Mosca acts incongruously towards his mistress' husband (and at that point to no one else). But Homer's contrasts extend indefinitely. We may set Hector against Achilles. Or Priam-Hector against Peleus-Achilles. Or Andromache-Troy-Hector, against Briseis-Phthia-Achilles. And so on. The poem does not invite us to stop. The smile of Aphrodite shines beyond Athene, and beyond the wound, to take in war (and peace), earth (and Olympus) in its implied contrasts.

Thus every incident has an interest in itself. Every incident instances the common character of a pitched human enterprise, and at the same time it throws into relief the specificities of individual involvement. Consequently, as Schiller[3] observed to Goethe, every incident in the *Iliad* has its own interest, and we tend to dwell on it. We do so not, as Schiller thought, because suspense is at low pitch; the uninformed reader surely drives to the conclusion in this tale as in another. Every incident has its own interest because its uniqueness shares in creating the overall epic view. Nothing is merely incident. The language of the poem, like the conception of the poem, keeps it on the same level with every other incident. Every act, though the poem selects one for its center, is at once episodic and crucial, like the numerous small combats, episodic for the victor who moves on to another, but crucial for the vanquished whose eyes are covered with darkness. The central action of the poem, Achilles' anger, is episodic in the whole war, and yet also crucial to himself, to Hector, and ultimately to everyone.

3

Looked at for its relationships, the *Iliad* offers an irreducible complexity of multiple contrasts. Looked at for its focus, it appears to view the world singlemindedly as one. Between the complexity of their allegiances and the simplicity of their functions the heroes act. None of them, by virtue of this total commitment, can know more than the others, or be aware more than accidentally of what the others do not know. They act pitilessly in a sphere where privacy of motive, Hamlet's or Othello's or the Ancient Mariner's, would be as inconceivable in action as in the diction of the poem. Forbidden to be secretive, they must be fully consistent.

This epic world is a large one, but is closed, and everyone, from his own angle, shares in it totally.

In a tragedy each character has a world unto himself. Polonius' world makes sense: he is not an old fool but a great statesman in decay. Yet Hamlet and Laertes, and Ophelia, and Claudius, each perceive depths Polonius knows nothing of.

> There are more things in heaven and earth, Horatio,
> Than are dreamt of in your philosophy.

This statement might be uttered by almost any tragic character to any other. It is an impossible statement for a character in an epic to make, even in the complex *Iliad,* where everyone moves in the even light of a total human condition. No one there struggles in inner solitude through nodal and cumulative actions of partial participation. Everyone is totally implicated. Everyone knows this and assumes the knowledge. Each has, further, a situation, which he also knows, along with everyone else. And a character lives his type, which everyone knows and some even predict.

Consequently, no one in this poem is stupid: all that Thersites says, makes sense. Diomede's assumptions and Ajax's have often been called shallow; how can they be when they coincide with those

of Odysseus and Achilles? Odysseus surpasses them in adroitness
and Achilles in prowess, but neither in perception.

Modern critics, too, have often distorted Nestor, as others used
to distort Polonius. But once an allowance is made for Nestor's situation as an old man, his garrulity—never once checked, as Polonius'
is—becomes not a foible but a prerogative of his honor in the
Achaean camp. Far from being stupid or slow, he often shows himself to be alert and wise. For example, it is Nestor who seizes the
advantage of Agamemnon's contrition and at once suggests the
embassy to Achilles, naming as its three members the most politic
possible trio, performing on the spot the skillful diplomatic move
of seeming to choose them by hazard.

In the uniform world of the *Iliad*, even the supreme persons,
Achilles and Helen, are determined by the situations of the common
war. "The God of War is common to all" (*xunos Enyalios*, 18·309),
"and kills the killer."

Helen, the devotee of Aphrodite, weaves on her loom what?
Scenes from the Trojan war. We miss the point here if we read
this as an exclusive irony (these lovely, guilty hands weave into
delicate fabric the carnage her own flight has caused); it is simply
a contrast; there is nothing sardonic in it. Nor can we attribute to
Helen pride, obliviousness, or any of the other traits such a scene
might suggest in a novel. If we speak of her as proud about what
she weaves, how can we reconcile this with her consistent piety in
the poem, to Priam and Hector, about the sacrifice of the Trojans?
Say that she has run away from Menelaus, that she is half adopted
into the family of Priam, that Aphrodite both favors her and presses
her—and this is her "character." We are given not a structure of
motive, but a set of relations. And beyond this, a beauty and a
delicacy that she possesses much as Achilles possesses prowess. It is
no cause of *nemesis,* the old men say on the wall, that for a beauty
so dreadfully like a goddess', Trojans and Achaeans could endure

pains so long a time. The beauty exists through its effect—an effect defined, as always, by the War.

Single and dread, Helen is caught in the same stresses as everyone else. Her mystery, Yeats's

> Homer that was a blind man,
> And Helen has all living hearts betrayed.

—this springs from our imaginations, not Homer's. The *Iliad* offers only a pitiless situation in which a supernaturally beautiful woman causes a war she suffers from as much as anyone, while preserving a luxury that attests, as always, to her situation: she is beautiful as Achilles is strong.

In reading the poem, we want to sidetrack the combatant and give him a character of the sort of privacy we latter-day city dwellers admire. Ajax is "plain-spoken." Then he is stupid, we say, and draw unwarranted conclusions from the simile in which he is compared to an ass driven into a field, (though we know Homer's similes usually hold only for one point of comparison. And what ground have we for assuming that Greek asses are thought to be as stupid as English? In the Bible, the ass allegorizes duty, not stupidity.) Diomede exults and fights: then he is the youthful hero, and in his encounter with Glaucus we pretend he is grimly ironic.* But Diomede calmly accepts this way out for Glaucus, valuing the armor more than death. Perhaps he is also rather tired of fighting. If we think of him as exulting, Hector too exults. Idomeneus also likes to gather spoil.

So does Dolon, who collapses under the accustomed stress of a situation. A wealthy man's son, he is a confused boy rather than a

---

* Unless we read that episode for a friendly handshake on the battlefield. Which we cannot. For, a) Glaucus' garrulity, and his initial reference to the leaf-fall mortality of men, gives away his dread—b) the guest-friendship is so remote that were it to keep combatants apart, the battlefield would be a maze of avoided combats—c) the poet plainly says that Zeus took away Glaucus' wits to change gold armor for bronze.

traitor, but we cannot call Odysseus especially "cruel" to deceive him, any more than Idomeneus is unusually cruel to taunt Othrioneus, Cassandra's bridegroom, that the Greeks will provide him with a Greek bride. War itself is cruel. Odysseus is merely caught in his situation; he gropes to defend the ships; he has stayed up all night; and he is desperate for the information Dolon gives. No one is exempt from cruelty. The range from freezing (*rigein*) to sheer delight (*charme*) in response to battle is possible for any warrior.

It cannot be said, either, that Glaucus is a coward. When he faces Diomede, he begins speaking of mortality and continues, endlessly, about the largely irrelevant story of Bellerophon. The garrulity betrays fear at that moment, as his situation might well induce him to fear: Diomede has just wounded two immortals and has shown his *arete* as that day invincible.

Even Hector willingly calls a battle on account of darkness, though on many occasions the heroes fight far into the night. Sarpedon upbraids Hector for cowardice; the reproach neither characterizes Hector nor merely formalizes an injunction: it is always a situational possibility for someone that the pressure of battle will become intolerable. No one remains permanently a coward, and even Paris later enters the battle. Glaucus himself, racked with pain from a wound, prays later for Apollo to remove his pain so that he can go on fighting after Sarpedon's death.

We sum up Sarpedon by listing his relations: son of Zeus, a husband and father, owner of rich Lycian lands. But we cannot go so far as to say he is abnormally sensitive to the code of battle, by citing his injunction to Hector and his famous speech of justification to Glaucus. Ajax likewise urges as much. Anyone, in fact, might speak what Sarpedon voices, because all exist in an equal depth of awareness, a common assumption of duty.

How then are the types individuated? How can Achilles differ from Sarpedon, who is also the son of a God? From Hector, also the nonpareil of his people? How can Priam differ from Nestor?

A person's situation itself individuates him. An individual is simply typified by his set of circumstances. The implications of the circumstances remain objectively the same, but each set of circumstances is unique. Sarpedon is the son of a god, like Achilles, but he is not the chief hero of a people destined to be victorious. Hector, a chief hero, leads a people heavy with the foreknowledge of defeat. Priam is a patriarch defending his home, a fact which itself differentiates him from Agamemnon without reference to the "character" of each. Nestor differs from him in lacking so much command, as Phoinix differs from Nestor by having been the tutor of Achilles.

Even Agamemnon and Achilles, for all their depth, are defined by their situational reactions to the complex, uniform epic code. The type gains its permanence against the uniform background. In a tragedy no such permanence exists, only struggle; Oedipus at Colonus is changed from Oedipus the king; he is led by an Antigone milder than the woman at the center of another play. But even Achilles does not change; he is only pressed superhumanly to exhibit the man-transcending structure of his type. Between Menelaus and Falstaff, Helen and the Wife of Bath, the Andromache of Homer and the Andromaque of Racine, lies the gulf of individuality. However closely you look at the Homeric characters, you cannot see individuality, though complexity of situation is apparent even in the smallest characters, Othrioneus and Medon, or Axylos in the one brief passage about him:

> Teuthras' son, who had been a dweller in strong-founded
>   Arisbe,
> a man rich in substance and a friend to all humanity
> since in his house by the wayside he entertained all comers.
>   (VI, 13-15)

"Friend" (*philos*) and "entertained" (*phileesken*) have the same root. Was Axylos mild, or equanimous, or kind, or sociable, perhaps even idle or over-confidential? The personal trait is lost in the amical function. The friendliness exhibits no nuance. It possesses the character almost of an epithet: "man-befriending" Axylos. The poem holds him to his exterior, he is his reputation, a distinct enough one for all the shortness of its presentation; and then he becomes like all the others who die in battle.

The two cardinal rules of dramatic speech are reversed in this epic, as in others; truths spoken anywhere in the *Aeneid,* the *Divine Comedy, Paradise Lost,* are general truths. In a play a speech holds only for the character, and only for the moment of utterance. Hamlet's questioning "to be or not to be" is limited by his particular character and by the scene, and circumstances, when it occurs. But every speech in the *Iliad* holds for the society as well as the speaker; even Thersites speaks permanently valid sense. And every speech holds generally, not just for the moment of utterance, but for any equivalent set of circumstances. The situation must change in a play: the play presents the change. In the *Iliad* the situation unfolds; but it is given, by fate, by decree of Zeus, and by the bearings of the characters. And so any speech, insofar as it offers general principles, applies to the whole epic universe. Hector, or any other hero, when the *charme* of lustful delight in battle is upon him, will feel himself equal to all his enemies, even Achilles. Odysseus' capping challenge in the embassy to Achilles is not only diplomatic: it is true.

Character does not determine a man's acts, but once again, situation does. The Hector who knows well that Ilium will fall is the same Hector who, in another situation, lights fires across the Trojan plain so the Achaeans may not steal away in their ships. Would he not seek their departure above all, rather than prevent it, if he knows they must win? Has he forgotten his own prophecy of doom? (But the very word "forget"—*lanthano,* does not carry our implications of cloudy imperceptions in the head. The Homeric hero does not think with his head but with his chest, as Onians[4] points out. *Lanthano* does not have the subjective nuances of "forget"; it can also mean "escape the notice of.") Hector is not inconsistent to prophesy doom at one moment and to light the fires at another; the two situations differ.

4

In the *Iliad* Homer has achieved a single view of a complex world, and he has done so through a verse style that is notable for its limpidity. The techniques of lyric analysis, again, will not serve to show how so transparent a style could render and unify such coordinated complexities. Homer stands at the head of the longest tradition of epic poetry, and his exemplary character appears nowhere so pronouncedly as in the style of his verse. Not that Vergil or Milton could adapt that style to their own purposes; Apollonius, among numerous others, had tried to do so and failed.

Homer's style possesses the attributes of any epic style: it is in its own way direct, and it is based on a simple rhythmic line which has not been precisely calibrated for small effects. In these characteristics it resembles the style of the *Cid,* the *Chanson de Roland, Beowulf,* and others. Beyond them, however, it has managed a much larger range of meaning, a finer ring of tone, a still loftier central conception. To see how he has managed to present all this in a style that is seemingly even simpler than any of these will take a great deal of deliberate critical discussion.

Otherwise we would be left with some shadow of Milman Parry's inadmissible principle of virtual equivalence among "oral" styles. "One oral poet is better than another," Parry says, "not because he has by himself found a more striking way of expressing his thought but because he has been better able to make use of the tradition."[5] But Homer has found a striking way of expressing his thought, because poems do have a meaning. How else could he have made a "better use" of the tradition to which Parry has opened all our eyes?

Being oral in origin, the style of Homer is rapid enough to carry the narrative along pointedly, and it is simple enough to allow its statements to be made without strain by a speaking voice. Its words and syntax have an initial plainness and directness.

These terms—rapidity, plainness and directness of thought and diction—have been provided, of course, by Matthew Arnold.[6] It remains to ascertain what is described by terms that, in effect, merely praise the quality of Homer's style. Finally we shall have to ascertain that attribute which lies at the heart of Arnold's four, "nobility." A newspaper account (to say nothing of Rieu's *Odyssey*) may be plain and rapid; only a great poet can be both, and noble at the same time. Homer is the only poet who so notably embodies all three attributes, with the possible exception of Dante. *Beowulf,* if noble, is certainly not rapid and in a sense not plain. The style of the *Cid* is plain and rapid, and also noble, but of a nobility far inferior to Homer's.

Nobility is of the Homeric essence; it may not be spoken of before some measure of his poetic world has been taken. We may begin by asking what distinguishes his plainness from, say, that of *Roland;* his rapidity from, say, that of the *Cid.*

Homer works with formulae, as Milman Parry shows us, and these formulae are surely far more elaborate than any the Anglo-Saxon or the Old French poet could have known. The formulae, too, have a fixity to them, and they fill out, or tend to fill out, much of a line in which they occur. Once "Achilleus" or "Troias" or "Diomedes" is placed at a given point in the line, only one epithet, usually, will serve, *dios,* or *chalkochitonas* or *boen agathos.*

The poet, then, binds himself when he chooses, but before he chooses the name, he is free to place it at any point in the line: he is free also to use an epithet or not. Crowding at the poet are the constant numerous possibilities of formulation, more fully fixed than were mere words, but equally disposable. The possibilities, we may imagine, crowd at his memory, and one can feel his mastery of that crowding by the very complexity of the story. How many facets may be picked up at any point of a many faceted story! At the beginning of the *Iliad,* we can almost feel Homer striving to get it all in and yet keep it all in one place.

Both simplicity and rapidity may be seen as a consequence of the poet's use of the formulae. The single line is set to one of several simple possibilities, and the one chosen keeps the line going on a limited course. The formula clicks in the memory, creating matrices of identity in the mind of the hearer. The formula is a vast simplifying device, resembling rhyme because the formula is tied to a given rhythmic possibility and thus constitutes an echo at a fixed point in the line. The formula also resembles a refrain—somewhat as a fugue resembles a round, though the formula's complexities of variation are even farther from the simplicities of the refrain than the two musical forms are from each other. But the poem does not structure itself fugally: only one formula comes at a time; each one can fully echo only itself and partially echo only those other formulae that use part of its sound (the same metrical length) or part of its sense (the same name). This amounts to a rhythmic and syntactical simplicity (as well as to a subtlety and delicacy of effect in the hands of a master like Homer): the refrain-like echo is always simpler than the manifold verbal possibilities that may fill out a given portion of hexameter. So two effects are felt to underlie the newness of the particular poetic sentence: the familiarity of a syntactic combination whose twin or cousin we have met before, and also a rhythmic recurrence (*nephelegereta Zeus* almost equals *ekaergos Apollon*) which produces a more striking identity than the always underlying similarity of one hexameter to the next.

Formulae also speed the movement of the poetry, linking it in larger units than the word alone would; the formulae act on the cadences much as a slope acts on a river: they allow it to flow faster. Nor do they hold it up at all, for the formula differs from any syntactic pattern in the crucial trait of not requiring a pause to distinguish it, while clauses and other syntactic units must be marked by pause to be recognized in their separability within the pattern. The ear takes the words of a formula together, in short, but there is no pause to make the ear keep them apart. We have a quickening effect, the union, with no corresponding rhythmic deterrent. This rapidity seems to reside in the very syntax, but it actually derives from the syntactic function of the formula. As for his syntax generally, Homer is a poet far less paratactic than the Hebrew poets of the Bible, and at the same time he is far swifter in his movement.

Moreover, the formulaic epithet is simple as well as rapid, because it emphasizes recurrent features. Herder asserts that early poetry generally does this, written as it is in a language young enough to keep excited at merely naming a sheep as "the bleating one," an Agamemnon as "the ruling one," ships as "dark-prowed." But Homer gets beyond Herder's primitive naming of obvious features: ships are no more obviously dark-prowed than the sea is wine-dark or the dawn rosy-fingered, and for an audience of men who have never met him, Diomede is not obviously "good at the war cry." The poet, in receiving his epithets, must relate them to his overall conception just because he must use them over and over again, because they refer to a single, recurrent feature, and also because some of them may have arisen in the convention as a naming of the obvious.

A kind of objective neutrality resides in the simple matter-of-factness of the individual elements in Homer's acts of naming, his words. In this neutrality, they lie more conveniently to hand for the poem's particular coordination of its presented world, for the epic *Gliederung*, to use Holthusen's term for the relation among the parts of an epic poem.* The overall scheme stands out more clearly from the point-for-point references when those references, the words of Homer, are not themselves worked up for the special rhetorical effects of lyric. Choosing among given elements of meaning, the poet achieves the great, but simple, leap from a simple, transparent naming to a larger-scale coordination, with little intermediate effort of emphasis. Instead of pressing for effect, he chooses matter-of-factly from a neutral vocabulary, whose sole slanted terms are the epithets. And any discussion of the unanswerable question as to whether or not Homer invented those must be posited on the

---

* "*Wenn die dramatische Darstellung das Sein der Welt in seiner Entzweiung, die epische es in seine Gliederung zeigt, im Gedicht wird die Welt geschworen als das Eine . . ."*[7]

phantom of an epic poet proceeding by lyric methods, opting for this or that lyric effect. Actually, invented or not, the epithets, by their very recurrence, assimilate easily to the neutrality of mere direct designation.

Initially Homer's diction itself is simple, operating on one level. If we look back, with the help of recent commentators, at the special properties his diction possesses, we may visualize what at their inception may have been the problems of style and composition he faced. For a style implies a diction; a style in the epic tradition implies a diction both traditional and poetic without prettification or undue rhetorical preselection.

A style itself consists of words, of certain words habitually found in certain kinds of order. Words come to mind only when they exist, and they exist only to say what has already been designated or thought. The poet will probably extend his language; he begins with it as it is. Bruno Snell[8] and more recently Max Treu[9] have found Homer's diction governed by his world view. Snell proceeds by distinguishing certain assumptions of Homer from our own, and he has made it clear, as critics from Vico to Owen Barfield had indicated, that distinctions we habitually make do not exist for him with quite the clarity that they do in our language.

First, Homer's words do not imply for their referents an unequivocal distinction between concrete and abstract, or between visible and non-visible. Helios means at once the sun, visible to the eye, and the god, in all the coordinated complexity of his various functions; just as for the primitive mind and language of, say, the Indian of Vedic times, the *fire agni* and the god *Fire Agni* are one and the same (and of course neither Vedic Sanskrit nor Homeric Greek uses the difference between capital and small letters). Men themselves, too, possess powers which are not distinguished as concretely physical or abstractly intellectual. Onians can make a strong case for the very functions of the mind in Homer's world as being essentially physical attributes. But while οἶδα, φρονέειν, θυμός, φρένες, and ψυχή have a physical effect we ignore in the modern words used to translate them, it would be a mistake to make, as Onians does, the contrary assumption that these expressions in Homer are primarily physical. They are "concrete" and "abstract" at once. In Snell's words, "Diese Seelenorgane unterscheiden sich nicht prinzipiell von den Koerperorganen."[10]

In Homer's Greek, which in one sense constantly presents abstract ideas, there has emerged no really clear-cut division between concrete and abstract—a simplicity and directness which, to a master, pose problems of style as difficult as those of a more complex civilized diction. Homer does not have to bypass such fixed categories of idea as concrete and abstract, but neither can he assume them: he must half-create them.

Homer had to contend with, or make poetry out of, another simplicity in his diction, the lack of terms that imply a distinction between general qualities and particular. As Snell points out, there is no Homeric word for a body before it becomes a corpse ($\sigma\hat{\omega}\mu\alpha$) beyond the "form" ($\delta\acute{\epsilon}\mu\alpha\varsigma$), as Aristarchus interpreted $\delta\acute{\epsilon}\mu\alpha\varsigma$ in his scholia. And Homer's substitute for our own general word, Snell goes on to show, designates the body only under particular aspects: $\gamma\upsilon\hat{\iota}\alpha$, the limbs in so far as they move, $\mu\acute{\epsilon}\lambda\epsilon\alpha$, the limbs in so far as they have muscular force. $X\rho\hat{\omega}\varsigma$, again, denotes skin as the limit of the body; and $\delta\acute{\epsilon}\rho\mu\alpha$, the skin as something that can be stripped off. So there is no general word for seeing, Snell asserts, only various modes ($\acute{o}\rho\hat{\alpha}\nu$, $\acute{\iota}\delta\hat{\epsilon}\hat{\iota}\nu$, $\lambda\epsilon\acute{\upsilon}\sigma\sigma\epsilon\iota\nu$, $\acute{\alpha}\theta\rho\epsilon\hat{\iota}\nu$, $\theta\acute{\epsilon}\alpha\sigma\theta\alpha\iota$, $\sigma\kappa\acute{\epsilon}\pi\tau\epsilon\sigma\theta\alpha\iota$, $\acute{o}\sigma\sigma\epsilon\sigma\theta\alpha\iota$, $\delta\acute{\epsilon}\rho\kappa\epsilon\sigma\theta\alpha\iota$, $\pi\alpha\pi\tau\alpha\acute{\iota}\nu\epsilon\iota\nu$).

It can be demonstrated, I believe, that even the most general words in Homer do not leave particularity behind. Even *Arete* we see through Aristotle's generalizing eyes. Adkins[11] reads competitiveness into Homer's *Arete,* and I would specify that *Arete* in the *Iliad* is always reducible to what the Homeric language understood not as general excellence, but as the particular sort of comparative prowess for one specific contest which we designate by the way we give odds on race horses for a given race, or seed tennis players for a

given match.* In all its uses of *Arete*, the *Iliad* offers no evidence
for interpreting it in a later sense as a pronouncedly general quality,
except in the negative way that Homer is not restricting himself to
the particularity which he implies; particularity can only be understood by contrast to generality, and Homer, who seems more "particular" with the word than we might be, is not dealing with words
that have jelled in their generality.

The point is an elusive one. To see how it affects the action of
the poem, we might consider the word *prophasin* in the striking
passage about Briseis' speech mourning Patroklos (XIX, 301-2):

Ὥς ἔφατο κλαίουσ', ἐπὶ δὲ στενάχοντο γυναῖκες,
Πάτροκλον πρόφασιν, σφῶν δ' αὐτῶν κήδε' ἑκάστη.

So she spoke, lamenting, and the women sorrowed around her
grieving openly for Patroklos, but her own sorrows each.

The modern reader is likely to take this for a striking psychological aperçu: the women mourn their own captivity, on the "pre-

---

* Even if we reject, with Boisacq,[12] the etymological connection between
ἀρετή and ἀρείων, ἄριστός; one particular case, this comparative notion of excellence can be seen to underlie all the occurrences of the word in the *Iliad*. For
example, in XV, 642 the word is used in the plural for the explicitly comparative
superiority of son to father in battle. In IX, 498, it expresses the superiority of
the gods over men, again with the comparative. In XX, 411 Priam uses it of
Hector's running speed, when in the previous line he has said that Hector can
run faster than all his other sons.

In XXIII, 571 it is used in a way that sounds general, but in a speech about
comparative prowess in a specific contest, where Antilochus has won by unfair
advantage; and in his next, shortly recurring use of the word, Menelaus makes
the comparative explicit (578). In XI, 90 the Danaoi turned the tide of a day's
battle: by their superiority (not "manhood" as Lattimore translates *Arete*) they
broke the battalions.

In XXII, 268 Achilles asks Hector to remember all his *Arete*, i.e., his highest
prowess, for this specific occasion. For, by the maxim of XX, 242:

Ζεὺς δ' ἀρετὴν ἄνδρεσσιν ὀφέλλει τε μινύθει τε,

In XI, 763 Nestor says, speaking of the comparative prowess of earlier days,
that Achilles will enjoy his *Arete* alone—a statement, as I interpret it, intentionally ironic, for there must be at least two contestants to prove *Arete*.

So the uses in VIII, 535; XIII, 237, 275, 277; XIV, 118; XXIII, 276 all
clearly have the comparative prowess of a specific contest in view.

text" (*prophasin*), of weeping for Patroklos. Leaf, however, follow-ing Heyne, reads *prophasin* not as false reason but as true:

> This passage has often been admired as an instance of truth to nature—a pretended lamentation for a stranger covering the expression of a real sorrow. Heyne, however, is not without justification in calling it "acumen a poeta nostro alienum." He is inclined therefore to take *prophasin* in the sense attrib-uted to it in 262, of a *real* cause; the grief for Patroklos is not a mere blind to cover what the women dare not express other-wise, but a grief really felt which arouses other and deeper sorrows of their own, exactly as in 338-9.[13]

Leaf's statement is penetrating, so penetrating in fact that it has almost led him back to the position he is controverting. In explaining the word, he is forced into spelling out a psychological complexity just as alien to the world of Homer as that he follows Heyne in rejecting. Turning to the other passage he cites, 262, the only other occurrence of the word in the *Iliad,* we find:

οὔτ᾽ εὐνῆς πρόφασιν κεχρημένος οὔτε τευ ἄλλου.

> that I have never laid a hand on the girl Briseis
> on pretext to go to bed with her, or for any other
> reason.

In Homer's world the "reality" or relative truth of the *prophasis,* the "pretext," cannot possibly be at issue. Agamemnon is disclaiming neither an honest nor a specious reason about Briseis, nor are the women in the other passage weeping either honestly or speciously for Patroklos. *Prophasis* will later take on the connotation "pretext" but here it is wrenching either passage to opt either for or against the Leaf-Heyne reading. Bed or Patroklos, these are simply the par-ticular circumstances Agamemnon would adduce or speak for (*pro-phan*) if asked, without any reference to whether or not he means what he says.

To express this critically is difficult, even if we remember that to read *prophasis* as a "noun" is itself half an Alexandrian idea. One could equally well read it as something like a preposition governing the genitive.

Returning to the passages, we find their immediacy of psychological freshness heightened rather than impaired by Homer's failure to provide for *prophasis* more of a general context of distinction than he provides for *Arete*. The women weep for Patroklos. And they also weep for their own cares. They weep for Patroklos ensemble, the plural verb: but for their own cares each individually, the singular pronoun. Homer's language in its particularity will not allow us to go any farther than that.

Of course Homer in a sense, by his very use of class words, does imply what for us would be a general notion. It is not so for him, however, because no classification is implied. *Eris* can be a particular quarrel, or it can be a force of quarrelling that moves in the train of Ares. Never is it the general idea of strife which it becomes for Empedocles. If there is one idea of it in the poem, we apply it from the poem to the word, not from the word to the poem: Homer may well have left Greek more abstract than he found it. As it is, all his "abstract" words have a ring of semi-concreteness and semi-particularity about them. They can occur in the singular or the plural almost indifferently; *eridas* occurs also in the plural (*eridas kai neikea,* II, 376), a use which becomes rare in later Greek.

Inheriting a vocabulary that is hazy at distinguishing between general and particular, leaves the bard faced with a diversity in his language which, from our point of view, he can unite only by making a coherent view of reality. Homer's problem is, in one way, exactly the opposite of the modern poet's; modern language diversifies into concrete and abstract, Homer unifies; and on the other hand, where it unifies particulars under an implied general heading, he offers an irreducible diversity.

The immediacy arrived at from the simple "identification" of concrete and abstract, general and particular, sets all the words in Homer's diction on a single level. Homer, more than Dante, creates here a *dolce stil nuovo,* where the language works closer to our ordinary designative prose—even than does the prose of fiction.

Moreover, in later poets, the literary history of the words weighs on them with a depth of association. In the *Iliad* nothing more than a simple, traditional, oral significance lies in the words. And the epic building blocks, the formulae of tradition, function in this regard like longer words, shiftable units of single designation.

How Homer's style differs from others' may be seen by looking at Vergil's stylistic adaptations of his received language. Here, for example, Palinurus is about to drop off to sleep:

> *cum levis aetheriis delapsus Somnus ab astris*
> *aëra dimovit tenebrosum et dispulit umbras.*
>
> (*Aeneid* v, 838-9)

Of course, Vergil is more stylized, more "sophisticated" than Homer. This stylization arises from an elaborate deployment of words in their ordonnance that arises from a skillful management of their histories. Vergil, as a post-Alexandrian, cannot, to begin with, handle belief in the gods with the candor possible to a simply believing Homer. And so he cannot handle *Somnus* other than "lightly," avoiding the facile solutions of Ovid, who limits himself as a poet by being too serious towards the Gods (*Fasti*) or too artificial (*Metamorphoses*). *Aether,* like its companion *aër* in the next line, comes to Vergil as a word existing in a poetic diction, with overtones of the Alexandrian astronomers and of Plato, not to speak of the pre-Socratic philosophers who first began, in poetry, to give a technical direction to these terms. *Levis,* in its ordered juxtaposition from *aetheriis,* retains a hint of its usage in classical physics; but it is, we may suppose, mainly a colloquial term. *Aetherius* displays, as a near anthimeria with *astra,* in syntax as in history, its relation to a series of high and largely foreign (Greek) usages; and the rhetoric is continued in the deft half-chiasmus which overstylizes the verbal connections in the next line (*aëra dimovit . . . et dispulit umbras*).

The verbs of motion become generalized here by the very usualness of habitual association: one always *dispulit umbras* and *dimovit aera; Somnus* always *delabit.* One can even see a highly stylized repetition-with-variation of the compounding verbs, close enough to echo one another as they are here coupled syntactically in the controlled coordination of the clause where they appear (*de*lapsus, *di*movit, *dis*pulit). The words in their heavy associativeness are made through a superbly thorough ordonnance to support the rhythms, and so to create Vergil's special, marvelously artistic, sculpturesque effect: *levis-aetheriis, aetheriis-delapsus, delapsus-Somnus, Somnus ab astris; aetheriis* distant from *astris* as *levis* from *Somnus.*

Such combinations of ordonnance, again, become possible because the very complexities of the words, taken singly, in their probably colloquial and certain literary associations, will bear such interplay. Without the overtones, such deployment of words would seem trivially arbitrary.

Dante, similarly, writing in a young Italian, introduces nonetheless a world of philosophical, theological, biblical, and even classical associations, when he combines the words *voluntade* and *pace:*

> *in la sua voluntade è nostra pace*

The interplay here is all in the line, the sculpture of Vergil reduced to a linearity whose simplicity, because of the considerable overtones of the words, remains Vergilian rather than Homeric. The poem, through the resonance of the words, reaches up and out from the verbal categories to the anagogic condensation it took him his whole life to achieve.

On the other hand, it increases the stature, and the poetic immediacy of Achilles, to see, as Homer's style shows us, that Achilles is subject not to some generalized *hybris,* but to a *menis,* a particular anger, as we would say, on a particular occasion. The characters in the *Iliad,* the immediate style indicates, are never responding to any theory of action such as is supposed by writers about Homeric soci-

eties. Their action rises out of the poem that views it, in the very
words of its style, as immediately, simply, and nobly, as Sarpedon
phrases to Glaucus—but does not in our sense formulate—his "motive" for entering this great imagined battle.

The particular limpidity of Homer's verbal sequences would seem
to be incapable of the grandeur attained by Vergil's frieze-like juxtapositions, or by the structured simplicity of Dante. And we should
expect the poetic effect of Homer, if a limpidity, to present its poetic
effects only in the mass like Spenser, or Claudel, poets notably limpid. We do not expect a limpid style to be capable of intense grandeur; or, in Arnold's terms, a rapidity of thought and movement
would seem, when combined with simplicity, to exclude "nobility."
Swiftness is most compatible with nobility in our stylistic expectations through such dense, complex lyric flashes as Pindar's.

Homer remains swift in his simplicity, and noble in his conception,
even when he most apparently manages his characteristic effect of
close momentary precision, as in these four lines from a passage near
the beginning of Book XXI:

> Meanwhile the other half
> were crowded into the silvery whirls of the deep-running river
> and tumbled into it in huge clamour, and the steep-running
> water
> sounded, and the banks echoed hugely about them, as
> they out-crying
> tried to swim this way and that, spun about in the eddies.

> ἡμίσεες δὲ
> ἐς ποταμὸν εἰλεῦντο βαθύρροον ἀργυροδίνην,
> ἐν δ' ἔπεσον μεγάλῳ πατάγῳ, βράχε δ' αἰπὰ ῥέεθρα,
> ὄχθαι δ' ἀμφὶ περὶ μεγάλ' ἴαχον· οἱ δ' ἀλαλητῷ
> ἔννεον ἔνθα καὶ ἔνθα, ἑλισσόμενοι περὶ δίνας.   (7-11)

The narrative line of the poem has carried it to this pitch; and
without the larger coordinated motions of the war, the description
of confusion here would be effective on a merely literal level. The

particularity of different kinds of sounds (παταγός, βράχω, ἰάχω, ἀλαλητός) gets a realistic grandeur from the fluid lack of implied comparison among them—the sort of comparison a modern stylistic critic would be tempted to see here. The extraordinarily rapid succession of sounds is a confusion which, if we look at it closely, becomes a fine and immediate sequence of momentary precisions. The reaction of the frightened troops arises from the pure moment of action, like the violence of Achilles. The deep swell of the river (βαθύροον), threatening only in the future, is followed in the description by a bright light, the silver eddy (ἀργυροδίνην). In a modern poet this would be a contrast of beauty (silver) against force (swell). But here each effect is purely momentary, and the language moves, for all the poem's larger contrasts, without smaller ones, from particular moment to particular moment. The sound of the man's armor at the moment is that of "things striking together" (παταγός [Autenrieth]),[14] in a pulsation [Ebeling].[15] Then in the water comes a different sound, (βράχω), one of a particular thin-echoing sharpness, not associated with the sound of metal but only with its pure auditory effect, and so "a word whose applications are difficult to reconcile" according to Autenrieth (applied variously to armor, axle, river, earth, doom). The poet's excited caesurae follow the seeming confusion closely. A new sound—(ἰάχω)—then seems to emerge from the edge of the solid banks (ὄχθαι), and becomes like the παταγός, μεγαλὰ; but now it appears in the neuter as an adverb, and so impersonalized (though presumably of shrieking persons). The word ἰάχω, again, is confusing to the modern lexicographer when applied, in Cunliffe's[16] list, to people, bowstrings, trumpet, hot iron in water, and fire; but it probably conveyed a precise indication of what the ear took in, a sound perhaps higher in pitch, more plangent, and more piercing than παταγός.

If plangent, the plangency changes. The troops that gave off παταγός as they entered the water, βράχω as they sank, and ἰάχω as they disappeared by implication behind the banks, now give off a yell, (ἀλαλητός); the reduplication suggests (as we still preserve it in the English word) an ululating yell, when, the next word tells us, they swim caught in the now plural and noun-formed eddies.

Since the consummate poet Homer, unlike the sometimes clumsy stylist who wrote *Beowulf,* almost never lapses into redundance, we may remark that ἀμφὶ and περὶ in the third line here are not redundant; and the repetition of ἔνθα here has the effect of noting, through a verbal identity, the levelling off of violent reactions; as, coming next to each other, ἀμφὶ and περὶ mirror immediately, in their succession, the very height of the confusion. 'Αμφὶ goes mainly with banks, περὶ mainly with ἰάχω.* Each has its particular momentary associations: 'Αμφὶ sees "about" from the point of view of something with two sides (which banks have), περὶ from the point of view of a circumference taken in by an eye perhaps just barely imagined, a supposed spectator.

In examining the compositional practices which Homer's particularity of vocabulary left open to him, I am implying not that he is formless, but the contrary. He must continually, word by word, or set phrase by set phrase, keep his action significant, and the existence of his action on a single, immediate plane demands that the poetic statements about the action do not simply embroider it; the style must present the action directly with the poetic content already distilled: so that one has the sense of the poet selecting one of several possible conjunctions from a verbal plethora, or as Homer puts it in another connection:

> στρεπτὴ δὲ γλῶσσ᾽ ἐστὶ βροτῶν, πολέες δ᾽ ἔνι μῦθοι
> παντοῖοι, ἐπέων δὲ πολὺς νομὸς ἔνθα καὶ ἔνθα.

The tongue of man is a twisty thing, there are plenty of
  words there
of every kind, the range of words is wide, and their variance.

(Iliad, XX, 248-9)

---

* Though, of course, it is a grammatical fiction to think of it as a "separable" prefix with ἰάχω; it could equally be called a separate adverb sometimes joined directly to the verb, and forming the so-called verb περι ιαχω—and Chantraine in his *Grammaire Homérique*[17] states that often these alternatives are indistinguishable.

To see Homer so does not impoverish him, it enriches him. It enables us to read the quick and flow of his action word by word—*entha kai entha;* "here, and here"—poetically.

5

In an epic poem, the hero tests the limits of a world that is alike for all in his society, and known to all, a stable world. The language of the poem evokes this stability in its directness, and also in its tendency to use formulaic phrases which remind the hearer through their recurrence that the elements in the presented action are likewise recurrent.

In ballads we have refrains, in *Beowulf* the *kennings,* and also such formulaic phrases as "Beowulf spoke, the son of Ecgtheow." In the *Cid* we have formulaic phrases now and then: "My Cid who was born in a good hour." In the *Chanson de Roland,* the burden of recurrent statement is carried by the near-refrains. In the more complex world of the *Iliad,* we should expect some feature of recurrence in the style correspondingly more ramified in its effect than any of these. This we do have, as Milman Parry has shown us, in the great stock of formulaic phrases which Homer presumably inherited from his tradition and out of which he very largely built his poem. Most pronounced among these formulae are the epithets, stable elements in the stable world of the epic poem, as Staiger[18] calls them.

If a god, or a man, or the sea, the city or a cliff, stands out momentarily, it gets designated by one of its known outstanding traits: ox-eyed Hera, ruling Agamemnon, the wine-faced sea, holy Ilion, the hard-to-scale cliff.

The formulae are adjustable. Gods and men, and the sea, city and cliff, may stand without epithet, or may get some other epithet. In their adjustableness, the epithets resemble other words, ready at hand in the poet's known language. But they are more fixed than ordinary words; they are fewer, longer, and more complex than other words; and they are quite limited in their range of possible attachment, while other words have all the freedom the laws of the language permit.

The epithets, then, are adjustable, but only within the limits afforded by the configured world of the poem. Since the configuration of the poem appoints the limits of the epithet, the epithet itself suggests in its very use the poem's configuration. Of course in a less configured poem—in any oral epic but Homer's—they would be less configured. And Homer's originality appears not in choosing them, for he may well have got them all ready-made from his tradition (or may well not). His originality consists in configuring them —a poetic task of a higher degree than that of inventing them.

The adjustableness of the epithet allows the poet to make the configurations fit without providing a special syntactical or rhetorical combination. So the epithet helps keep the poem simple: the structure never gets more than linear at one moment. And the epithet, in its singleness of reference, reminds of its recurrence without binding the language to structural reminders of the recurrence; so it speeds the movement of the poem. The epithet typifies in its naming; at the same time it remains plain and direct: the types remain those configured in the action of the poem.

Even when it seems to evaluate, the epithet, we may presume, deals with an attribute that is conceived of as existing in the object prior to the naming. When Homer calls the Ethiopians "blameless" (whatever *amumon* may designate exactly!), he does not hit on the designation by a felicitous personal insight, as Shakespeare designates England "this demi-paradise." In a language that does not distinguish clearly between concrete and abstract, "blameless" exists on the same plane as "shadowy." Or to put it in Kantian terms, all attributions made by Homeric poetry, including the epithets, are something like analytic judgments—of the type "the table is solid," and not synthetic judgments—of the type "the table is beautiful." In lyric poetry, on the other hand, one could define all attributions as synthetic—

Thou still unravish'd bride of quietness,
Thou foster-child of silence and slow time,
Sylvan historian . . .

Not only the metaphor of "bride" and the trope of "sylvan historian,"
but every word in its role as a rhetorical choice—"thou," "still"—
builds one synthetic judgment into another. Homer, contrastingly,
works with an analytic language in which everything said is traditional, taken for granted and predigested.

An object in the Homeric world—and in the world where there
are no firmed abstractions everything named may be regarded as an
object, even a Destructive Dream sent by Zeus—may be thought of
as faceted with many stable attributes. In this the object resembles
the Homeric hero, faceted with the points of his situation (father,
son, warrior on the losing side, husband of rescued woman, brother
of war-cause: Hector). And it also resembles the Homeric event,
faceted in its multiple and stable contrasts.

Even less than the kenning does the epithet encompass the whole
object. The kenning picks an attribute: whale-path. And that *is* the
ocean. But the epithet is an adjective, not a substantive. It merely
modifies. So we have "the barren ocean" at one time, and "the wine-
faced sea" at another. Epithets in Homer are far commoner than
kennings in *Beowulf,* and they shade off into mere adjectives (is
stugeros, "hateful," in the phrase "hateful darkness," an adjective or
an epithet?). In the half-lines of *Beowulf,* the verse-unit dwells on
the kenning. But in the long impetus of the hexameter, the epithet
crops up as it comes along, usually as the verse is rounding out.

Of the attributes that the epithet may momentarily fix on, it chooses
the one determined by the situation of the moment. For Homer does
choose and place his epithets, Milman Parry notwithstanding.* One

* Parry has shown that Homer's epithets are metrically unique, or nearly so.
Therefore, he argues, at a given place in the line only one epithet will fit. To
interpret an epithet as if it were chosen in place of another (when there is no

can always interpret the epithet Homer has chosen for its congruities in the poem, and the epithet will always bear our scrutiny. Take, for example, the beginning of Book Sixteen:

> So they fought on both sides for the sake of the strong-
> benched vessel.
> Meanwhile Patroklos came to *the shepherd of the people*
> Achilles
> and stood by him and wept warm tears like a spring
> dark-running
> that down the face of a rock impassable drips its dim water;
> *and swift-footed brilliant* Achilles looked on him in pity,
> and spoke to him aloud and addressed him in winged words.

At the point of the second line Patroklos is seeking relief and guidance. The pastoral image fits, and fits better than would the more glorious epithets applied to Agamemnon, because Achilles leads a smaller group and regards them more modestly.

Patroklos expects that Achilles will respond as a king should respond and suggest some way out—perhaps for the shepherd to lead his people. He is weeping because in the given circumstances he can see no way out, precisely as Agamemnon wept at the beginning of Book Nine. And the identical simile is used there of Agamemnon, with the exception that Agamemnon weeps merely tears, not warm tears. (He is not a friend, but a king; his tears come harder.) Patroklos expects his tears to move the shepherd of the people. And

---

choice, he claims) is to "find beauties where none can exist."[19]

Against this view it may be argued that one can make the given place in the line bigger or smaller in many cases by merely adding or removing a particle, and that one may also move the epithet and its noun from the given place. To assume that all the line is fixed but the "blank place" of the epithet, is to imagine Homer as composing with all his line frozen but the epithet. But surely the line shapes itself simultaneously in his head, and no one part may be thought of as fixed before the rest. Moreover, to think of this illustrious poet as bound by the exigencies of the metrically unique epithet, would be comparable to thinking of Dante as bound by the exigencies of *terza rima* or Shakespeare as bound by the sonnet form. No one but a provincial versifier (such as the inferior writers of primitive epic) may be thought of as so constricted by his form. The hardness of his marble does not hamper Michelangelo.

Achilles is moved; but not in that role. Rather, it is as the *swift-footed brilliant* Achilles that he takes pity, and then not on the fighters but on Patroklos himself. Their own fathers Peleus and Menoitios are still alive, Achilles says, and so why weep? And Achilles shortly calls the tears "soft," not "warm," making the relation between bodily feeling and emotion a little more remote; for "warm" is the more sensual word. The *shepherd of the people* is no longer there, only the *swift-footed brilliant* one, with something of a god's inaccessibility (*dios,* a rather vague word, means brilliant and also godlike). By his next speech Patroklos realizes that the shepherd has withdrawn; then he merely addresses his friend, with the remoteness of the patronymic but with undiminished praise, as "Son of Peleus, far the greatest of the Achaians."

The epithet refers the action of the moment to that known attribute of the object which happens to be uppermost at the given point. Each epithet indicates contrast and complexity within the stability the very recurrence implies. The mountains are shadowy when Achilles thinks in his mind of the distance to Phthia, across "shadowy mountains and sounding seas." When the aspect of clarity stands out, the view of Olympus to the gods, the mountains are "snowy," the word evoking their visible tops on a sunny day.

An epithet involves more than a mere literal designation: its choice as a particular facet of ship, of sea or person, and its recurrence too, make it more, conjoining it to the poem's constant adaptive configuration. Within each epithet reside two and possibly three significations: the literal one, "a ship is descriptively well decked;" the configured one, "it is well-decked with reference to the action of the moment; resisting assault and fire." To these we may also add an absolute one: "well-decked" is a recurrent property, mysterious as the "dimness" of water is mysterious, transcending its function of resisting attack. But these three significations are not levels of allegory in Dante's sense. Homer's plainness keeps them all bound into the unitary and unrhetorical fact of the word's designation. The lack of metaphor and trope in the Homeric language binds the word to a full directness of implication, and the three significations converge in an absolute and unabstracted union.

Often we get two epithets in a single line. When we do, the relationship between the two begins to carry the complexity of the poem's configuration. Agamemnon, looking at the wounded Menelaus (IV, 171), says that if Menelaus should die, he himself would

> return *a thing of reproach* to *overthirsty* Argos

> καί κεν ἐλέγχιστος πολυδίψιον Ἄργος ἱκοίμην.

Elegkistos, "least of all": least in the sense of reproach, perhaps, as Lattimore here renders it: small in the eyes of the people. But the smallness, by syntax and metre, is also opposed to the great thirst (*polydipsion*) of Argos. Nature continues on in the great thirst of that country which elsewhere Agamemnon calls an "udder of the land." In one sense man is "least of all" when compared to that richness. Agamemnon in particular, prompt to catch a real or imagined slight, thinks of himself as dwarfed while looking at the wounded Menelaus. His imagined dwarfing goes beyond Menelaus and the moment, and also beyond Argos. For where could this ruler be "least of all?" Even as a shade, in the *Odyssey,* he is not "least of all."

The land lies outside, as well as beyond him: its thirst is purely natural; if this were a metaphoric poem we could call Agamemnon analogous to his land, "very thirsty"—he could be thinking of it as very thirsty, projecting his own unquenchableness on his domain. Here, again, we have a contrast, almost an antinomic contrast, and yet the formulaic character and justness of the attribution keeps *polydipsion* from being contained in just this one aspect of contrast.

Or take the famous phrase that caps Helen's wonderment about where the Dioscuri may be; perhaps they are at home, she says; or perhaps they are reluctant to go into battle out of shame for their sister.

So she spoke, but the teeming earth lay already upon them

Ὣς φάτο, τοὺς δ' ἤδη κάτεχεν φυσίζοος αἶα   (III, 243)

"Already the *life-giving* earth held them." They are underground
in the land of the dead. But the earth that holds them is, by contrast, a life-producing one. The phrase is the more striking because
it brings up Helen's ignorance; she is unaware of what has happened to her brothers; the natural process that has brought them
underground transcends her knowledge, just as the life-giving process of the soil transcends an individual death. A contrast is set up
between the facts and her knowledge, and also between life and
death, earth and men. We do have, to be sure, a dramatic irony
against Helen; but it is muted by the fact that in life as the *Iliad*
conceives it, all men are comparably limited.

The epithet derives its force here from these antinomic contrasts,
which coexist with what from another point of view is a likeness.
(Man also possesses the life that earth gives.) And so they resemble
the configured contrasts of the whole poem. But at the same time
there is something absolute about "life-giving," a permanent facet
of the earth which exists unnostalgically, independently of their
death or of her ignorance, in the absoluteness, the objectivity of the
Homeric epithet. Matthew Arnold[20] insists on Homer's objectivity
in rejecting Ruskin's interpretation of "life-giving":

> "The poet," says Mr. Ruskin, "has to speak of the earth in
> sadness; but he will not let that sadness affect or change his
> thought of it. No; though Castor and Pollux be dead, yet the
> earth is our mother still,—fruitful, life-giving." This is just a
> specimen of that sort of application of modern sentiment to
> the ancients . . . It is not true . . . that Homer called the earth
> *phusizoos,* because "though he had to speak of the earth in
> sadness, he would not let that sadness change or affect his
> thought of it," but consoled himself by considering that "the
> earth is our mother still."

Arnold is right initially in rejecting for this verse the "tender
pantheism" of Ruskin. And yet Ruskin is right to hear sadness, I

feel; or at any rate I hear it in the end of every hexameter as it rounds out, formally unfilled, in the musical disappointment of the *syllaba anceps*. *Aia*, falling on the *syllaba anceps*, carries the sadness for my ear, while *phusizoos* by itself does not. The contrast may well be there that Ruskin hears; but the epithet has both a literal and an absolute side as well, and so it is not confined to sadness. The sadness is present only in the whole condition of the Homeric world,—of which, to be sure, this line, with any other, partakes.

6

In the *Iliad,* indeed, a superelegiac sadness clings at every point to all the heroes; their life involves their death, the imagined peace never is realized, all mortals are transient. Not only in the lines that say this:

οἵη περ φύλλων γενεή, τοίη δὲ καὶ ἀνδρῶν.

Like to the race of leaves is also the race of men.

(VI, 146)

but throughout, one hears the elegiac note rising in the verse.

In Homer's hexameter, the words are forced into a foot which is somewhat longer than an average word: they are poised and held in the voice as it fills out the necessary dactyl or moves on into half a spondee. In thus suspending its words, the hexameter produces an elevation that serves as a vehicle for Arnold's "nobility," Aristotle's "stateliness" and "swelling emphasis." The measure holds the long epithet straitly, the short particle buoyantly, in its sweeping variation. The same six-foot line moves swiftly on, and each line is free to form in its rush an improvised variation.

The metricians[21] find thirty-two kinds of hexameter in Homer, as against nine for such an Alexandrian as Nonnos. (The kinds are distinguished by the count of caesural positions, of dactyls as opposed to spondees.) But the verse of the Alexandrians is heard to be far more structured than Homer's; he "allows" verses they do not, such as the trithemimeral caesura (after the first syllable of the second dactyl) and the bucolic diaeresis, found often in Homer but elsewhere mostly, as the name implies, in the elegiac measure. Homer also "allows" a spondee in the fifth foot, as the Alexandrians and the post-Alexandrian Vergil almost never do.

Which is to say that Homer permits just about anything; his varieties come not from his great complexity, but from a freedom of metrical composition comparable to that of a ballad writer. Vergil deploys his quantitative measures, and counterpoints them, in W.F.J. Knight's[22] view, with the Roman accents of the Latin words. In the rush of his measure, however, Homer lets his accents—and his quantities—fall where they may. That is to say, he improvises, in consonance with his oral method.

It is even possible that Homer would not have felt his measure as other than a slight heightening of pitch and ennobling of accompanying vocabulary, very much in the spirit of what we are told of the Yugoslav bard who unconsciously slips into meters when asked to recount a military episode. To speak of Homer's use of the caesura, for example, and to show that he "varies" it more than an Alexandrian poet, is to turn him into the kind of super-Alexandrian Vergil succeeded in becoming.

Homer flows more readily than Vergil because he is not formulating precise variations and obeying elaborate laws (such as the avoidance of the fifth foot spondee). His hexameter moves freely ahead, coordinating with his syntax, providing a variable cadence which holds the sentences to a felt rhythmical norm. So free is his movement that he can sometimes lengthen or shorten his syllables at will.[23] He can even depart from the usual hexameter in the defective *stichoi* which were classified in antiquity by Athenaeus.

His linear construction moves freely in avoidance not only of hypotactic subordination, but even of the sort of stiff coordination a primitive parataxis calls to mind. In this freedom the line rings clear for a poetry whose impression suggests not figures sculptured on a frieze, like Vergil's, or bits of radiant glass in the giant pattern of a rose window, like Dante's, but the fluidity of an improvised music. Yet Homer's *syllaba anceps* rings at once freer, and less tonally qualified than Vergil's (or Callimachus'). It rounds out imperfectly and moves along in the improvised flow.

Since sound is indissolubly wedded to sense in verse, it is the poem's coordinated sense that allows us to hear, in the hexameter of the *Iliad,* an improvisatory power, and not the indecisive chaos to be heard in the more inferior medieval chronicles of warfare. Yet correspondingly, without that sounding hexameter, the level world of Homer, where all men and gods, feelings and objects, exist on the same plane, would seem not a unity but merely the sort of flatness of impoverished reference that characterizes what we have of Ennius' verses.

7

The epic poem has a solemnity about it—a "high seriousness" in Arnold's phrase—which derives from the totality of the hero's struggle. An unusually strong pathos clings to the solemnity of the *Iliad;* a pathos created by the unnatural pressure of the war, conceived as an unnatural but expected demand on the heroes. And their mortality is thought of as coming on with seasonal swiftness. Helen does not know that the life-giving earth already holds her brothers dead. Beowulf holds out for fifty long years, but Achilles knows he is to die young.

> Like to the race of leaves is also the race of men.

Taking the pathos from the sense of the poem, we can hear it in the sound as well, in every hexameter's dying fall. The heroes are pathetic as they die, clutching at life with empty hands. They are pathetic while they live under the necessary and intolerable burden of fighting. Often they are frozen stiff (*rigein*) at the thought of battle, even Hector; or weep copiously about it, even Agamemnon.

Battle "wears them down" is a verb recurring so much (*teirein*) as to be well-nigh formulaic. And battle is the human condition. Achilles' choice is a choice for all: to go home and live ingloriously or to die young sacking Troy. Even back home, as Sarpedon says to Glaucus, a man gains property and honor through his willingness to fight. Glory comes of the war. The peaceful land may be prosperous in the nostalgic memory of the fighters; the peacetime woods themselves are ravaged by the lions and boars of the similes. In peacetime, too, Glaucus says, ten thousand fates of death stand ever at hand.

If Argos, in Agamemnon's wet-eyed formulaic description, is an *outhar aroures,* an udder of the land, then the life of the warrior is a perpetual weaning. We learn in the *Iliad,* Goethe says, that we are reenacting Hell on earth. In the poem war is a hell. A man is vexed, Odysseus tells us in the poem's initial council, if he but sail away from home a month on stormy seas. How much more so if he is fighting away from home for nine years! The Achaians long "like boys or widows" to return home (II, 289). Yet Odysseus speaks only to say they must stay still longer. Everyone knows that no one can escape the double threat of death or defeat. There is pain for the conquered; and also for the conquerors, pain.

Moreover, an obscure wrongness dwells in the whole exploit: Hector (VI, 265-7) cannot go pray to Zeus with gory hands. The helmet is frighteningly unnatural to Astyanax. If Helen had not been abducted, there would have been no war at all. If Agamemnon and Achilles could get together the calamity of the war would be immediately over:

> If ever we can take one single counsel, then no longer
> shall the Trojans' evil be put aside, not even for a small time.

If the powerful did not lust for more power and the wealthy for more wealth, cities would not be sacked. But they are sacked, and one cannot leave off. Even if everyone wants to return, the return is "beyond what is fated" (II, 155. *hypermora nostos*).

There is pathos in the very instigator of the war, Alexander: he cannot enjoy the "lovely home he has built himself . . . on the peak of the citadel." Pathos constricts Hector in a farewell to his mother: pathos lies so close to the surface that he cannot even enjoy the refreshment of wine for fear of losing heart altogether:

> My honored mother, lift not to me the kindly sweet wine
> for fear you stagger my strength and make me forget my
> courage;   (VI, 264-5)

and there is pathos when he asks the women to pray:

>   if only she will have pity
> on the town of Troy, and the Trojan wives, and their innocent
> children,   (VI, 275-6)

This is what they do say in their own pathetic prayer to Athene. And the goddess of reason need not even formulate a reply, so irrational is their request in the logic of war (and so pathetically human is it to pray for what cannot be granted):

> She spoke in prayer, but Pallas Athene turned her head from
> her.   (VI, 311)

Pathos inheres not in just this person or that, this loss or that, but in the loss of the whole war, brought into any particular focus through the actual contrasts that are perpetually being drawn: Hector to Alexander, Helen to Andromache, the childless guilty against the innocent parents, the dutiful losing Trojans against the brilliant winning Achaians.

Andromache's pathos springs from another, similar battle. Achilles sacked her father's city and slaughtered her father Eëtion. Yet his horrible action had limits he will now exceed: there resides in the prophesying scene between husband and wife a prophetic contrast with Achilles' slaughter of Hector:

>   He killed Eëtion,
> but did not strip his armour, for his heart respected the
> dead man,

but burned the body in all its elaborate war-gear,
and piled a grave mound over it, and the nymphs of the
    mountains,
daughters of Zeus of the aegis, planted elm trees about it.
                                          (VI, 416-20)

Later it is Patroklos who will get the mourning nymphs, and not
Hector. Despoiled of its war-gear and unburned will be the body
Priam is to ransom. When the embassy comes to Achilles a little
later on, he will be playing war-lays on a harp taken in the sack of
Eëtion's city. Hector's own pathos resides in his very role, the heartbreaking contrast between glory and certain defeat, underlying the
heartbreaking contrast of the family not left to itself, when the husband is spoken of as his orphaned wife's sole consolation, their
son's sole mainstay.

Either some man well-skilled in prophetic arts had spoken,
or the very spirit within themselves had stirred them to the
    onslaught.   (VI, 438-9)

So the wife says, in conclusion, of the sack that is to widow her. The
husband, by pathetic contrast, himself possesses this prophetic skill
—he evidences it on the spot. And he also has the spirit for attack
—he will shortly drive the Achaians to their ships. Yet neither prophecy nor prowess can stave off the further, ultimate orphaning:

Then tall Hector of the shining helm answered her: "All
    these
things are in my mind also, lady; yet I would feel deep shame
before the Trojans, and the Trojan women with trailing
    garments,
if like a coward I were to shrink aside from the fighting;
and the spirit will not let me, since I have learned to be
    valiant
and to fight always among the foremost ranks of the Trojans,
winning for my own self great glory, and for my father.
For I know this thing well in my heart, and my mind knows it:
There will come a day when sacred Ilion shall perish.
                                          (VI, 440-8)

"All these things" that Hector knows well are no less in everyone's mind than in his. In his particular situation he voices them. And the son screams for fright at his father's helmet: war is unnatural, but all men must fight, and Hector may doff his helmet, but only for a minute. It is through tears that Astyanax smiles, the baby's situation an image of the human condition. Hector, ceremonious as his role dictates, prays to Zeus that his son—for whom he has prophesied captivity—may be a better warrior than he, that he may:

> bring home the bloodied spoils, and delight the heart of
> his mother   (VI, 481)

as he knows Astyanax is destined not to do.

The world perishes, and the world is always the same. "Like to the race of leaves is also the race of men." Castor and Polydeuces lie dead beneath the life-giving earth. Heroes die, and other heroes replace them; their situations having vanished from memory, they have become a mere procession of names recited by Nestor. The name of a bygone hero, filling out the line of poetry along with other names, reminds us at once of the perennial nature of battle, and of the vanishing mortality of the fighters. The past resembles the present, and the poem may compare this war to the wars with the Amazons or the Arcadians, or the Seven Against Thebes; to the exploits of Laomedon or Bellerophon or Meleager. One may draw lessons from the prowess and strategy of the past because of the resemblance. Except that the differentiating conditions are lost, save in dim memory. And it must be the memory of someone whose present situation directs him to draw the analogy. Priam is as old as Nestor, but his situation never calls him to speak of past wars. Phoenix too is old; but he touches on his personal history of suffering, and on the analogy, implied rather than stated, between Achilles and Meleager. The situation evokes these, rather than any of his own past exploits. The past may be a straw grasped at to cover fright: so Bellerophon serves the recounting Glaucus. Agamemnon reminds Diomede of Tydeus' prowess so as to urge the man's son into battle. The past's representatives stand always near, themselves either victorious, like Nestor's comrades, or vanquished, like the parents of Andromache. The complexity of relations passes as the life is superseded, and the patronymic has a formality, a mere formality, on which the poetry never expands while it is given: the father is a name, but only a name.

Hector, like everyone, knows he will die, and Achilles knows he will die not long after Hector. To die is to leave the complexity of one specific involvement in the total exactions of the epic world. This is almost inconceivable for those who must define a transitory life in terms of what is permanent to it, struggle and mortality. Helen can barely imagine the past at the very moment when its full nostalgic force bears in upon her:

> kin he was to bitch-faced me, if indeed it ever was.
>
> (III, 180)

In the world of the *Iliad,* as in other epic poems, Hamlet must appear in the guise of Fortinbras; everyone marches to war. The whole being of a hero rests on his willingness to risk what will annihilate that being, the death that lies beyond his situation, intensifying it. Death comes in the first sentence of the poem: the wrath of Achilles has brought myriad pains on the Achaians and sent many stout souls to Hades. The last event of the poem is a funeral. Time after time after time some hero encounters what he perpetually fears, one of the ten thousand fates of death that stand perpetually at hand.

So Sarpedon says to Glaucus, urging him into battle. The life of peace itself is based on the hero's willingness to be a warrior. The life desired and the death standing near at hand: this is the one great contrast of the poem; and into it all the others are configured.

Everyone acts under the possibility of death, too transfixed by its risk to give way to the moods about it that lyric verse can entertain. Moreover, death does not dominate a tragedy in this way. To begin with, tragedy involves nobility in life, and not in death. Death is merely a possible end for a tragedy. Only the hero necessarily dies, and when he dies or others die in his train, it is understood that he has died prematurely because of the play's chain of events. Death comes to him as a surprise, and comes perhaps to him alone, or at least only to those he has personally entangled. Death results from a set of events and choices. It results directly from his flaw.

In an epic poem, the converse holds for all these conditions. Death is not a surprise, not the lot of one man alone, not conditioned by choices, not incurred through personal flaws. Achilles' flaw does not bring his death: it removes him from the risk. Working out the flaw endangers him again, as he steadily knows. He is no tragic protagonist to die alone; ultimately everyone must die eventually and anyone may die in the poem.

No specific set of events, the limited causality of drama, engenders the catastrophe. While the poem centers on the specific occasion of Achilles' wrath, the war exists beyond the wrath; it would continue without the wrath. It has and it will. The heroes are mortal all through the war, though the wrath intensifies their mortality. The pattern of the world's complexity in the poem is larger than any character can fully measure, even the central hero.

Everyone knows this. In an epic, once again, everyone is equally aware of everything, and everyone stands in the same light. Mortality sums up what everyone knows. "War is common to all," (*Xunos Enyalios*). Each hero moves in the doomed awareness, and the poetry rings with that awareness in every line. But Hamlet, when he asks himself about suicide, does not speculate about the certainty of death: on the contrary, he may choose to die, and this is what an epic hero cannot do. He may only choose to fight; though if he does not make this choice, he ceases to be a hero. And once he has chosen, he may die at any time. Achilles and Hector both know they are to die; but Coriolanus and Othello do not know this: they cannot know it in the very conception of their tragic independence.

There is no way out. If Paris had not run away with Helen, there would have been no war. But men's wills do clash, and so they fight. The poem offers us again and again the comparatively elaborate syntax of a contrary-to-fact condition, as if on the threshold of the war lay always a more benign possibility that is fated never to be realized. So an easy way out always tempts the heroes; Agamemnon proposes they sail home, perhaps as a trick; and everyone jumps at the possibility. Both Hector and Ajax are eager to call the battle for darkness. Both sides, against all probability, are willing to pitch the entire outcome on a combat between Menelaus and Paris, but this is really unreasonable, and so the Goddess of Reason intervenes. The oaths made before this duel are themselves unreal, as is implied by the unusually elaborate sacrifices for ratifying them made to both Chthonic and Olympian deities.

The poetry centers on the killing. With pitiless clarity the wounds are delineated, and with such precision about the organs mutilated in each wound that Homer has been thought by some to have been a physician. The individual organs of wounding instance the presence of the ten thousand fates of death that stand perpetually at hand.

A wound in the poem entails death. This contravenes what we know—and probably Homer knew—of actual battle. For in modern war, under our far more shattering weapons, few men still die at the instant of wounding. They go back for treatment, and their wounds linger. If they do die of wounds, it happens a day or two later. But in the fiction of this poem, to be wounded is either to be killed at once or to survive wholly. The wound may linger with all the sharpness of Agamemnon's wound, which is compared to the pangs of childbirth. (The strangeness of the simile, for all its literal vividness, highlights the unnaturalness of war.) But Agamemnon survives, and Glaucus survives his wound. No one dies of wounds behind the lines: to be wounded in combat brings, if not survival for the rest of the episode, death right on the spot.

The poetry that recounts the wounds is enumerative, unremittingly visual in its pitiless confrontation of a fate which it invents, a fate which may well have been a departure from the actual conditions of a Homeric battle.

There is no half-way condition in the *Iliad;* mortality always presses. A fate, when it descends, is ultimate, just as involvement is always total, and always transcends the will and the power of the hero. But not his knowledge, for he is aware of this, aware in his breast; even while his eyes, like the poet's, take in the organs of his own dread piercing. If he is pierced, darkness covers his eyes.

8

Above and to one side of the combatants exist those who are not subject to death, the non-dying (*athanatoi*), the gods. They carry on the serene life of peace which man glimpses only through remembrance, or in the imagined comparison of a simile.

In the *Iliad* the gods do impinge on the lives of mortals, singly and in groups. In *Beowulf* God stands off in the unknown as a calm ruler and measurer (*Metod*). But he is not directive, like Zeus; he orders no doctrine and no policy. In *Paradise Lost* the good and the bad angels, embattled over the soul of Adam, do not exhibit the checks and balances of the *Iliad*'s Olympian deities. In the *Divine Comedy* everyone stands in a permanent way towards the Divine Mover: the definition is part of the past, and the poetry sums up a total order.

The total order of the *Iliad* includes the gods, but problematically. At any point they may enter, or they may not: the mere mention of Athene's name by Menelaus (XVII, 570-2) causes her to fill him with as much boldness as a fly bent stubbornly on blood; but at another time she ignores the full formal sacrifice of the Trojan women.

In the language of the poem no distinction is made between the visible woman goddess Aphrodite and the abstract attraction to love. And so we cannot say Aphrodite metaphorizes love, or Athene thought. To say "Athene" is not a pre-conceptual way of saying "mind,"—the goddess simply stands there over the rationale of an individual, Odysseus, or over a whole society: it is rational that the bronze-greaved Achaians should defeat the long-gowned Trojans; and hence Athene is seen favoring the Achaians.

Aphrodite, while standing for the appeal of love, and beauty, the sex act, the libidinous force in human affairs, at the same time, exists as a lovely and a somewhat irresponsible goddess; the person and the "abstract" force belong on the same level in the Homeric language and in the action of the poem. Ares is the summed-up pitch of battle and also a real, divine warrior. Xanthos, who enters the fight, is at once an armed hero and the watery, swollen river that frightens even Achilles. To go beyond this is to overphilosophize Homer, or to change his angle of vision: he is not a Vergil to harmonize the intellectual overtones of deities half-disbelieved; nor is he a Dante to give us even the allegorical level. In Homer's world, using Dante's terms, everything works on the literal level, and on that alone: the language provides no other.

The god's obscurity may seem to border on chaos, and we may not see the god's abstract quality for his seemingly capricious personality. And yet the chaos dissolves into a pattern the minute we inspect it. It makes sense for Athene to curb a wrought-up hero, for Aphrodite to accompany an appealing woman, for Hera and Athene to be working together, for Apollo to curb Aphrodite, and so on.

The gods are incalculable; they embody that unknown which inheres in epic poems as a kind of finality, an impetus toward broaching the unsayable. They may enter at any moment, upset the balance of forces at any point, favor a man or threaten to withdraw as Aphrodite threatens to withdraw from Helen. They are visible, too, the unknown and the incalculable made visible. In the *Iliad,* living on the real mountain of Olympus across the sea, whose snowy peaks can be seen from Troy still on a clear day, they may look down over the sea and with their own eyes watch the fighting. When they descend, they themselves may be seen.

If a god is recognized, he is recognized at once. Aeneas' slow-wondering birth of half-recall—*O quam te memorem virgo!*—is impossible in the even light of the *Iliad*.

When all comes through direct and clear, even the unknown must have a nameable form, an aspect of clarity. The whole prime cause of the action is lost, but assignable: a plan of Zeus brought it about and brought it to a conclusion (*Dios d'eteleieto boule*), as we learn in the opening invocation. Sometimes it is not known what spirit has acted—the hero merely names "demigod" (*daimon* XV, 467). Or a fate intervenes, *ker,* or the Erinyes, who stop the horses of Achilles from uttering further speech. Always it is something that can be named, a god, and the named may be seen.

Gods differ from men in their immortality; they resemble men in form and appearance. Helen, the old men say, looks fearfully like the immortal gods. The gods may be wounded like men, but then they bleed an invisible fluid, ichor and not blood. They are visible, but they may be invisible or disguised at will. They eat, but a different food. They live in society, but a carefree life.

The gods speak a language like men, and it names the same objects, a bird or a river: but the names are different names. They can see farther than men, all the way from Olympus to Troy. Yet they are not omniscient: something may escape their attention, which in the *Iliad's* sunlit world means it has escaped their vision.

In one sense they are more limited than men: each is circumscribed within the singleness of his single function. Apollo says—as it is the part of the god of success to do—that Aphrodite should not be fighting in battle.

The gods stand always at hand to incite action and deflect human purpose. Apollo, the god of success, keeps Patroklos from taking Troy. To say that the logic of events, or the inner appropriateness of strategy, "really" keeps Patroklos from taking Troy, is to rationalize the poem, to allegorize the gods. It is, ultimately, to put within the realm of the known but invisible—an internal strategic principle—something that the poem embodies in an exactly contrary aspect: the acts of the gods are visible, not invisible, in the poetry (though not to the participants always); to the participants whether visible or invisible, the gods are always bringing the unknown to pass.

In the great sphere of this life, another sphere like it, holds the deciding sway. The incalculable gods alone can start a large motion; Aphrodite has induced Helen to run away with Paris. And they alone can resolve a large impasse: the gods, after deliberating the dilemma, decide to send Priam as an ambassador to Achilles, not only to rescue Hector but also to set Achilles back in the human context from which he seems irrevocably alienated. This time they do not intervene directly, but through men, through Priam.

The gods, again like men, work in combination: Hera and Athene oppose Zeus and Aphrodite; Hermes works with Thetis, Poseidon with Hera. And they work at cross purposes, again like men: Athene against Aphrodite, Zeus against Hera. The whole cosmos is divided among the brothers of Chronos, as Poseidon insists:

> All was divided among us three ways, each given his domain.
> I when the lots were shaken drew the grey sea to live in
> forever; Hades drew the lot of the mists and the darkness,
> and Zeus was allotted the wide sky, the cloud and the
>   bright air.
> But earth and high Olympus are common to all three.
>   Therefore
> I am no part of the mind of Zeus.   (xv, 189-94)

Earth is common ground, on which they may battle, as men must; but they may withdraw from it, as men may not.

If a god acts alone, he does so with the tacit consent of Zeus. Zeus himself tends to solitude; in this, as Cedric Whitman[24] points out, he resembles Achilles. But this is only another one among many aspects of contrast, as always; he also resembles Agamemnon in his sensitivity to prerogative. From the council of the gods in the first book to the council in the last, the gods characteristically act in groups, like men, consulting each other, operating in combination, or deceiving each other, bypassing each other, checking each other. Athene, coming to help the Danaans at the beginning of Book Seven, is immediately joined and questioned by Apollo; and the two of them together are invoked by Zeus to a somewhat different end.

The poem renders the gods who guide and transcend the action of the poem with the same pitiless and martial clarity that fixes and reveals the life of man. If the poem understood or ordered the gods, they would be less problematic than it presents them; if it hid the gods, they would be less clear. In the *Iliad* they are at once incalculable and visible, problematic and clear.

9

The serenity of the gods' perpetual peace contrasts with the perpetual tribulation of warring mankind. Man remembers a world of peace, and the poem expands on that world chiefly in the similes. The similes, then, often constitute a contrast, and one which goes farther than the simple juxtaposition of war and peace, just as the contrasts in the situation of an episode go farther than a mere juxtaposition of two heroes. The similes often deal with the violence of lions and hunters; so peace is like war in its violence as well as different in its ease: the contrast, taken in another aspect, becomes an analogy.

In lyric poetry such contrasts and analogies derive from the intensity of the metaphors and other tropes, coiled economically for their effects. In Homer, however, the simile is casual; it may ramble on and on, it may repeat itself; and it corresponds in no tight symbolic way to what it describes. In Homer, and in early epic poems generally, the simile need not set up a field of metaphorical correspondence, as in a lyric poem. It merely takes a point of comparison and spins it out with open, independent detail. The very form of the traditional epic simile encourages this independence.

The incidental details of the simile more powerfully parallel the details of the narrative by not being fully exploited within the simile itself:

> But at that time when the woodcutter makes ready his supper
> in the wooded glens of the mountains, when his arms and
>   hands have grown weary
> from cutting down the tall trees, and his heart has had enough
>   of it,
> and longing for food and for sweet wine takes hold of his
>   senses;
> at that time the Danaans by their manhood broke the
>   battalions,   (XI, 86-90)

While this is not a simile in grammatical form, it is one in structure: the time they broke the battle line was the time before supper. We are not to infer here that the Danaans at this particular point have not eaten; in fact, the insistence of Odysseus and others on regular meals for the troops, the necessity of a full stomach for courage, would argue that they had. We cannot even say that the Danaans have had enough of killing, as the woodman has of chopping, for the very next action shows Agamemnon rushing on in battle-lust "like a lion seizing fawns." Not applying the comparison to the particular scene, we may apply it the more forcefully to the general cosmos of the poem: war is unnatural, pressing on just at the time when the man of peace goes home to supper.

On the other hand, Dante, who expanded an epic style out of a lyric one, always works his similes lyrically to the full in their immediate context:

> *Era già l'ora che volge il disio*
> *Ai naviganti e intenerisce il core,*
> *Lo dì ch' han detto ai dolci amici addio;*
> *E che lo nuovo peregrin d'amore*
> *Punge, se ode squilla di lontano,*
> *Che paia il giorno pianger che si more;*
> *Quand' io incominciai a render vano*
> *L'udire, ed a mirare una dell' alme*

It was already the hour when desire turns
For navigators and makes the heart tender,
The day they have said to their sweet friends goodbye;
And the hour that pierces the new pilgrim of love
If he hears a bell from far away
That the day seems weeping because it dies,
When I began to render vain
My hearing, and to admire one of the souls . . .

(*Purgatory,* VIII, 1-8)

This twilight stands metaphorically for the particular place in purgatory and for the particular time; the voyage, the mountain landscape, the new pilgrim, the twilight bell heard afar . . . all these borrow the clarity of purgatory, while purgatory borrows their piercing tenderness. Morally, too, the state of the souls, and of the Dante who is about to rest, is figured in the metaphor. Anagogically the metaphor expresses one whole purgatorial situation in a picture that has never left the literal base of a complex emotion explained in a complex simile—an emotion that Dante, a living man, shares with the striving but resting dead.

This immediate fullness of complex and exhausting reference, in this particular twilight, coordinates with other lights: a superior one, the perpetual noon of Paradise; the far inferior ones, the twilights of the Inferno:

> *Lo giorno se n'andava, e l'aer bruno*
> *Toglieva gli animai che sono in terra*
> *Dalle fatiche loro;*

> Day went away, and the brown air
> Took from the souls that are on earth
> Their burdens.　　　　　　　　　　(*Inferno,* II, 1-3)

As critics from Aristotle to Hugh Kenner have pointed out, any metaphorical expression contains four terms, not two: a man is not compared to a lion: the boldness of a man is compared to the boldness of the lion. In this fourfold union, boldness is the point of contact, and the metaphor may act in a number of ways towards uncompared attributes of the vehicle and the tenor: the yellowness, swiftness, impatience, hunger, deep-voicedness of the lion; the tallness, intelligence, nimbleness, tenacity, color of the man. Dante takes the uncompared attributes and configures them in his fourfold senses. And in lyric usage generally, we expect the uncompared attributes to be pulled into the comparison:

> My days are swifter than a weaver's shuttle.

The point of contact is speed. But the compactness of the comparison, its elusive intensity, seems to reside in the implied similarity of uncompared attributes: Job's days also resemble the weft from a weaver's shuttle in the monotony of the fabric that is built up, in the even relentlessness with which that fabric progresses. One may even see, in the flickering of the rapid shuttle, an illusory appearance that would correspond to an illusion in his days: he feels them now to be vanity. Passivity enters the picture, too: there is nothing Job can do about his days, he has been plagued. He can only sit passively and watch them build up swiftly on the loom.

Job's days resemble the shuttle in monotony and relentlessness, in flickering and passivity, in the progressive building up of a fabric; as well as in swiftness. The uncompared attributes lie beneath the surface to enrich the point of comparison; they need only to be noticed to be recognized as appropriate, and therefore present.

In modern poetry the uncompared attributes can figure so importantly as to predominate over the main point of comparison:

> Take this sea, whose diapason knells
> On scrolls of silver snowy sentences . . .   (HART CRANE)

The comparison of waves' sound to the sound of a diapason, of that to a funeral knell, then of the ridgy sand (or waves?) to a scroll, of water to silver, of foam to snow, and of a wave to the sentence—the points of similarity here (loud sound, whiteness) have dwindled;

they merely serve to permit the multiple associations arising from the fact that a knell (like the sea) has a sound.

Or, in still another usage, the main point of the comparison may be implicitly ruled out as grotesque, at the very moment it is stated, adding an irony to the richness of the overtones in the uncompared attributes:

> Crénelé comme la mâchoire d'une vieille,
> Son toit

> Crenelated like the jaw of an old woman,
>   Its roof.

(CORBIÈRE)

The contumacious poet's tower resembles an old woman's jaw more in its impotence and in its superannuation, than in its actual look. The comparison may also suggest the useless gossipy wind that plays through the tower, and its pride for having had its legend in its time (which the poem presently mentions) . . . crenelation is ridiculous in precisely the same way that Corbière ridicules his own contumacy.

In the epic simile, as used by a poet like Dante writing in a lyric form, the uncompared attributes may take a vigor of immediate application. Milton and Vergil, in their own ways, also work the immediate context hard. But Homer's similes are simpler than all these, lyric and epic alike.

Homer uses his language in the similes much as he uses it elsewhere. He does not build special tropes beyond the main point of contact in the simile, and even that point of contact serves first to illustrate: it is initially explanatory, not evocative, like the repeated simile in the *Cid* that compares parting between people to ripping a nail from the flesh, *come uño de la carne*. The poet of the *Cid* merely explains a mental pain by a physical one: he does not set up a matrix of correspondence in which our attention is directed metaphorically to the physical nail and the physical flesh. "Rosy-fingered" dawn, for all the impressiveness of this epithet built on a simile, also

works in an explanatory way, particularly if we remember that
"finger" may be too precise a translation of *daktulos,* a word of
vague meaning (jointed member?) never occurring separately in
Homeric Greek. The metaphoric epithet makes no implied comparison between the rosy, slenderly jointed structures of light in the
morning sky and the personified fingers of Aurora, goddess of the
dawn; it simply names the rosy structures of light. The epithet aids
the hearer to visualize an action of light. Just so the similes help to
visualize actions that happen to be visually complex:

> As along a great threshing floor from the broad blade
> of a shovel, the black-skinned beans and the chickpeas
>   bounce high
> under the whistling blast and the sweep of the winnowing
>   fan, so
> back from the corselet of glorious Menelaos the bitter
> arrows rebounded far away, being driven hard back.
>   (XIII, 588-92)

The arrows bounce like chickpeas. Yet arrows resemble chickpeas
in no subsidiary effect, and the modern reader may be struck with
an oddness in this simile, a tonal effect not to be attributed to it. If
one tries to visualize the bouncing arrows instead of to compare,
with his eyes and not his mind, the simile falls into place and the
visual effect sharpens.

But Homer mentions black-skinned beans too, and the threshing
floor, the blade, the winnowing fan, the blast: the simile permits
such an unrelated excursion into the field of harvest, an implied
general contrast to the field of battle, but here not a specific one.
Often, in his noted circular method, Homer will go out from the
tenor of the simile and after such an excursion return to it: the tour
has been a window on a contrasted world.

But the simile always hinges initially on the likeness of the way
the eye takes in the objects compared. The old men on the Trojan
wall are seated "like grasshoppers." While the mind fumbles to

formulate in just what respects the resemblance holds, the eyes grasp it at once; it is a visual comparison of lean, hunching figures.

Homer's similes rise out of the action, at heightened moments, to explain the physical character of the action. They draw on the animal world or on peacetime activities not, as some critics have thought, for rhetorical expansiveness, or even initially for contrast, but in order to have a different groundwork by which to explain what is seen in the eye:

> As before the blast of a fire the locusts escaping
> into a river swarm in air, and the fire unwearied
> blazes from a sudden start, and the locusts huddle in water;
> so before Achilles the murmuring waters of Xanthos
> the deep-whirling were filled with confusion of men
> and of horses.   (XXI, 12-16)

Homer compares the men to locusts as a recipe books says "a piece of butter the size of a pea," simply to illustrate the type of physical (and also psychological) action. I believe it would be turning this simile into one of another kind to press the implied comparison of Achilles here to fire.

The simile, as well as delineating the action more precisely, pauses to indicate that this particular act has an importance; emphasis and delineation imply one another too, insofar as that which calls for emphasis is also likely, as here, to be complex enough to need delineation.

The change from one descriptive simile to another carries forward, through the illustration, the same sort of momentary progression in an action which can be traced in the particularity of verbs and other words in the narrative. Water, through the comparison, has become a native element: instead of fire and locusts, the poet goes on to give us dolphins and other fishes. But this acclimation of men to water is developed precisely as in the action verbs of the narrative: the simile functions like a long explanatory phrase, and the comparison of men to fish we might wrongly call almost surrealistic.

Overtones may abound in Homer's metaphors, obscuring their visual base. Thetis proceeds like mist, Apollo like night. Imperceptibility and swiftness are perhaps in view here; but first, as always, in the eye: the modern habit of setting up symbolic echoes will falsify such similes if the abstract overtones in any way take over from the main, visual note. Apollo comes on suddenly, as night comes on for us. Night comes every night. We are not meant to bring the first statement (Apollo sudden as night) to bear on the second (night's inexorable recurrence). The two coexist as a small complex in a cosmos made up, wherever we turn, of small complexes. The hero himself is a small complex, totally caught in the larger complex of his society at war. And this itself is a small complex seen in the perspective of immemorial time, a perspective that Nestor opens up for us. The structure of the similes, then, resembles the imaginative structure of the poem.

Any psychological effect in a simile of Homer's follows on the visual effect; of course always in Homer's world the psychological is not clearly distinguished from the visual, the abstract from the concrete. Men crouch "like fawns": they are seen to do so. Hence they are fearful like fawns; but to be fearful and to crouch are the same thing.

> As when a cloud goes deep into the sky from Olympus
> through the bright upper air when Zeus brings on the
>   hurricane,
> so rose from beside the ships their outcry, the noise of
>   their terror.   (XVI, 364-6)

We might catch our breath in admiration for the emotional mood which is surely conveyed through this comparison between a storm cloud gathering away deep into the sky and an onrush of terror. But the emotional effect resides totally, as always, in the physical motion; because the language of the poem, in similes and otherwise, does not distinguish between the emotion and the effect. The emotion is the effect, an identity we have to state and theorize, because the opposite is possible for us, but not for Homer: only that unitary mode of thought stands at his disposal.

The *Iliad* holds itself to its narrative line, and not to a figure. The similes brilliantly expand the reference of the narrative line at brilliant points of action; they do not construct any sort of interlocking metaphorical structure, yet neither would it be precise to say that they fail to construct such structures: this would be to make Homer naive, and Homer is naive only in retrospect.

10

The epic world where Achilles finds himself is a vastly complex one, and he is caught up in testing its limits of complexity. Yet the poem centers on him so completely that its structure may be described through his development.

The code demands that the hero fight, pitting his own mortality for the honor of the group, so that he may himself gain honor. His honor flouted, Achilles asserts that honor by withdrawing from the only ground where honor can be achieved. Self-contradictory, he asserts self-consistency, putting himself above the group when he depends totally on the conditions of the group.

In this poem man is as he acts in society. Achilles asserts his full manhood and also the weakness of his irascibility in refusing to put that manhood into performance. He remains godlike, brilliant Achilles; and his preeminence as the prime hero of the poem is a fact. He cannot himself act on that fact; to do so is to begin undermining it. The fact of his singularity exists, but in the human condition it can be acknowledged only by and through others. Achilles' wrath arises when the head of the group uneasily withdraws the acknowledgment: this amounts to an assertion of his singleness from the group, and he is then logically undermined by a process of events in which his tenderest point of contact with the group, Patroklos, meets death.

To the conditions which the brilliant Achilles exceeds he is at the same time subservient; the deadly paradox of his character matches the deadly paradox of the whole society, whose only honor is in self-destructive and wearing war.

Directly because of Achilles' anger does Zeus, incited by Achilles' divine mother, send the destructive dream that has Agamemnon marshal the troops. This act, in turn, after an interplay between the bitter side of Achilles' property assumption (Thersites) and the honorable side (Odysseus), brings the entire forces of both Trojans and Achaians into focus. Through the leverage of the anger the whole conflict is moved into view.

The situation progressively deepens. In the combat between Menelaus and Paris, Athene has Pandaros wound Menelaus with an arrow, the prophesied instrument of Achilles' own death. Then Diomede, like Achilles later, bests the very gods in his prowess. He takes armor from an old guest-friend instead of refusing ransom, as Achilles does, from a new one. His force brings Achilles' Trojan counterpart into the battle, and Hector leads the Trojans right up to the ships, lighting the signal fires that blaze across the plain.

By now the pressures are so intense that Agamemnon, weeping like a dark-watered spring, sends the embassy to Achilles. The embassy offers both restitution and reparation. When Achilles refuses these, he reveals a new, private and irrational depth to his anger. The war darkens correspondingly, beginning with a night exploit of espionage and pillage, interrogation and execution. Battle now involves groups of heroes working together, and not the single combats that characterized the first eight books. All the main heroes of the Greeks are wounded, along with the very physician who might heal them: they take their wounds with them back to the fighting.

Patroklos is urged back into battle by a self-contradicting Achilles who imagines the impossible exploit of a Troy taken by the two of them amidst universal death.

The seed of Achilles' irrationality is made explicit in his answer to the embassy. In the complexity of his situation his response is necessarily complex, and in his loneliness after the embassy he works out, as do the wounded Greeks and the doomed Patroklos, all the consequences of his paradox.

The paradox, to insist on the point, does not rest on character. And here I must take issue with the most profound discussion of Achilles that I know, Thomas McFarland's "Lykaon and Achilles."[25] McFarland posits for Achilles a character that has "the sort of intellect able to abstract principles from particular cases, and able to abstract these principles so clearly that they become motives of action . . . the sort of intellect that prizes the spiritual above all else . . . always looks with horror upon war as the triumph of force."

But Achilles nowhere looks with horror on war, not even in the passage uttered at the height of his vexed frustration when he re-enters the battle:

> I wish that strife would vanish away from among gods
>   and mortals,
> and gall, which makes a man grow angry for all his
>   great mind,
> that gall of anger that swarms like smoke inside of a
>   man's heart
> and becomes a thing sweeter to him by far than the
>   dripping of honey.   (XVIII, 107-10)

What Achilles rejects here is not war but strife, *eris,* quarreling among allies; and specifically his own personal anger. Individual, not social quarrels inspire Achilles' condemnation. In giving way to that kind of *eris* he has caused the death of his best friend.

Achilles, furthermore, is found by the embassy in Book Nine singing *klea andron,* the glorious military exploits of heroes, on a lyre captured in the sack of Andromache's father's city.

"Nothing is won for me . . . in forever setting my life on the hazard of battle." McFarland reiterates this statement and claims that it "invalidates another possible motivating factor: that of material gain." But this statement to the embassy is based largely on an insistence about material gain. Achilles is saying again what he implies in the first book, that since no distinction of booty is made between bad heroes and good, why should he risk his life?

And in saying this, he has involved himself in contradiction, as Odysseus has already pointed out in the intentionally shocking exordium of his speech:

> Your health Achilles. You have no lack of your equal
> portion
> either within the shelter of Atreus' son, Agamemnon,
> nor here now in your own.   (IX, 225-7)

This is exactly the case, for Agamemnon is now offering back Briseis, and an abundance of other compensation, for the flouted honor of Achilles. Achilles can persist in his anger only by a kind of self-contradiction.

Achilles in his speech obsessively comes again and again to his old point; since Agamemnon refuses to honor him, he will refrain from fighting. With this point he keeps trying to ignore the plain fact of Agamemnon's reparation. He involves himself in a further self-contradiction, by basing himself on an earlier, now superseded, state of affairs. This amounts to his wishing for the earlier situation and preferring anger to honor. The anger consequently loses its equivalence to the cause; it becomes all-embracing and perverse. As Achilles later says after the death of Patroklos has made him capable of introspection, anger is like honey in its sweetness, like smoke in its obscuring of response.

The only terms which remain for Achilles to proclaim his isolation from the group are the same terms which hold for all. And so his long speech to the embassy (IX, 307-429) is the falsest to fact of the poem: in a sense it is the only really false speech in the poem, the only one that flies in the face of plain fact.

Now Achilles forces himself to act so against the given universal facts of experience; he cannot distort or rend or take odd positions, as can Hamlet or Othello or Timon. He can only take the square universal assumptions of every warrior and by setting them against one another contradict the plain facts of the case. He speaks his heart, but his heart is shrouded in the smoke of anger.

He must be described, in turn, with the terms of the society, like everyone: described not by new words or strange situations but by a simple negative of the code. Nestor defines such an impossible condition before the embassy, in the light of a failure to respond to the group tie (IX, 62-3):

> Out of all brotherhood, outlawed, homeless shall be that man who longs for all the horror of fighting among his own people.*

Achilles, in effect, does homage to the very fact of his irrationality by his reiteration of the refusal, by his extravagantly unfulfilled threat to return home, and finally by his recital of the choice Thetis has given him: "If I return home I have a long life." By not returning home—and he never makes any gesture of preparing to return—he in effect makes the other choice, the choice to fight. Since his refusal hinged on lack of reparation, there would seem to be no way to get him back into the battle. On the other hand, he is precisely waiting to go back into the battle. His later mild answer to Phoenix implies as much:

> I think I am honored already in Zeus' ordinance which will hold me here beside my curved ships as long as life's wind stays in my breast.   (IX, 608-10)

His anger from this point on exhibits all the anguish of the contradictory tension between refusal and anticipation.

In his comparison between Helen and Briseis he tries to formulate —to come as close as a Homeric hero can to formulating—McFarland's principle of the "sanctity of human relationships."

---

* aphretor, athemiston, anestios.

[Let him lie beside her] and be happy. Yet why must the
   Argives fight the Trojans? . . .
Was it not for the sake of the lovely-haired Helen?

                                        (IX, 336-39)

If Agamemnon keeps Briseis, he contradicts his reason for the
whole expedition. But Agamemnon offers Briseis back. And Briseis,
herself, as Achilles goes on to say, was captured in the sack of a
city. To be the consistent pacifist McFarland urges that he is,
Achilles should not only return to Phthia at once as he threatens to
do; he should also give up Briseis himself.

But the Homeric assumption offers nothing for the denial of force
to rest on in a world wholly founded on force. Force is a fact, and
not by his subservience to force but by his denial of it does Achilles
bring himself ultimately to "destroy pity," as the gods say of him
before the embassy of Priam in the last book.

The contradictory anguish of his bile (*cholos*) has left his initial
anger (*menis*) in the background. From now on, in their anguishing
and fumbling night exploits, the Achaians objectify a state of war
that corresponds to Achilles' internal state. This state is constructed
of the same assumptions it is denying, and so it is doomed to failure.
Achilles, born of a god, begins the process through which Patroklos
will kill another born of a god, Sarpedon.

Achilles' lingering near Troy contradicts the absoluteness of his
refusal. Consequently, Patroklos cannot quite believe it. Tending
the wounds of Eurypulus in the absence of the wounded surgeon, he
declares that perhaps he can urge Achilles to battle. A battle scene
intervenes, and by the time he meets his friend (XVI, 1-5), he is
weeping for the Achaians. Phoenix, too, at the embassy had been
moved to shed a tear for the ships. Achilles is pierced with pity
(*oiktir*) for his friend's grief, though not for his people's suffering.
Still, his bluff of implacability condemns him to conceal even this
emotion, and so he reproaches his friend for crying like a girl—for
crying at the deaths in combat precisely as the water nymphs and

the female slaves will accompany his own weeping at the death of Patroklos.

The object of Achilles' feeling retorts by accusing him of having been born without all feeling. He asks for Achilles' armor, and he gets it. And from that point he mimes Achilles' prowess in what Whitman[26] perspicuously calls a surrealistic montage of the two heroes' qualities, Patroklos transcending himself to become like Achilles inside the shell of his friend's armor.

Achilles sticks to the consistency of his self-contradiction; forgetting anger, he has committed himself to acting as though he were angry. Dead to all but his friend, he wishes all lay dead and they alone survived to capture the battlements.

So his friend alone dies, committed by the extravagance of acts that the armor on his back inspires in him. The friend slaughtered, the armor is lost after a battle involving multitudes on both sides.

Achilles, having mourned and fasted, receives a substitute suit of divine armor. Henceforth he dominates the battle; the worlds of peace and war, surrounded by the cosmos, are emblazoned on the shield the poem devotes half a book to describing. He has been armed by the intervention of the overseeing powers, whose protection closes him in and stands before him on his shield.

The hero of an epic poem is bound to awareness and confrontation of death; Achilles' sense of his own death reemerges as his anger subsides:

> Now I shall go, to overtake that killer of a dear life,
> Hektor; then I will accept my own death, at whatever
> time Zeus wishes to bring it about, and the other immortals.
>
> (XVIII, 114-6)

Like Hector, he is caught in the pitiless logic of force. He has come full circle and brought the society with him. But the circle is not closed by the death of Hector. Achilles, killing the foremost of the enemy, justifies his society but not Society. The anger he ceased to hold towards the Achaeans is now brought to bear on his enemies, and on anything involved in the death of Patroklos, including the Briseis of whom he has spoken with such affection to the embassy:

> I wish Artemis had killed her beside the ships with an arrow
> on that day when I destroyed Lyrnessos and took her.
>
> (XIX, 59-60)

Odysseus perceives this double-edge to Achilles' return; he recommends that the troops eat, and that while they are eating the ransom be transferred to the tents of Achilles, making the reparation a *fait accompli* before the anger can take some other dread form.

Achilles will not eat. He goes out hunting Hector, and his rage appears in the extravagance of his challenges to Aineias and Hector, in his slaughter of the unarmed Lykaon whom he once spared, in his taunting the corpse of Lykaon.

His slaughter alters nature and the gods; the river swells with the corpses and threatens his very life. All the gods are called into play, and the river is finally dried up by a fire of the corpses Achilles has slaughtered.

Killing Hector, he drags his corpse around the tomb of Patroklos, abandoning food and sleep in the attempt to vent his now limitless rage.

All is satisfied, yet nothing is satisfied. He has returned to the Achaeans, he has killed and outraged Hector, he accepts the impending necessity of his own death. Still, he is brought to a condition of utter alienation, a condition which, as always, the poem can define only in its negative terms. These are physical ones, the deprivations of simple food and sleep that ultimately no man can sustain and live. Achilles must be harmonized with a total human society, and not through malnutrition or sleeplessness. The delicate courtesy of his arbitership in the funeral games over Patroklos, an attempt to play out his tensions, only perpetuates the tensions, leaving him equally overwrought. The games abound in strange fumblings and misses: no one gains relief from them, least of all Achilles.

What to do about Achilles becomes a problem to the very gods themselves. They might steal the body of Hector, but they will not, Apollo says, because:

> No, you gods; your desire is to help this cursed Achilleus
> within whose breast there are no feelings of justice, nor can
> his mind be bent, but his purposes are fierce, like a lion
> who when he has given way to his own great strength and
>   his haughty
> spirit, goes among the flocks of men, to devour them.
>
> (XXIV, 39-43)

"Achilles has destroyed pity (*eleos*)," he says. "There is no *aidos* (shame or respect) born in him." (44-5). Presumably he has lost pity and shame not just by mourning Patroklos (does not this testify to pity? But Apollo cites it), and not just by dragging Hector, but in the whole cycle of his acts, trapped in the dead end of mourning, abstinence, and outrage.

To work out of the deadly circle he has closed around himself, he must show a pity and respect fully commensurate with the pity and respect he has slighted. There is no Achaean, and no group of Achaeans, on whom he might work out the necessary therapeutic piety. He has already apologized to them, he has already judged the games; he has already fought for them; he has even been brought to acknowledge the limits of his prowess by his terror of drowning in the swollen river.

There is one man whose pity he has utterly outraged, to whom he has shown none of the *aidos* he gave the enemy Eëtion. That man is the head of the enemy camp, Priam. Zeus solves the gods' dilemma: Priam himself shall evoke pity and respect in Achilles by going to his tents to ransom Hector.

Now the predictable response of any Trojan toward Achilles is Hecuba's; she would like to tear out his liver with her teeth. But Priam alone measures up to the call of the god; he kisses Achilles' hands, swallowing an outrage so deep that he enables Achilles to swallow the total frustration in which he has trapped himself.

Achilles, in his situation, is the only one of all the Achaeans who would not slaughter Priam on the spot. The poem dwells on this point. Priam himself realizes it so forcibly that his hair stands on end for terror as he approaches Achilles' tent.

In the all-embracing social logic of the poem these two, fixed in opposition to each other, are also the only ones from the two camps who might approach each other.

Priam speaks: he succeeds in the great effort of imagining what it would be like to be Achilles' father, and then how Achilles would feel towards his father. Finally he is able to speak frankly of his own emotion, of the extreme suffering figured in their confrontation:

> I have gone through what no other mortal on earth has
>   gone through;
> I put my lips to the hands of the man who has killed
>   my children.   (XXIV, 505-6)

Achilles pushes him aside and ponders, thinking first of his own father, then of Patroklos (the sound of the mourning moves in the background); then, finally, of Priam. He, in response, is able to imagine what it is like to be Priam. Alone of the Achaeans to perform so great an outrage, he alone of the Achaeans stands out and above them enough to match so great an effort of the imagination.

By giving back the corpse of Hector, Achilles wakens again to pity and to respect. And by promising a share of Priam's ransom to Patroklos, he duplicates in a funeral ritual the piety towards property which his original anger had exaggerated.

To refuse Priam's ransom—an inconceivable touch in Homer's world—would be to perpetuate the exaggerated conditions to which he had condemned himself.

Finally, Achilles breaks his long fast by eating with Priam, and he promises to hold the Achaians off twelve days so that the Trojans may give Hector the full funeral rites that conclude the poem.

At Hector's rites, the ritual statements of Andromache and Helen, Hecuba and Priam, stand in their own superb objective rightness,

feelings proper to the situation of each without regard to the side
they are on: in this Achaeans and Trojans are alike; so have the
Achaeans mourned for Patroklos. And these ritual statements stand
tonally for the restful resignation of Achilles, precisely as the battle
scenes had figured the stages of his wrath, the earlier ones with
Diomede and Hector, the later ones with the wounded chiefs and
Patroklos.

> So they surrounded the tombing of Hector, tamer of horses.

Taken in this light, the last line of the poem, in its culminating position, has the effect of encompassing more than Hector. Achilles,
too, is tamed, the tamer whose own horse uttered the miraculous
words prophesying his death. The anger of Achilles is subdued to
the force of the world it masters. Force dominates the *Iliad*, but
force is superseded. Force, finding its end in death, in death is null:

> They piled up the grave-barrow and went away and thereafter
> assembled in a fair gathering and held a glorious
> feast within the house of Priam, king under God's hand.
> Such was their burial of Hector, tamer of horses.

II

Force dominates the *Iliad;* yet man in his very piety towards force
may express a principle of equanimity that nullifies force without
at all diminishing it. Achilles is to die, the Trojans are to be defeated, Hector is mourned; these events take their ultimate poetic
character not from the universal principle of force but from the
quiet piety, the *aidos,* that allows the force its order; without that
aidos the very force could not be coordinated as a central view of
combat. There would be merely chaos and raw slaughter.

Without it, too, the poetry would lack nobility: without that
piety no quiet would be heard in the inner ring of the hexameter.

All the action of the poem comes to a head in that piety: the
scene between Achilles and Priam. Only through that piety can

Achilles become released from the intolerable self-contradictions of his persisting rage into the piety-centered limits of his mortality. By virtue of that piety, the last line of the poem need only imply a force and a transcendence of force. One matter-of-fact sentence produces but a single flourish, the *ge* of slight emphasis elided so as to take up not even a short syllable of the measure:

Ὣς οἵ γ' ἀμφίεπον τάφον Ἕκτορος ἱπποδάμοιο.

So they surrounded the tombing of Hector, tamer of horses.

It is *they* who surround and tend the burial; the "ge" italicizes the Trojans, setting them off against the Achaians, and so Achilles against Hector. Different in their destinies, alike in their mortality, they are left at a single point, the burial of Hector, that extends to all.

The temper of the last line's understatement can be heard through the onward surge of the entire poem. Wholly resigned to grimness, the *Iliad* is founded on a wholeness that sees grimness in an even pious light of mortality.

Fire, for example, means violence (to violate Homer by translating his ordered integers into metaphors). And yet it also means peace:

> So with high thoughts these sat night-long by the outworks
> of battle, and their fires blazed numerous about them.
> As when in the sky the stars about the moon's shining
> are seen in all their glory, when the air has fallen to stillness
> and all the high places of the hill are clear, and the shoulders
>   out-jutting,
> and the deep ravines, as endless bright air spills from the
>   heavens
> and all the stars are seen and the mind of the shepherd
>   gladdens;
> such in their numbers blazed the fires the Trojans were
>   burning
> between the waters of Xanthos and the ships, before Ilion.

A thousand fires were burning there in the plain, and beside
   each
one sat fifty men in the flare of the blazing fire.
Standing each beside his chariot, champing white barley
and oats, the horses there awaited well-throned dawn.

(VIII, 553-65)

The fires are lit for a violent intention: Hector is forcing the
Achaians to stay on the plain. But these fires in their appearance
evoke the air's stillness. The brightness by which the rivers and
ships along the plain may be seen is set into comparison with the
way a shepherd gladdens to see mountains and endless bright air.

The improvisation of the surging syntax almost but not quite
corresponds to the single line: it is too adaptive to be called simply
paratactic. The unrhetorical repetition of "stars" and "fires," insists
on the peace by the very sameness. The scene is held, the poetry
rushes forward. Time, too, rushes forward evenly. The horses (Hector tames them in the poet's ultimate epithet) await the dawn, a
dawn to bring deaths; and, finally, the truce of Hector's burial. The
barley they eat is white, a contrast to the darkness, a likeness to
dawn; but contrast or likeness are dim overtones beside the inviol-
ably concrete whiteness of the barley. Dawn is well-throned as men
never are; but like men it has a throne.

The words, by virtue of their seemingly casual usage, let each
object stand out for itself. Yet each stands in a dramatic relation
to the moment and what lies beyond the moment. Each suggests
violence and peace. The horses stand beside the chariots; together
they will be violent, but now they are peaceful. The scene is beau-
tifully clear, but the clarity is of a violent intent. Later fires will
burn the ships of Hector, and also of Patroklos; but later still, fires
will ritually consume their corpses.

The mind *(phren)* or heart of the shepherd gladdens. And the
Trojans have been thinking *(mega phroneontes)* high thoughts.
Presumably the sight of the fires across the plains may buoy them
up to something like the gladness of the shepherd looking at the

stars; but the poetry neither pauses nor builds to insist on this point of the comparison. Just so it lets its caesura come with the flowing verse; just so it enjambs now and then as occasion offers.

The last two lines of this passage and the book leave the scene to look ahead into a well-throned light. For even if we ran the poetry on here and ignored the perceptive book divisions of the Alexandrian editors, there would still be an equal break in the sense.

This poetry moves ahead simply with its simple words. Every line, at the same time, keeps an easy wholeness in view, a wholeness of which grim force would be too strict a formulation; but the other, the peace of piety, cannot be said to counterbalance. It only transcends. Piety and force are the sole pair of elements blended in the poem without being contrasted.

Violence always predominates: peace always transcends; yet dominance and transcendence stand in no fixed balance. Violence is held more in view by the comparable simile that crops up to heighten the crown of fire Athene gives Achilles before battle:

> As when a flare goes up in the high air from a city
> from an island far away, with enemies fighting about it
> who all day long are in the hateful division of Ares
> fighting for their own city, but as the sun goes down signal
> fires blaze out one after another, so that the glare goes
> pulsing high for men of the neighboring island to see it,
> in case they might come over in ships to beat off the enemy;
> so from the head of Achilles the blaze shot into the
>   bright air.   (XVIII, 207-214)

The ominousness of violence is heightened, but a clarity of something else remains to which the violent do homage, the piety of defensive fires set against the force of the fire round Achilles' head. It is Athene who has kindled this blaze, an Athene who has elsewhere held back Achilles' sword. The air is bright and high, the divisions of Ares are hateful. Men set fires so as to fight for their own city, a value that exists over, and at once impossibly and triumphantly beyond, the fighting.

CHAPTER THREE

回回

The Man of Many Turns

THE epic poem is all-embracing; it is comprehensive, rather than encyclopedic, in character. It is their focus, more even than their lack of verse form, which deprives *Finnegans Wake* or *La Comédie Humaine* of an epic aura, and which almost gives one to *War and Peace*. The distinction, while elusive, is nicely illustrated by the contrast between the encyclopedic *Tesoro* of Dante's master Brunetto Latini and the comprehensiveness of the *Divina Commedia* itself.

The code that is to press the mortality of the hero, the verse style that is to sound the depths of his objectified feeling, though they must derive from tradition, cannot simply be received from it, even if the tradition be that of the man's earlier work.

An epic poem must find its embodiment in a wholly adequate fable. The test of adequacy is not to be found in some generality such as War, the subject of many long poems, or Wandering, the subject of many others. An epic adequacy, moreover, cannot be said to be guaranteed by the resonance of an archetypal plot. Poems with stories, short and long, in all conventions, draw as heavily on the archetypal situation as they do on the rhythmic emphasis of a meter —that is to say all but universally—and perhaps for related reasons.

It may be said, in brief, that epic adequacy resides in some myth

that can unify all the incidents of a given poem into a view of experience large enough to pose completeness for the life of the protagonist. The poet's great task of invention is finding the myth for
his particular poem, a problem that Homer had to solve by centering on Achilles no less than Milton did by centering on Adam.
Such adequacy may not be gained by merely choosing a subject
which superficially resembles some other adequate myth. Each epic,
to possess its own universality, must fully articulate the view it en-
visions on ground it wins for itself. It is the poet of *Beowulf* who
makes his myth superior to that of the *Waltharius*. Looking at epic
poems after the fact, we can remark on the aptness of the invention: if such aptness were completely bound up with generic laws,
we would have more epic poems than we do. Getting the right myth
and a "classic line" together at full pitch is one of the rarest of literary acts.

So Homer—if we may conceive of the same man moving on with
the same traditional equipment from *Iliad* to *Odyssey*—did not repeat himself by selecting some similar myth. He did not go on to
the Seven Against Thebes or some other war, as Apollonius superficially chose Jason because Odysseus had been done, as Statius and
so many others opted for their own or another national myth of
war, aping the *Iliad*. Nor did he handle his verse in quite the same
way.

Homer managed the complexity of the *Iliad* by coordinating an
entire society at war. This achievement was unique, and since it
was, it could not serve him for a poem which presents a like complexity in the sequential experience of a single hero.

Achilles stands at the center of the *Iliad*, but his world measures
him. Odysseus, however, measures his world as he moves through
it. And it does not alter him; he remains the same from first to last,
not only in the actual time span of the poem, but also, essentially,
over the twenty years of his wanderings.

In his dominance of the action he resembles Beowulf, Roland, and
the Cid. But their experience is also single, while Odysseus goes

through varieties of experiences that intimately mirror his complexity while testing his mind and emotions. In its characteristically light and subtle way, the *Odyssey* exhibits a hero whose experience is internalized; whose psyche is plumbed. So the heroes of the best epic poems after Homer—Aeneas, Dante, Adam—resemble Odysseus more closely than they do Achilles. And Pound has taken Odysseus in *The Cantos* for the persona most fit to mirror his varieties of experience.

The actual fable *(logos)* of the *Odyssey* is short, as Aristotle[1] points out. And yet the poem is complexly interwoven *(peplegmenon)*. This is because we have recognition *(anagnorisis)* throughout, he says, and this simple term serves as well as any other to describe Homer's mediation between his single hero and the hero's manifold experience.

The poem insists on this singleness, and this complexity, in its very first line:

Ἄνδρα μοι ἔννεπε, Μοῦσα, πολύτροπον, ὃς μάλα πολλὰ

Tell me, Muse, about the man of many turns, who many . . .

Man, the first word. Complexity is named twice, in *polutropon,* "of many turns," and also in *polla,* "many."

Odysseus' situation deepens in time, and the situation of the poem deepens as it progresses; yet Odysseus' adequacy remains everywhere the same in all its aspects *(polutropos)*. Only by a kind of alteration of the substance of the poem can we accept Cedric Whitman's[2] reading of a developing self for Odysseus. His wholeness appears from the beginning in the memory of friends and comrades about him, in the persistence of his return, in his adroitness at meeting the enigmas of societies so variable that beside them the forms of Proteus which Menelaus must master seem simple indeed.

Through all the "change" of the poem—the term is Whitman's—

Odysseus, by intelligence and striving (as the opening tells us) copes consistently with minds and peoples:

> Tell me, Muse, about the man of many turns, who many
> Ways wandered when he had sacked Troy's holy citadel;
> He saw the cities of many men and he knew their thought.

The variations of scene in the Odyssey involve a progression from the young to the mature (Telemachus to Odysseus), from the old to the new (Ithaca to a Phaeacian present), from the single to the complex (Nestor to Menelaus; Calypso to and through Circe), from the hostile to the hospitable (Ciconians to Phaeacians), from the natural to the fantastic (Ciconians to Hades, to the Oxen of the Sun groaning on the roasting spits), from the known Troy far from home to the remote Phaeacia whence Odysseus may soon sail for Ithaca.

Underlying these progressions is the psyche of the hero, broad because we have narrow ones (Nestor, Telemachus) for comparison. And since everyone's experience is appropriate for his character, the experience becomes a figure of the extent and complexity and subtlety of his inner life.

Applying this principle of congruence between a man's self and his destiny to the smaller characters, to the other peoples, we may apply it *a fortiori* to Odysseus. In this principle lies the canon of unity for the whole poem. Character in the *Iliad* is a given affirmation of a man's stable situation. In the *Odyssey* the situation is in flux, which means not that character changes, but that the flux of situation itself is seen to rest obscurely on the predisposition of the person or persons involved, character as fate.

The heroes return from war on voyages that are revelatory to us of their very selves. The simple Nestor had a straight return, the proud Agamemnon a disastrous one. The subtle and elegant Menelaus, a slighter of the gods, finds a return which tests his subtlety. Prompted by a nymph, he must first grapple with Proteus' sleepy noon disguises on lonely Pharos; then sacrifice in Egypt to the gods.

Far more various are the wanderings of Odysseus, and consequently far more famous is Odysseus himself. He is outstanding in all virtues (IV, 815: *pantoies aretesi kekasmenon*).* And the fullness of his humanity is mirrored in his wanderings.

Telemachus, too, voyages to learn to become like his father, to overcome his excessive respect (*aidos,* III, 24). He already has too much of what Achilles had too little. As the disguised goddess of wisdom says to him:

> Few are the sons who are equal to their fathers;
> Most are worse, but few are better than their fathers.
> If you would not be a coward hereafter, and senseless,
> If the counsel of Odysseus has not forsaken you wholly,
> Your hope in that case is to bring these deeds to pass.
>
> (II, 276-280)

Telemachus passes over into his manhood; it is through him, as he moves into the present of the poem, that the narrative begins, evoking both memory and futurity in the longing for Odysseus, and also the dim sense that the father who has been gone so long may have come to his mortal end.

Telemachus, risking a voyage to learn the facts about his father, learns that no simple facts are forthcoming, because facts undergo the alteration of memory; the glorious Trojan war that Nestor tells about, in which he and Odysseus were equal counsellors, does not seem the exploit that subtle Helen and Menelaus remember, focusing as it does on the deceptions of the wooden horse.

How a man sees things depends on who he is; Intelligence is the presiding goddess. These gods are not objective, standing for the unknown-and-visible, as in the *Iliad*. They are clear in the *Odyssey*, and yet they too vary according to the observer, who is then himself objectively presented in the foreground of the poem. To Menelaus they are beings who must be propitiated. Nestor sees them as stubborn (III, 147), Helen as capable of great favor (IV, 220-222), the

---

* The plural here forbids our reading *arete* in anything like a Platonic sense.

Phaeacians as always benign. At the same time this particular people takes the gods with sophisticated familiarity and humor, laughing at Demodocus' tale about Ares and Aphrodite; adultery occasions mirth for them—the very evil that Penelope has been avoiding for twenty years.

Character is fate: who a man is also determines how far he goes, how widely he is tested, what sort of a home he has made his own. In this sense men get exactly what they deserve, a moral transparently presented at the very outset in Zeus' speech to Athene and the other gods:

> Well now, how mortal men do accuse the gods!
> They say evils come from us, yet they themselves
> By their own recklessness get pains beyond their lot.

The Phaeacians are near to the gods (V, 35); they dwell far away from other mortals, having been close to the challenging Cyclops. Their location and their way of life are taken altogether for a total character that compasses Odysseus at this stage, but does not absorb him.

Each man is closed in the world of his own perceptions, and so is each people. Each place visited is an episode for the variable Odysseus, as in a lesser way for his searching son. Nestor lives a simple life, his boys doing his work for him. It is a comfortable life, too; there are smooth stones before his palace. Beyond his imagination, overland from his territory, lies the elegant court of Menelaus, come upon characteristically in the midst of a wedding celebration. In that court there is a dominance of ceremoniousness all but total. But neither of Telemachus' hosts exhibits any trait so surprising as the near-supernaturalism of the Phaeacians, who also marry their cousins; or the out-and-out incest of the forever dining children of Aeolus.

Pain* befalls man, but the gods have taken pain away from the

---

* George Dimoff[3] finds pain the pervasive theme of the *Odyssey*, deriving Odysseus' name from the verb for suffering.

Phaeacians. With pain, the gods have taken away the sort of wholeness exemplified, as always, by Odysseus, who lands naked and
hungry on *their* shore just before finally going home. Nestor can
face pain in nostalgia, but Menelaus can stand little pain. His "heart
breaks," he tells us, when he learns from Proteus that he must sail
the relatively little distance from Pharos to Egypt. And he has small
patience for combat, as his words imply:

> quick is the glut of cold lamentation   (IV, 103)

Helen passes to her guests a drink with a nepenthe in it, to make
the drinker so forget all his pain that:

> He would not shed a tear down his cheeks the whole day long,
> Not if his mother and his father were both to die,
> Not if right in front of him his brother or his dear son
> Were slaughtered with bronze, and he saw it with his
>   own eyes.   (IV, 224-7)

Through the formality of Helen and Menelaus there is felt a certain coldness. And to Odysseus the Phaeacians display a childish eagerness, for all their own elegance. Menelaus has the servants bathe
Telemachus, a task Nestor assigned to his own daughter. Anxious
about their cleanliness, Menelaus orders the bath as soon as they
arrive; Nestor has had it done as a send-off. Such coldness, in this
poem of heartfelt pain and joy, may evidence cruelty. Menelaus
mentions casually that if Odysseus should care to settle nearby, he
would gladly sack and depopulate a city for his old friend.

Each character, of place and society, becomes objectified in the
comparing eye of the visitor; Telemachus, like his father, can compass the varieties by encountering them. Home is the norm, and
Ithaca—unlike Aeaea or Ogygia or Phaeacia or Pylos or Argos—
has no special features other than the chaos into which it has fallen.

Odysseus discovers himself on his way home. The wideness of the
way, the wideness of the character destined for so much turning, be-

comes apparent by comparison with the briefer ways of others, and by the more circumscribed societies, each of which objectifies a whole moral attitude and destiny: a character (*ethos*) of the sort Aristotle asserted this poem to be woven from (*peplegmenon*).[4]

Ithaca lacks the heightened felicity of Lacedaemon and Phaeacia, their ordered painlessness and easy delight. Subject to pain and chaos, it is the more rooted in the human variety known and sought by its absent overlord, and it stands waiting in memory, changing in reality, for his rearrival. When he does arrive, his reinstitution must be so deliberate as to take nearly half the poem. While Odysseus wanders, Ithaca stands in unseen relation to him, though from the beginning it is portrayed in its changed reality. Perpetually the poem holds his biased and unswaying nostalgia in a comparison, often unexpressed, between home and the place of sojourn. Explicitly he declares that Calypso surpasses Penelope in appearance and form, but such ideal excellence pales before the real rootedness of his mortality. Telemachus, in refusing Menelaus' gift of horses, admits that Ithaca affords poor pasturage; but he persists in his superlative praise of the island:

> In Ithaca there are no broad courses or any meadow;
> It has pasture for goats and is pleasanter than a horse pasture.
> But none of the islands that lie by the sea has good meadows
> Or a place for driving horses, and Ithaca surpasses them all.
>   (IV, 605-8)

So he feels; and so does his father, enough to strain his ingenuity to return there.

This epic hero substitutes supple intelligence for the courage and prowess of the Cid, Beowulf, and Achilles. He follows not a code but the course of his own longing, an inner canon the poem sets out as equally to be trusted. Consistently, then, he does not gather all he knows in order to face the unknown. He acts on hunches (Lestrygonians) or social canniness (Phaeacia) or a surfaced feeling (Calypso) or luck (Circe) or improvised plan (Cyclops). In a sense there is nothing he can rely on as known, because he always copes with a wholly new situation in utter ignorance:

> For I have arrived here as a long suffering stranger
> From afar, from a distant land; so I know no one
> Of the men who conduct this city and its fields.
>
> (VII, 22-25)

He faces not the unknown but the new, not death but transience. Transience, itself a consequence of mortality and a kind of figure for it, replaces death in the imaginative vision of this epic. Longing for permanence drives the resourceful Odysseus round the changing seas and years.

Home itself changes, in the relentless metamorphosis of a third of a life-time. Permanence and change, satisfaction and longing, joy and pain, foresight and happenstance—these never get fixed in hard opposition because Odysseus moves too fast and copes too variously. His fable allows him to embody all these complexities without setting one stiffly against another; without overembroiling himself in any, and also without slighting the real difficulty or allure of a single one.

It is not death he must face. From the present time of the poem on, that risk is slight. In this epic, a life rounds itself out by return to an original mature circumstance that the very course of life has altered.

Change brings pain, and yet the joy of changelessness among the lotus eaters or the Phaeacians lacks the fullness of changeful life. Death may be taken as a fearful circumstance and at the same time as bland fact. The death of his mother Anticleia is spoken of matter-of-factly (XIII, 59) in a salutation wishing joy.

In the seeming universality of transience, arrival seems forever debarred, and Odysseus comes back a second time to Aeolus, who will not help him; to Circe, who greets him with a warning. Back again he comes, also, to Scylla and Charybdis. Death lies as a test in the future. Though the hero's own death is vague and remote, he must risk it and pass its country in order to return. Odysseus can get back only by visiting the dead, all the way past the eternally shrouded Cimmerians. Even then it takes the escort of the Phaeacians, who are near to gods, to get him back. The Phaeacian vessel, moving like a star, unerringly and effortlessly swift, bears Odysseus in a sleep "most like to death" (XIII, 879-92) to the home he has not been able to sight for twenty years.

Odysseus has changed so much himself, and Ithaca has become so remote to him, that he does not know where he is when he wakes up there. Of the disguised Athene he asks a question at once obvious and profound: are the inhabitants hospitable or wild?

All is old, and all is new. If Odysseus did not recognize old elements in any new situation, he could not exercise his many wiles. If he did not have to confront the new, there would be less need for any wiles at all.

The need dwindles at the end, but it has not disappeared. At the end of his life he must undertake another journey across the sea and set up a tomb to Poseidon among men who do not know the sea (IX, 120 ff).

Odysseus stands midway between the easier returners, achievers of a simpler permanence, Menelaus and Nestor, and those who have died on the return, the victims to change, Agamemnon and Ajax, not to mention all his own followers.

Permanence brings joy, transience pain. The living sustain a subtle balance between permanence and transience, and so between joy and pain. The sea is sparkling but treacherous; to the solitary Odysseus Ogygia is joyful for its unearthly beauty but painful for its not being home. Pain coalesces with joy, or else a life is shown to lack the epic wholeness: if pain becomes total, one is to die; if joy fully dominates, one enters the lifeless permanence of the Lotus Eaters and the Phaeacians, whom Odysseus' long tale of suffering fills not with tears like his own but with a feeling of charm, the poem twice says (*kelethmos:* XI, 334; XIII, 2).

To return brings joy but causes pain. It is of the joy of return that Agamemnon speaks (IV, 522)—he who least of all would have cause to remember that joy. Yet the pain of becoming reinstated in a changed home offsets, precedes, and intensifies, the joy of restitution.

In his coping, Odysseus works his way through contrarieties; pain and suffering he names at once when he is asked what his wanderings have brought. Joy can be as much a trial as pain; heartbroken with longing on Calypso's isle, he refuses her blissful immortality but enjoys her in the cave. He lives a year with Circe. The Lotus Eaters, the Phaeacians, and the Sirens all promise—the first could even fulfill—a painless existence wherein the pain might be obviated and even the longing be gone. But the fullness of life demands the wholeness of longing; and Odysseus, delighted and also pained, pushes on to his return. All the sufferings of wandering are told, after the tears of a delightful song, to the banqueting, hedonistic court of an Alcinoos who has already promised escort home. The habit of Ithaca counters the novelty of the strange delights, and yet habit too is the enemy of the remembered home: Odysseus stays seven years on Calypso's island.

Within its scheme of variety, this broad poem can vary the key of an alteration between joy and pain without changing its tone. Each episode has a different flavor of joy or pain. As Odysseus sails away from Cyclops, he gets exulting delight in exchange for teeth-gnashing despair. Aeolus occasions first impulsive gladness and then a resigned, fearful despondency. An ocean of moods for the longing hero is held in the single vision of the poem.

2

The poem sustains a sense of the hero's fine equanimity in transience and permanence, in sorrow and joy, by having placed him in a flexible situation where he transcends every person and every people he meets. The equanimity of the hero also enters the verse, for example in its descriptions of the visible world through which Odysseus moves.

A fine veil of poetry, simple and delectating, limns the changing landscapes, none so fully described as Ithaca, and all consequently more immediately redolent of an almost lyric singleness, a seemingly mythic signification. But the significance merely impresses in passing, and does not construct allegories. What are the Cimmerians at the bounds of the deep-flowing ocean, shrouded in darkness and cloud, who never see the beams of the sun or the starry heaven? They are far (Ithaca is nearness) and shrouded (the mists part often in the clarity of the Adriatic sun; Ithaca sees sun and starry heavens). They stand before the underworld, sharing some of its obscurity.

As Stella[5] points out, the fruits and trees of this landscape are described more realistically than the fabulous vegetation found not only in the jewelled forests of Gilgamesh, but in such Greek legends as the Golden Apples of Hesperides. Yet as Max Treu[6] says, we cannot distinguish between fairytale and real in the landscape descriptions of the *Odyssey*. Its epithets are at once evocative and descriptive, far looser than those in the *Iliad*:

> The sun arose, leaving the *lovely* lake,
> Into the *much-bronze* heaven, where for immortals it shone,
> And for mortal men upon the *life-giving* earth.
>
> (III, 1-3)

All the grandeur of the *Iliad,* as Longinus says, but less intensity. *Polychalchon,** much-bronze, sets off no contrasts between "lovely" and "life-giving." The attributions are not faceted situationally, as they are in the *Iliad*. They merely rise to their seemingly haphazard descriptiveness, and their rightness seems to reside somewhat in a mythic resonance. The real and the fairy-tale are mingled in the

---

* Even if this word carries a memory of an Aegean primitive concept of a bronze heaven, as Stella[7] asserts, we must decide what the epithet denotes in the poem.

memory of the recounting Odysseus and the perceptions of the
poem's hearer. Against the joy of a given place stands the hero's
own pain; against the beauty of life the hard risk of death, and the
difficult, losing battle against time. At the end of all the easy hos-
pitalities of Phaeacia, of the checked Circe, of Calypso, lies the
difficult restitution in Ithaca. The transience of an arriver's longing,
of the guest's contingency, clings to the poetry, for Odysseus' longing son as for himself:

> And they came to hollow Lacedaemon full of ravines.
>
> (IV, 1)

This is a new sight to Telemachus, a temporary one; his enjoy-
ment of the visual loveliness, the presence of this poetic line in the
narrative, is tinged with his fearful search for light about his father.
Helen's nepenthe does not last for him, though it may for the
Lacedaemonian court.

> They when they saw it
> Wondered at the house of the king nourished by Zeus;
> Like the beam of the sun it was or like the moon.
>
> (IV, 43-5)

But the sun goes down, the moon rises, and by day or night there
is toil. Lacedaemon for the son, like Phaeacia or Ogygia for the
father, is a delightful interlude, something unreal in the reality of
life. A man who has a full life on his hands can see the loveliness,
along with some of the unreality. His eyes enjoy the glitter, but his
heart is in his mouth; the words catch the glitter, the rhythm moves
wave on nostalgic wave in the total feeling of the poem.

The hexameter—lightly!—bears the burden of sadness, reiterating
in its "disappointed" last foot the sorrow of the total fable. Poetry
makes people weep in the *Odyssey,* even finally in the Phaeacian
court. Odysseus himself weeps to hear of Troy, though he weeps
behind his veil.

"The accents of the Homeric hexameter are the soft rustle of a
leaf in the midday sun, the rhythm of *matter*"—Spengler's fine ear[8]
has picked up the characteristic rhythm of the *Odyssey.* Not, I feel,

of the *Iliad*. In both poems, of course, quantity determines the main rhythm, and not accent. Where Vergil patterns the subordinate accents, Homer lets them fall where they may. This randomness in the *Iliad* produces a surging afflatus, rather the way the free meter of the ballad does. In the *Odyssey*, I do not hear these free syllables as surging. The unaccounted accents play, as it were, over the surface of the statement, as the words themselves seem to do. In the *Iliad* the unaccounted accents do a more strenuous work, and yet are closer to prose in their lack of emphasis; in the *Odyssey* they twitch the veil of the poetry, rhythmically carrying a sense of the variety of life.

The poetry reveals its lightness in the very particularity of its designations; it touches lightly on literalness, and quite haphazardly (*pace* Auerbach[9]). All is known, but the known is a mystery. Home remains the same, but time changes it. Take the line about the constellation Bear, "which they also call by the name Wagon":

οἴη δ᾽ ἄμμορός ἐστι λοετρῶν Ὠκεανοῖο·

And it alone has no share in the washings of Ocean.

(v, 275)

The statement conveys a literal piece of astronomical fact, but with a light resonance that lies in each word. "Oie," alone, echoes the aloneness of Odysseus. "Has no share," or "unfated" *(ammoros)*: in the very negation lies a whole sense of fate, at once specific and general. The "washings" *(loetroi)* are carrying Odysseus too; he is caught in the wash of the ocean stream above which gleams the Bear. In its suggesting of analogy, though, the line is not meta-phoric. It merely speaks of the natural world, the stars and the sea, in words that usually apply to man, and so it hints at a participa-tion in a total situation which is not patterned but merely moves ahead in its predictable but incalculable alterations. This hint is absent from the line when it occurs in the *Iliad* merely to describe a point of Achilles' shield.

And the tone of the poem, the fine veil of what, for lack of a more delicate term, we may call irony—that tone veils all the actions and the landscapes. The hexameter carries that tone, forbidding, as it were, even the most dire incident from carrying a tragic cast. The elegiac becomes a delectated likeness. At the height of the grisly Cyclops episode, a joke: Odysseus is "no man." Homer may have got this joke from a folk-tale or not; it has the same effect in the poem, the consonant presentation of an exultant joy within a crushing sadness.

Through its tone of equanimity, the verse conveys pain and joy without setting one paradoxically off against the other, as the *Iliad* somewhat schematically sets the actuality of pain against the memory of joy. The veil of mystery covers everything in the *Odyssey;* yet everything also shows through the tonal veil. Deception comes up again and again, the host of disguises and feints and subtle unmentioned calculations and adjustments which every character makes, and preeminently the resourceful Odysseus. Even gods deceive; right at the start in Book I they quickly hold their committee meeting about Odysseus, while his enemy Poseidon, the opposition, is conveniently far away among the Ethiopians.

For all the deceptions, clarity. For all the caprice, justice. For all the wanderings, return. Here the world is utterly clear and whole, and utterly mysterious. Its clarity is its mystery, the poetry is declaring. The same blue Aegean washes real and miraculous shores, and the real and the miraculous differ only in incidental, equally perceptible details, which the poetry proffers:

> On the hearth a big fire was burning, and the smell from afar
> Of cedar and easy-split pulp was exhaled to the island
> As it blazed. She within, singing in a lovely voice,
> Going to and fro at the loom, wove with a golden distaff.
> Wood was growing around the cave in abundance,
> Alder and black poplar and well-scented cypress,
> Where the birds with their long wings went to sleep,
> Horned owls and hawks and, with their long tongues,
> Salt water crows, who are busy with the things of the sea.
>
> (v, 59-67)

A superlative place, but with a quality finely perceptible as of itself; distinct from the superlative of Lacedaemon or Phaeacia or Aeaea. The cave, the trees, the birds, and later the springs and meadows, characterize the physical world of Calypso, which is at the same time her world of spirit, just as the deepness of Ithaca resides for the poetry, as for the naming Telemachus, in the very physical home-liness and roughness of the place.

Often we are given designations for the sea, wine-faced or grey, Protean as the numberless lands are different. Yet each is clear and whole unto itself, each capable of receiving at times the enumera-tive detail Auerbach claims is typical of the *Odyssey* generally.

Homer, however, is not so enumerative in his verse as Auerbach claims. The poet does tend to linger over detail of the narrative, as Auerbach follows Schiller in asserting; but not utterly for the sake of the detail. If we cannot read some other significance into the detail—the ritual use of Calypso's trees, for example—we cannot obliterate significance either. Certainly to assert that Homer tells "everything" would be to make him inarticulate. He must select, though more abundantly than the inspired author of *Genesis*.

Nor can it be said, with Auerbach, that the *Odyssey* has no "back-ground," no hidden depths of motive. It is all foreground, to be sure, but a light irony holds all the detail. That light irony consti-tutes the background, the delicate and profound sense of success in transience, of unfinality in any terror, which renders the epic sense of life to the *Odyssey,* lightening the poetry and unifying the fable; so that the poem stands as something at once close to what we ex-pect from a novel in its incident, and yet utterly different from a novel in its final bearing.

3

In all the alterings of circumstance, in all the pains, the hero's self remains wholly adequate in its adaptability *(polutropos)*—and with-out being defined. To take Odysseus' wanderings as deepening him, the way Cedric Whitman does, involves reading the significance of the places he visits as allegory or symbol. They do have the ring of archetype, and they do figure a total spiritual condition, each of them, mysteriously. Yet to read their significance as symbol or allegory is to pierce the veil of mystery. The depth is all on the surface, a sunlit mystery. No totality glides like a Moby Dick in the darkness beneath these waters. To interpret the surface of this poem metaphorically is to translate the surface as gaining significance from some depth; but the significances are all there on the surface, embodied simply in landscape and lightness of gesture.

Achilles develops and realizes his manhood. Odysseus moves ahead with his into time, changing only as he ages, while events at once tax and fortify him. He simply exists. No coordinated social world can deepen him; there is only the series of unpredictable surfaces, each complete and partial in itself, which he shows himself capable by meeting, and whole by transcending. Intelligence attends him from first to last, and the manifestation of Athene at his landing on Ithaca attests no special consideration, no final success, but only a momentary embodiment, as the world of his striving has actualized itself under his feet without his being aware of it.

When Odysseus speaks to himself, as he does after having set out from Ogygia (V, 299ff), the soliloquy explores no motive but merely develops and estimates the incidence of misfortune. Once again, it is all on the surface: the depth inheres in the irony with which it is presented, an irony so slight as to seem transparent, vanishing at a breath.

The irony may at numerous moments emerge into event. Odysseus slights Calypso in his account to Arete, falsifies his contact with Nausicaa, and delicately implies a refusal of Alcinous' marriage offer by mentioning in the course of his narrative how he has often refused such offers elsewhere. Menelaus, who had to wander years because he had slighted the gods, gives Telemachus a libation bowl! So, the poem hints, he has learned his lesson. Athene sacrifices to her enemy Poseidon. But the events need not be ironic; they may be deadly serious, and irony is still conveyed in the uniform tone of the verse.

Without the *poetry,* the flexible Odyssean hexameter, the humor would be episodic, and so would the nostalgia. The variety of incident would then merely add up to a superficial romance of the picaresque with some fine detail and occasional lyric moments, rather like the *Lusiads.* But in the *Odyssey* nostalgia comments on humor. Humor and nostalgia blend but do not fuse in the epic unity of this poem, lighter than the *Iliad,* but no less profound.

Suffering, even the dark terror of Cyclops or Odysseus' wholesale slaughter of the suitors, is kept serenely in vision, as it is not in even so equanimous a comedy as the *Tempest.* Only loosely can the *Odyssey* be called a comedy, or even a comic epic. It is an epic whose lightness compasses comic events, and also tragic; that allows of both tragic and comic events without inventing a whole philosophic relation for them (or a Dantesque justification) beyond the unitary tonal feeling of myth and verse.

Part Two

CHAPTER FOUR

The Refined Style

T HE epic poem, whatever balance it strikes between single line and all-embracing fable, retains a normativeness and directness of presentation to which lyric poetry in its most brilliant tradition does not aspire. In the epic, life is a mystery which the poem manages to take whole by placing the mystery at its center: the unknown inheres in the known. In the lyric poetry of Blake and Rimbaud, or Pindar and Sappho, life is a mystery the poem harmonizes in nostalgic flashes: the known takes a single emotive (and intellectual) leap at the unknown.

Poets, like all who use language, by choosing what they will say, limit it. By setting it necessarily into syntactic, and rhythmic, order, they organize it. A poem is inclusive, insofar as it contains chosen materials, and in a kind of order. It is exclusive, insofar as other materials and other kinds of order are left out. We should ask of a poem not how much is included, but what, and in what way; and what is excluded, and in what way. A principle of exclusion implies a principle of inclusion, and vice versa; Wordsworth, in the *Preface to the Lyrical Ballads* wants poetry to include certain material one way and this involves excluding a specific kind of material handled another way.

The "diaphanous" epic, while highly inclusive, is not more so than the "prismatic" lyric. (The terms are those W. P. Ker uses, without applying them to specific genres.) Blake's "The Sick Rose," includes as much in its reference as does the *Odyssey*, and with comparable profundity:

> O Rose, thou art sick!
> The invisible worm,
> That flies in the night,
> In the howling storm,
>
> Has found out thy bed
> Of crimson joy;
> And his dark secret love
> Does thy life destroy.

The way in which this tremendous poem is inclusive allows us to bring all the traditional equipment of critical analysis to bear on it: image and metaphor and symbol are there, rhetorical stance and organization, logical statement, deployment of connotation, modalities of tone, orders of rhythm and meter, implications of doctrinal system, all interpenetrating of course. Though not so obviously as the highly wrought work of Donne and Pindar, Rimbaud and Crane and Keats, this poem has all the richness of indirection, not to say idiosyncracy, in which Coleridge, again, finds "the specific symptoms of poetic power." Taking this "prismatic lyric" and noticing its quick fluidity of language and ruminative delicacy of perception, we may speak, with Staiger,[1] of vivified "memory," *Erinnerung,* the term he uses to characterize all lyric poetry.

Staiger, however, when he implies that lyric poetry must display his *Erinnerung,* is too exclusively romantic and modern (though a classically trained translator of *The Greek Anthology*). There is a kind of lyric poetry other than the "prismatic," which, like epic poetry, tends to be direct and normative in style, to avoid Staiger's *Erinnerung* and Coleridge's "specific symptoms," to eschew metaphor or else to use it for mere rhetorical condensation instead of Blake's apocalyptic overtones or Baudelaire's correspondences. This "direct" kind of lyric poetry is less inclusive than either epic or prismatic lyric. It does not attempt to embrace or suggest as much as possible of some apprehended whole; instead it contents itself with trying to set forth some understood part with maximum objectivity and control, and in such a moderate way that it comes to seem like stylized prose. A speech so controlled in manner gives an impression that is cultivated and purified: refined.

It is this "refined" style, common to both epic and lyric for over a millennium, that Vergil learned before he became an epic poet. He transmitted it to Dante, who made of it something sweet and new in the vernacular tongue, a *dolce stil nuovo;* and to Milton, who force-fed it to become a near-equivalent of "prismatic" lyric. But usually the refined style has qualities that Staiger attributes largely to epic poetry. It attains to a "thereness" of simply represented objects and ideas; to *Vorstellung* or representation. By calling this style refined I should like to suggest it is not only a neutral style (Coleridge's word for it), and not only a common style (the way Eliot[2] speaks of Dante's style).* This is a style whose purity is notable because it has put the common diction through a selection process. The style is pure by being *refined.* Arnold meant something like this by both his terms of praise, *grand,* and *academic*— though neither word puts its finger on the Dantesque excellence, too common to be grand, too *dolce* and also too *nuovo* to be academic.

Poetry in the refined style moves within limits, masterfully. When successful, it conveys an impression of "classic" inevitability which cannot be attributed to rhetoric or diction alone, to say nothing of metaphor, when the full play of metaphor lies beyond its limits. The refined style is always more remarkable for the exquisite bal-

* He says it evolves from the Italian dialects; I would say it recaptures through Vergil this postHomeric heritage.

ance it achieves among its elements than for the predominance of any one of them—something that in fact it rather avoids. One hears this refinement in the verse of Robert Frost, from time to time, when the prismatic, and the idiosyncratic too, have been shaded out:

> Why make so much of fragmentary blue
> In here and there a bird, or butterfly,
> Or flower, or wearing-stone, or open eye,
> When heaven presents in sheets the solid hue?

> Since earth is earth, perhaps, not heaven (as yet)—
> Though some savants make earth include the sky;
> And blue so far above us comes so high,
> It only gives our wish for blue a whet.

Verse of this firm, even tone cannot allow even so much modification as, for example, Blake's "dark secret love," so strong a coloring as "crimson joy"; nor can it begin to give its central image free rein. In this style, a word like "whet" would be too idiosyncratic in any position but one of full rhetorical emphasis; it is too curious a word not to be assigned a job of special prominence under the set normative conditions of the classic voice Frost adopts, to keep his central metaphor in full rhetorical control. Attributions are made to classify along broad simple lines, "earth is earth," "blue so far above us comes so high," or, even more simply:

> Sea waves are green and wet,
> But up from where they die,
> Rise others vaster yet,
> And those are brown and dry.

To find a voice of comparably classic calm, so unmodulated as this, one would have to go all the way back to *The Greek Anthology;* as perhaps the classical student Frost has himself done. Even when the voice rises toward dramatic or near dramatic speech, or when it shades into lyric privacy, the refined style can be heard, bringing

Frost closer to the Augustans than to most of Eliot or Tennyson;
and closer yet to Horace:

> You went to meet the shell's embrace of fire
> On Vimy Ridge; and when you fell that day
> The war seemed over more for you than me,
> But now for me than you—the other way.
>
> .   .   .   .
>
> Back out of all this now too much for us,
> Back in a time made simple by the loss
> Of detail, burned, dissolved, and broken off
> Like graveyard marble sculpture in the weather,
> There is a house that is no more a house
> Upon a farm that is no more a farm
> And in a town that is no more a town.

The voice is as though purged of personality; an "objective" voice
like the voice of epic, speaking in a style whose refinement is as
"pure" as that of "pure poetry" without any of the clean musical
emotive drift to which that particular style aspired. In this essential
quality alone—and it is enough to give both the same tonic ring—
Frost resembles Rilke more than he does any of his English contemporaries. It is a ring that gives Rilke, too, the sound of objective
inevitability:

> *Aus Drang, aus Artung,*
> *aus Ungeduld, aus dunkler Erwartung,*
> *aus Unverständlichkeit und Unverstand:*
>
> *Dies alles auf sich nehmen und vergebens*
> *vielleicht Gehaltnes fallen lassen, um*
> *allein zu sterben, wissend nicht warum—*
>
> *Ist das der Eingang eines neuen Lebens?*

The last phrase is Dante's, and the note itself; or rather, the note is
one Dante shares with the refined poets of two millennia. It is a

note, this note of refinement, that can be heard through the different
key signatures of English poetry once it became civilized:

> Your ÿen two wol slee me sodenly;
> I may the beautee of hem not sustene,
> So woundeth hit thourghout my herte kene.
>
> And but your word wol helen hastily
> My hertes wounde, while that hit is grene,
> Your ÿen two wol slee me sodenly;
> I may the beautee of hem not sustene.   (CHAUCER)
>
> False hope prolongs my euer certaine griefe;
> Traytrous to me and faithfull to my loue:
> A thousand times it promis'd me reliefe,
> Yet neuer any true effect I proue.   (DANIEL)
>
> Sweet, be not proud of those two eyes,
> Which Star-like sparkle in their skies:
>
> .   .   .
>
> When as that *Rubie,* which you weare,
> Sunk from the tip of your soft eare,
> Will last to be a precious Stone,
> When all your world of Beautie's gone.   (HERRICK)
>
> Then *Sinne* combin'd with *Death* in a firm band
> To rase the building to the very floore:
> Which they effected, none could them withstand.
> But *Love* and *Grace* took *Glorie* by the hand,
> And built a braver Palace than before.   (HERBERT)
>
> O could I flow like thee, and make thy stream
> My great example, as it is my theme!
> Though deep, yet clear, though gentle, yet not dull,
> Strong without rage, without o'er flowing full.
>
>   (DENHAM)
>
> A milk-white *Hind,* immortal and unchang'd,
> Fed on the lawns, and in the forest rang'd;
> Without unspotted, innocent within,
> She fear'd no danger, for she knew no sin.

Yet had she oft been chas'd with horns and hounds,
And Scythian shafts; and many winged wounds
Aim'd at her heart; was often forc'd to fly,
And doomed to death, though fated not to dy.
                                                        (DRYDEN)

I am a part of all that I have met;
Yet all experience is an arch wherethrough
Gleams that untraveled world whose margin fades
Forever and forever when I move.   (TENNYSON)

No, there is not a dawn in eastern skies
To rift the fiery night that's in your eyes;
But there, where western glooms are gathering,
The dark will end the dark, if anything:
God slays Himself with every leaf that flies,
And hell is more than half of paradise.   (ROBINSON)

In evenness of voice, though the last two rise slightly from it, these poets all have the ring of classic refinement, a dominant likeness we may tend to forget in pointing out the distinguishing differences: Chaucer's courtly French form or Daniel's intellectualized Italian one, Herrick's miniaturization and Herbert's almost emblematic allegory; the more Spenserian allegory of Dryden, tempered as Denham tempers the metaphysical extension of his thought-metaphor. We have to look through the purity of this style to see, faintly, Tennyson's nostalgia or Robinson's despair.

It would be difficult to enumerate briefly the traits of this style, beyond a tendency to logical play in word-repetition, a certain predilection for monosyllables and abstract or generic words, and a perhaps unconscious care *not* to follow the Romantic injunction "load every rift with ore," so that the statements carry a large breathing space around them. Mainly, we may remark, in every one of these passages, a sure reining-in of any stylistic device which would make the voice run away and break the even pace of refinement. The diction is kept from excessive oddness or particularity. Word qualification or logical progression are not permitted to take over the poem, as they do in Donne. Denham differs little from Daniel or Chaucer, or Robinson, in the control of his logic; the temperateness into which he has moderated a metaphysical convention defines him more clearly than does that convention, and makes him more distinctly a poet in the classic tradition of refinement than a late and faint follower of Donne and Marvell. As for the principle of inclusion, all these verses are simple, not to say conventional. If one accepted Cleanth Brooks' scale of merit according to degree,[3] and especially complexity, of inclusion, all would rank very low indeed. None exhibits the "language of paradox" markedly enough, even in the notable lines of logical qualification, to illustrate what Brooks asserts to be the distinguishing attribute of nearly all poetry (as indeed it is of much romantic and modern verse).

All these poets resemble for these moments at least, in the evenness of their refined style, more the Augustan poets who followed, or preceded, them, than they do the poets of prismatic paradox and metaphor. And they all share with the Augustans traits which are sometimes supposed to characterize just the Augustans themselves: the logical play of the metaphysicals neutralized into normalcy, the abstractions and the antitheses, the witty but unhurried movement of statement. The tools we use for Keats or Donne are as ill-adapted to Chaucer and Daniel, Rilke and Robinson, as to Pope and Dr. Johnson. And to isolate any one element critically, as Rosemund Tuve did the logico-rhetorical structure of argument, carries with it the danger of confusing Donne, whose glory is an extreme reliance on a distortion of his components, with Herbert and all these others, for whom the rhetoric is only one element in a balance artfully sustained without distortion. And poetry, for the refined style, lies in the balance more than in any one element of it.

The refined style may still be discerned as a ground bass when other elements begin to blend into it, as in the passages from Tennyson and Robinson above, or often in Burns:

> We twae hae paidl'd in the burn,
> Frae morning sun till dine;

But seas between us braid hae roar'd,
Sin auld lang syne.

The traditional lyric meditation here is quite alien to the ballad;
diction and tone are kept in a refined balance. And only the powerful admixture of the ballad stanza itself keeps the refined note from
being as pure as in Horace. The Scotch dialect alone, in this style,
attains a well-nigh Tuscan normalcy when handled thus, though not
always in Burns.

While Villon's rhythms have the splendid evenness and precision
of refinement, his diction shades away from the refined style into
somewhat too easy repetition, as in the first and sixth lines here, or
into mere denotative particularity, as in the second, third, and
fourth:

> *Dictes moy ou, n'en quel pays,*
> *Est Flora la belle Rommaine,*
> *Archipiada, ne Thaïs,*
> *Qui fut sa cousine germaine,*
> *Echo parlant quant bruyt on maine*
> *Dessus riviere ou sus estan,*
> *Qui beaulté ot trop plus qu'humaine,*
> *Mais ou sont les neiges d'antan:*

Repetitiveness and particularity, of course, derive from the central
conception of the *Testament* itself, and to say that Villon is less
refined than Horace or Herrick leaves him still a greater poet than
either.

He is greater, partly because he does pitch his voice higher. He
wants to take in more, while the refined style is a style of contentment *par excellence*. It wishes to master a part of the world, rather
than to raise large questions about universal mysteries. But the mastery it attains is itself full enough, that the refined style, in the hands
of Vergil, Dante and Milton, could be stretched to master an epic
wholeness.

This means was not possible for Homer, to begin with because he lacked a tradition of precise rhythmic modulation, and lacked also a wealth of class words on which the refined style depends so heavily to keep its semi-abstractions in control of its marshalled material. In Greece, as the refined style developed, the poet tended more and more to use general words, for "seeing," say, and not the specific modes, though as the heir to Homer's vocabulary he had available to him all the specific and modal words, not only as speech but actually in the stock of poetic vocabulary.

After Homer came the birth of philosophic considerations that produced a notion of generality—of classes—at just about the time when philosophy abandoned poetic discourse for prose. At just about this time, too, the rhythms of poetry in hexameter and elegiac couplet became more precise. Xenophanes in his own practice epitomizes the two movements of thought. He is a philosopher—a specifically anti-Homeric one—and throughout his practise he is a poet with subjects more special than those of other philosophers, than Empedocles* and Parmenides. In fact, Xenophanes' short poem about the gods constitutes in all particulars an epigram in the style that Callimachus and his contemporaries even further refined.

Homer, seen from the vantage point of philosophy, lays the elements of his experience out in a kind of encyclopedic apposition and mimes it orally rather than interpreting it. The effect of paratactic syntax and particularizing diction on the hearer is to bind him in a kind of knowledge which accepts experience without analyzing it. Hence, in Havelock's[5] interpretation, the necessity Plato felt to break Homer's hold before he could analyze knowledge. Charles Olson[6] stresses the availability of the sequential, unanalytic method of Homeric parataxis to modern poetry, and perhaps renders possible for the first time, at least since Aristotle, the assimilation of something like Homer's unmetaphoric and ungeneralizing style to

* Perhaps by the time of Empedocles, who is a century later than Xenophanes, the verse itself was felt as merely the sort of external ornament to philosophic conception that Lucretius, following among others Empedocles, declares it to be. Perhaps this is what lay behind Aristotle's remark[4] that Homer and Empedocles have nothing in common except meter.

poetry. But as a free choice, in the syncretic historicizing culture that is our own, and not in any way on terms like Homer's.

Neither our free choice, nor Homer's own terms, were possible right after the birth of philosophy. Language, once it had become analytic and grown abstract, could only be accepted on its current terms, and the refined style resulted as a means to organize an abstracted segment of experience poetically. For the original ideas put into verse by Xenophanes and Empedocles, or later Epicurus and Lucretius, the elegiac poets substituted a rhetorical strictness and normativeness of diction that struck a peace between received ideas and ordered invention. From Callinus and before to Catullus and after, Greek and Latin poetry in its shorter and unspecialized forms exhibited the rhetorical strictness, even-toned normalcy, and tendency to abstraction of the refined style, calling to mind Pope and Jonson— or Dante and Vergil—far more than Pindar and Sappho, or Aratus and Empedocles.

Our most sensitive historical critics, Wimsatt[7] on Pope and Donald Davie[8] on the eighteenth century generally are able to find in Augustan poetry some of this representative normalcy in diction and syntax (Davie), in rhyme and metre (Wimsatt). Still, the faint residuum of idiosyncracy in the poets they discuss imposes a sort of strain on their critical practise. The quality they seek critically—the quality which the Augustans sought—is to be found, as the Augustans thought, in exemplary and unidiosyncratic fullness chiefly among the classical poets. Pope gets this quality as an echo from Horace; Horace from the Alexandrians.

The refined poets temper rhythm and diction, syntax and structure of idea, adroitly enough to make the style finally accessible as a means to the poet who will manage a scope greater than it usually affords. Vergil goes to school in that rhythm, that diction, that syntax, that structure, before he attains a poetic breadth sufficient for the *Aeneid*. So Dante and Milton go to school in lyric—specifically through Vergil the elegist as well as through Vergil the poet of the *Aeneid*.

As for rhythm,—to take the most elusive, and most essential element first—the very openness of the total subject in an oral epic, the very simplicity of diction and syntax, permit a freedom of metre to the surging cadence. The Homeric hexameter is not bound by the elaborate laws to which the Vergilian hexameter conforms. The choice of spondee or dactyl in a given foot, the fall of the caesura, seem accidental.

In the refined verse of the elegists and epigrammatists, and also of the pastoral poets, the whole poem is drawn tight. Diction and syntax sharpen their focus in consonance with the sharp focus of the subject, and the metre follows suit. It was a keen ear for poetry that led scholars till recently to date Tyrtaeus in the third century rather than in the sixth. They heard his measures—correctly—as closer to the Alexandrian precision than to the Homeric abundance. But the focus of the poetry's subject and not the precise historical time, made for the rhythmic difference.

Every syllable is felt to fall exactly, every caesura to be measured, in the firm order of the tighter classical line. The elegiac couplet dominates this tradition because it serves such a tightness. In Coleridge's exemplum, "The Ovidian Elegiac Metre Described and Exemplified":

> In the hexameter rises the fountain's silvery column;
> In the pentameter aye falling in melody back.

The pentameter, with its caesura fixed by rule, arrests rhythm and syntax while rounding it out. The fullness of the "silvery column" is not allowed to surge on: it is checked in the shorter and (because of the fixed caesura) stiffer second line. The pentameter's very shortness, too, leaves a tonic gap that prepares for the dominance of the succeeding hexameter, producing a measure even more supplely adaptable to the rhetorically delimited subject than the French Alexandrine or the end-stopped couplet.

The caesura is placed precisely in these lines from Propertius (I, 3: 1-6), so precisely that the rhythm of the hexameter sounds

scarcely less fixed than that of the pentameter, for all the rigidity
of its ruled caesura:

> *Qualis Thesea/ iacuit cedente carina*
> *languida desertis/ Gnosia litoribus;*
> *qualis et accubuit/ primo Cepheia somno*
> *libera iam duris/ cotibus Andromede;*
> *nec minus assiduis/ Edonis fessa choreis*
> *qualis in herboso/ concidit Apidano;*

The simple regularity of caesural recurrence suggests, in the very
rhythm, a tightness of application for the simile—correctly, for this
simile is much tighter in its reference than the Homeric simile (I
shall expand this point later), just as its caesurae are tighter than the
Homeric caesurae. Over the large cadence the rhythm falls back in
the neat doubled units of the elegiac couplet, held further in step
by the calculated regularity of caesurae.

Line by line, too, each caesura forces the words to dance their
logical countersteps of rhetorical neatness, within the smaller cadence
of the word-by-word modulation. The image of separation—Ariadne
on the shore, Theseus sailing away—inheres already in the juxtaposition of the first two words: *Thesea,* an adjective that suspends
the expectation of its noun; and *iacuit,* the verb whose subject,
Ariadne, does not come till the next line. The caesura insists neatly
on the lovers' separation by cleaving the adjective of Theseus with
the verb of Ariadne: *Thesea/ iacuit.* The voice bears down the
more for the spondaic movement in *Thesea,* chosen for that reason
instead of some dactyl.

The next line, the pentameter, emphasizes Ariadne's relation not
to Theseus (whose departure was insisted on in three words, all
trisyllabic, of the first line's five) but to the shores. She is *languida,*
they are *desertis;* she is *Gnosia,* from Cnossos, they are *litoribus,*
shores (Naxos) that here remain nameless; she knows where she
comes from, but not where she is. The caesura, coming between the
two pairs of words, insists on the identity already objectified in the

inflectional likenesses. A nominative is paired with a dative, another nominative with another dative; the two nominatives also go together, and the two datives: but this syntactical juncture must ride over the mid-line pause, and the pause neatly insists on it. The pause at once joins and separates likes: at once separates and joins opposites.

Each pair of lines has a similar rhythmic (and syntactic) structure, and the caesurae, as well as the elegiac couplets themselves, insist on the multiple junctures, held almost statically in place for the poetic juxtapositions of this particular elegy. By such a tightness of rhythm are the words held in and ordered. A singleness of effect, a precision of statement, is gained, for a subject as circumscribed as the one-pointed epithet. The singleness of the point remains for this style, even when the poem is as broad as that Callimachean compendium of mythology, the *Metamorphoses*. Ovid displays a virtuosity of rhythmic effect equal to his resourcefulness in stringing his poem out artificially on the single strand of physical change.

A ballad, in its free-wheeling rhythmic flow, must continue for some little while to round itself out. In the firmly measured rhythms of elegiac epigram, the poem can be both full and precise in the single range of two lines:

> *Odi et amo:/quare id faciam,/fortasse requiris.*
> *Nescio, sed fieri/sentio et excrucior.*
>
> I hate and love: why I should do that you may well ask.
> I do not know, but I feel it done and am racked.
>
> (CATULLUS, 85)

The poetry hinges not only in the paradox of ambivalent emotions, but also in the exact rhythmic deployments, brought to a head in the last and longest word of the epigram, *excrucior*. The torment of the ambivalence may be heard, as well as understood, to move in that word, the last of a series of three verbs. *Excrucior* is united with the second verb, *sentio,* by being on the same side of the caesura; and

with the first, *nescio,* by not being broken up into two units across
the caesura (*fieri/sentio*). Not to know and to feel happening is to
be excruciated: *nescio* plus *sentio* equals *excrucior,* and the final
word has its accents bent on the rack of the (for Latin) artificial
dactylic movement. *Fieri* is a passive form to the active *faciam,* but
excrucior is the only indicative passive of all six verbs applied to
himself by the poet (*fieri* is an infinitive; we have *odi, amo, faciam,
nescio, sentio,* and finally the passive *excrucior*). The other verb,
requiris, ends a line as *excrucior* does, and balances its heavy suffering by a light, active questioning.

Rhythmic precisions enrich the psychology, neatly circumscribed
within its paradox.

The classically controlled rhythm can build an utterance impassioned enough to seem to burn these special effects away, while
actually using them:

> *Vivamus, mea Lesbia, atque amemus,*
> *rumoresque senum severiorum*
> *omnes unius aestimemus assis.*
> *Soles occidere et redire possunt:*
> *nobis cum semel occidit brevis lux,*
> *nox est perpetua una dormienda.*
> *Da mi basia mille, deinde centum,*
> *dein mille altera, dein secunda centum,*
> *deinda usque altera mille, deinde centum.*
> *dein, cum milia multa fecerimus,*
> *conturbabimus illa, ne sciamus,*
> *aut ne quis malus invidere possit,*
> *cum tantum sciat esse basiorum.*   (CATULLUS, 5)

This masterly lyric has not left the tradition of epigram very far
behind, rhythmically or in diction and syntax. Its tonal range is
constructed through a precise weighing of syllables and pauses, varying between the high pitch of the first six lines and the breathless
haste of the last six, between the double pause of "Vivamus/ mea

Lesbia/ atque amemus" and such effects as the unified sweep of "nox est perpetua una dormienda."

The very sureness of the Alexandrian range allows it the impassioned sound, a range fuller than that accessible to, or at least attained by, the nearly translating Jonson:

> Kiss me, sweet. The wary lover
> Can your favours keep, and cover,
> When the common courting jay
> All your bounties will betray.
> Kiss again; no creature comes.
> Kiss, and score up wealthy sums
> On my lips, thus hardly sundered
> While you breathe. First give a hundred,
> Then a thousand, then another
> Hundred, then unto the other
> Add a thousand, and so more:
> Till you equal with the store,
> All the grass that Rumney yields,
> Or the sands in Chelsea fields,
> Or the drops in silver Thames,
> Or the stars that gild his streams,
> In the silent summer nights,
> When youths ply their stol'n delights;
> That the curious may not know
> How to tell 'em, as they flow,
> And the envious, when they find
> What their number is, be pined.

Leaving diction aside, speaking only of rhythm, Jonson's poem is at once simpler, and more disintegrated, than Catullus'. The Latin poet gains his singleness of sweep by the very range of precise effects he has learned in the school of Callimachus and the other anthologists. They, in turn, get their rhythmic precision from the numerous poets—among them Callinus and Tyrtaeus and Xenophanes—who had bent the Homeric normativeness to a more precise, but smaller, end.

This tradition, for all its precision can, of course, be polyphonic at other hands than those of Vergil:

> *Ecquid te mediis cessantem, Cynthia, Bais,*
> *qua iacet Herculeis semita litoribus,*
> *et modo Thesproti mirantem subdita regno*
> *et modo Misenis aequora nobilibus,*
> *nostri cura subit memores a! ducere noctes?*
> *ecquis in extremo restat amore locus?*
>
> (PROPERTIUS I, 11, 1-6)

In this harmonically controlled flight of the voice, every syllable is accounted for. The rhythmic complexity does its work, and indicates the limits of its precision, through its control. The exclamation of the next to the last line—"a!"—builds to a rise of pitch level and a suspension of voice juncture; and yet the very formal artifice of the exclamation is underscored by its position at the most conventional point for pause in the elegiac hexameter, the so-called bucolic diaeresis.

In the diction of this poetry, as well as in the rhythm, resides a comparable precision and control. This diction exhibits both "purity" and "strength," to use the terms by which Donald Davie[9] indicates the effects to be found in—and sought after by—the Augustans. And yet this purity and strength do not derive from metaphor, even in the enlivening of buried metaphor that Davie finds to underlie these qualities in Augustan verse:

> Kingdoms by thee, to sickly greatness grown,
> Boast of a florid vigour not their own: . . .
>
> This is an attempt to revivify the dead metaphor of "the body politic," the metaphor which Burke spent his time bringing to life; and it is most nearly successful with the prosaic epithet "florid."

Davie finds an implied metaphor even in such generalized nouns as "grove" and "gale": "But a grove is planted, and to see all groups of trees as groves is to see them all in the park of a creator-god."

Still, metaphor, even buried metaphor, is too intermittent an effect to account for any constant quality in a diction. Nor can such a term as "concrete universal"—devised by Wimsatt through applying Aristotle to modern practise—cover a poetry so little specially concrete.

If as little specially concrete as Homer's diction, that of the "classical" is much more universal, or general. For instance, the words of Propertius in the passage above can be felt to fund their common associations. They can be felt as a poetic diction, and an abstract one. *Mediis, cessantem, mirantem, regnum, nobilis, cura, memor, nox, amor, locus*—these words are all heavy with the weight of poetic tradition, a tradition that includes philosophy (*cura, memor*), science (*locus, medius*), and political theory (*regnum, nobilis*) without referring specifically—metaphorically, concretely——to philosophy or science or political theory.

Now words, of course, are signs, and to account fully for the character of a diction, one needs a fully responsible theory of signs, and also of what signs refer to. One needs, that is, a whole epistemology and a whole ontology, and these oblige a full-dress and full-scale philosophical presentation. Fortunately, however, some aspects of words in poetry may be noticed without being fully accounted for. We may then somewhat summarily apply Davie's term "purity" to the diction of Propertius (and also to Callimachus, and Ovid, and Catullus—to all the poets in this tradition). We may also apply the word "strength." Now purity implies selection or exclusion; the word has been chosen for its normative value from others that are somehow less normative:

> *odi et amo* . . .

These are the bare normative words, redolent at the same time of associations that go back to (but do not specifically evoke) Empedocles' dualistic theory of a universe pulled together by love and apart by strife.

"Strength," on the other hand, implies inclusion: many senses of the word are packed or fused together into the condensed sort of expression the eighteenth century referred to as "strength." Purity and strength: exclusion and inclusion.* The "concrete universal" will not account for this process: it is itself only a special instance of selection (concrete) and inclusion (universal).

The common diction of the refined style has a "purity" by virtue of its having been selected for normative value. What "strength" the diction has, however, derives not from the packing of meanings so much as from the singleness, and also often the abstractness, of the poem's central theme, a singleness the precision of the metre has drawn tight. In Catullus' epigram, again:

> *Odi et amo: quare id faciam, fortasse requiris.*
> *Nescio, sed fieri sentio et excrucior.*

all the words are abstract or general. None are packed with implied metaphor, except possibly the last. Their strength comes, rather, from their generality, as their purity comes from their normativeness. Knowing its limits, the poem fills itself out word by word to their very edge; a set area with broad exclusions invites, within the set area, words of maximal inclusion.

As Davie reads it, "grove" in eighteenth century verse implies the metaphor "park of God," because to call all groups of trees planted evokes the Great Planter. More appositely, grove is the most general word for a group of trees that carries with it an implication of order in the group, as well as the closest translation for the Latin word *nemus,* itself somewhat more general than the handful of English words by which it could also be translated. The diction of the Latin language lends itself to generality, as does the diction of French. Yet the Latin poets, whom the Augustans imitate, learned how to manage such effects of consistent abstraction from

---

* It is not even so simple as that, for strength, as a packed group of meanings, may govern a special kind of words: those capable of packing; and strength, like purity, may therefore instance exclusion (as well as inclusion).

Greek poets who were dealing with a language as particular in its way as English. Catullus' master, Callimachus, gets his effect through diction of a similar generality:

> Εἶπέ τις, Ἡράκλειτε, τεὸν μόρον, ἐς δέ με δάκρυ
> ἤγαγεν· ἐμνήσθην δ' ὁσσάκις ἀμφότεροι
> ἥλιον ἐν λέσχῃ κατεδύσαμεν· ἀλλὰ σὺ μέν που,
> ξεῖν' Ἁλικαρνησεῦ, τετράπαλαι σποδιή·
> αἱ δὲ τεαὶ ζώουσιν ἀηδόνες, ᾗσιν ὁ πάντων
> ἁρπακτὴς Ἀίδης οὐκ ἐπὶ χεῖρα βαλεῖ.

> Someone told me, Heraclitus, of your doom, and led
> Me to tears: I remembered how often both of us
> Had brought the sun down in chatting. But somehow,
> Halicarnassian friend, you are ash since long ago.
> Still, your nightingales are alive, on which the seizer
> Of all things, Hades, shall not put his hand.

This epigram insists on the nature of human speech, with the very first word, *eipe* (told). Its last statement is about the permanence of poetic speech. It insists on generality by the very second word, *tis,* someone. What its central statement introduces by a line and a half, and does not say till the final word comes,* is that the Halicarnassian friend is ash, *spodie.* Not friable or gray or buried or light or dry ashes, but simply ashes, of "fourfold" age (*tetrapalai*). Fourfold is, of course, itself generic, referring to a round and not a given number.

Metre reinforces the generality. This metre does not get the specific, thought-miming effect of fluid lyric. It is what Arnold Stein calls an "abstract vehicle," and is needed to carry these semi-abstract statements. Without the rhythmic precision of the epigrammatic couplet, this poem would risk—inconceivably for an Alexandrian poet with his traditional common style—becoming the sort of doggerel into which it was translated in Victorian times:

> They told me, Heraclitus, they told me you were dead . . .

---

* This in itself a characteristic of epigram, to which the "delayed climax" is a basic device. The effect is of snapping the lid tight on the contained matter of the poem.

This diction has been maintained constantly on a level of generality which gives a sense not only of common style, but of a common style heightened, the effect Vergil was to inherit from Catullus without being enamored of it for its own sake, as Ovid was. In it, through general words and precise rhythms, every statement has an air of being lucid and purified.

The terms in this diction have been selected for a degree of generality, one similar to the kind sought by the Augustans, in W.K. Wimsatt's view.[10]

In discussing the Augustans' concern for a similar generality, Wimsatt arranges three kinds of words on a scale, with reference to the concept of species, and implicitly to that of substance:

1. The abstract or less than specific-substantive style: e.g., *implement.*

2. The minimum concrete or specific substantive style: e.g., *spade.*

3. The extra-concrete, the detailed, or more than specific style: e.g., *rusty garden spade.*

Now Augustan poetry sometimes calls attention to its adherence to Wimsatt's second level: it calls fish the "finny tribe," sea "watery plains," and the like. But when it leans too heavily on such periphrasis, it gets as removed from the refined style as from Homer, or from that English master of the refined style, Walter Savage Landor:

> I strove with none, for none was worth my strife.
> Nature I loved, and, next to Nature, Art;
> I warmed both hands before the fire of Life;
> It sinks, and I am ready to depart.

Landor's diction here, like Catullus'—or Callimachus', Horace's, Propertius'—holds itself easily but firmly on Wimsatt's first and second levels, and without abnormal expressions like "finny tribe" or even "grove." Words on Wimsatt's second level, in any case sound normative for poetry because poetry tends in general—as Elizabeth Sewell[11] shows—to use generic words like *spade,* instead of for example a word like *mattock.* It tends to say, not just in the refined style but in any, *horse* instead of *Percheron, dog* instead of *Pomer-*

anian, sun, moon, sea, road, instead of *nova, asteroid, fjord, boule-vard.* In fact the words in Wimsatt's third-level extra-concrete example are already closer to his second level than *mattock* would be for *spade, rubiginous* for *rusty, arbor* for *garden: rusty garden spade,* his third level example, is actually made up of words from the second level.

No words are closed to poetry, but any poetry tends to select some group out of the total dictionary, and the normative style in poetry, of which the classical refined style is the clearest example, tends to select normative words, a diction that quietly, at every step, insists on its generality, but a limited generality.

Even metaphor in this style—as in many—must remain a simple generality avoiding strictly in its figure the connotations* that are welcomed in other lyric styles. Its ordinary words, firmly based on their medium denotation,* manage connotation as a descant. But metaphorical connotations would upset the balance and break the limits of the refined style, which consequently rules them out. Hence one cannot describe the desired "classical" quality, as Davie and Wimsatt do, by discussing metaphor explicit and implied. In the refined style, metaphor is itself only a specially cogent means of making a generic statement. The metaphor of the "nightingales" in Callimachus's epigram is really just a trope for "poems," or rather for "pure song of poems," and calls up no Keats-like bird: it is a generic word which serves mainly not for association (between bird and poem), but for generic economy: it is the only way one can refer to several abstract features of poems in a single word. The same may be said of Landor's "fire of Life" above. This is a pointed way of making a generic statement, and the reader suppresses rather than evokes (as he would in Blake or Pindar) any concrete association, any flowering analogies between fire and life.

The diction of the refined style never gets too far from the sub-stantiveness of Wimsatt's second level into the abstraction of his first. Nor does it allow more than a key excursion now and then into

* I use these words in their colloquial critical sense, and not, as Wimsatt would, in their logical definition.

the diction of the third level, particularity. Catullus may use a word now and then with the violent particularity of popular speech—*irrumo;* or one with the diminutive subtlety—*phasellus,* or all the feminine turns in the Attis poem. In these particularities of usage, much of the strength of association results from the pull of this kind of word against the firmly held norm of general substantive words. As in other ways, the refined style seeks for its diction balance above all.

The pull—of the firm, precise meters, of the normative, refined diction—can be felt even in such colorless words as the particles. Homer lets the particles flow thick and fast in the grand and rapid sweep of his improvising measure. In the context of exactly calibrated metres and words selected for refinement, the one particle sequence in Callimachus' epigram partakes of exactness, and also of a coordinated general effect, in a way Homer's do not. To put it differently, we pause on this group of little words, *alla su men pou* in line three, because the refined style implicitly invites us to pause on all words by exhibiting its precision of rhythmic and syntactic ordonnance.

Each of these small words separately, or all taken together, has a generalizing rhetorical effect. They come at the key point, at the introduction of the middle term between two opposing statements, underscoring that the epigrammatist cannot blink the fact (which *pou* resists fixing on) of a friend's now being *ash.* Metre and the influence of the surrounding diction combine to make the particles at once more precise than Homer's: each particle carries an exact rhetorical weight, while Homer's merely aid the flow; and each is more general than Homer's: each one invites categorization, while Homer's merely provide a running and faintly qualifying modulation. One might, in fact, come on this exact sequence of particles in Homer, but the force of the surrounding and including metrical and verbal conventions would give them a different bearing.

A style comes into being in order that it may render a certain sort of subject. The precision of metre, the generality of diction, which characterize the refined style, characterize also its subject matter, which is always precise both in its clarity and its limitations, and which always has an abstractness about it.

In the normative poetry of the refined style, life is knowable but in part. So in the refined style, as metaphors tend to be mere tropes, myths are not resonant wholes but compact instances, the way Propertius uses them. The refined style sees particularities not as dazzling instances but as members of a class. For example, Propertius speaks of the particular traits of Cynthia which will be forever lost if he dies before getting them into verse. But he does not render her particularities. He merely holds them in the clear focus of classifications, within the substantive but general diction of the refined style:

> quam si perdideris, quis erit qui talia cantet,
> (haec mea Musa levis gloria magna tua est),
> qui caput et digitos et lumina nigra puellae,
> et canat ut soleant molliter ire pedes? (II, 12, 21-5)

He gives us head, fingers, black eyes. He speaks of how her feet were wont to go *molliter,* a word which includes "softly" and "gently," but is more general than either. And that is all.

Lumina nigra, dark eyes, or more literally *dark lights,* is an oxymoron in rhetoric, a paradox in logic. Antithesis, oxymoron, and similar figures, characterize the refined style. And yet this poem holds in view by these two words not the paradox of the mysterious reconciliation of opposites, but the lucid union of opposites. This oxymoron produces not Keats' or Pindar's or Rimbaud's fluidity of varied suprarational nuances, but a clear fixity of rational substances, opposed in the smaller part of two words (the oxymoron) while joined in the larger part of the poem.

The prismatic lyric intimates a world larger than itself: elegy and epigram resign all of the world but the roped off coherent part of the single statement. Now the epic poet wants a large, not a limited, scope. But he wants coherence, and the refined style offers a form for coherence. So Vergil goes to Catullus rather than to Ennius for style; the young Vergil goes first to Theocritus and not to Pindar.

Even the *Aeneid* reads more like the *Aitia* of Callimachus than like the *Argonautica* of Apollonius—in style at least; but what element of a poem cannot finally be included in style?

The restricted subject matter of the small, refined poem intensifies the poem's diction. Subtlety and richness can come through in the strong and pure line that the refined style achieves at its best:

> *O fons Bandusiae, splendidior vitro.*

The comparison, of fountain to glass, is commonplace; all of Horace is commonplace. The richness of this strong line inheres in the controlled rise of the voice in the two middle words, long words expanded as well as heightened from the shorter ones of the beginning and end. (Alexandrian poetry, Wifstrand[12] tells us, favors the use of long words.) All the words except *Bandusiae* exist on Wimsatt's second level; and all four are commonplace. Horace's limitation of the subject matter is felt to harness fully the precisions of rhythm and diction.

A whore fades as fast as the roses she wears, Propertius says to Cynthia, and so a whoremistress is accursed. Such a statement, single and limited in itself, cuts across a rich field of human emotion, without quite matching the satire of Juvenal or the lyric of Mimnermus. It remains rational, and its richness is compounded from generalities focussed sharply to attain a richness far greater than that of such ultimate descendants as Waller's "Go, lovely rose," (Waller's poem, of course, itself being in the refined style.):

> *dum vernat sanguis, dum rugis integer annus,*
> *utere, ne quid cras libet ab ore dies!*
> *vidi ego odorati victura rosaria Paesti*
> *sub matutino cocta iacere Noto.*

> While the blood renews, while your time is whole from lines
> Use it, lest tomorrow the day cull somewhat from your face.
> I have seen myself the rosebeds of odorous Paestum
> That should have lived, lying cooked under the morning
> south wind.
>
> (PROPERTIUS, IV, 5, 59-63)

Sanguis, annus, dies, Notus, most of these are the general and substantial words of Wimsatt's second level. The intensity of *vernat* and *cocta,* in their near-metaphorical specificity and their condensation, rises partly out of their departure from the norm of the other words. The refined style allows departures from class words to be contributory richnesses. And the prevalence of class words suggests classification even for other words. *Rosaria Paesti,* two particular words, evoke not just roses or even Roman horticulture generally, but also the action of flowers anywhere in the seasons, which are called into play by the reference to just one season in *vernat.* The particular words do not etch in any particularity, the way Baudelaire refers to the Pont du Carrousel: by wrenching from the norm of class words, they instance the controlled vividness of the poet's encompassing and categorizing emotion.

The rational pattern of syntax, in which the refined style excels, permits it to deploy its generalized words in a controlled and rational frame of reference, very much as the abstract vehicle of the rhythm does.

The rhetorical operation of this rational pattern, as it appears in syntax, can be seen pointedly in chiasmus, perhaps the most widespread of the syntactical devices on which the refined style concentrates, along with the rhetoricians who dwell on these devices from Alexandrian times right to the Renaissance. Chiasmus is itself only a special instance of syntactic contrast set up between words close in position and words distant in grammatical relation. Remembering that chiasmus is defined *ex post facto* by the grammarians, we may see its trick in many places that we cannot strictly label chiasmus:

> *et mala desertos/occupat herba deos.*
>
> (PROPERTIUS, II, 6, 36)

The positional identifications (*mala-desertos; herba-deos*) set off the syntactical ones (*mala-herba; desertos-deos*); and while strictly we may not label the order as chiastic, the effect is one that chiasmus itself is only a special way of getting. Moreover, a contrast resembling a chiastic one is set up between the exact rhythm and the exactly controlled syntax. This pentameter line rhythmically divides at the strong and ruled caesura after *desertos*. But by suspending till after the caesura the two nouns with which the adjectives before the caesura agree, the speech cadence of the line sends out powerful (contrasting) shoots of unity over the dividing abyss of the caesura.

The syntax may hold diverse objects in a rational framework; Ovid, whose *Metamorphoses* exhibit an interest at every point in diversities for their own sake—a *metamorphosis* is nothing else— abounds in extreme examples of these syntactical devices, such as the triple chiasmus:

> *carmina digna dea! certe dea carmine digna est.*
> (*Metamorphoses*, V, 345)

The contrast of regular chiasmus lends itself well to the fixed presentation of the incongruities that metamorphosis entails:

> *Occupat hic collem, cumba sedet alter adunca*
> *et ducit remos illic, ubi nuper arabat:*
> *ille supra segetes aut mersae culmina villae*
> *navigat, hic summa piscem deprendit in ulmo.*

> One man takes a hill, another sits in a curved skiff,
> And pulls the oars there where before he plowed.
> That one sails over sheaves or the tips of his sunken farm,
> And this man catches a fish from the top of an elm.
> (*Metamorphoses*, I, 293-296)

More than of contrast, the chiasmus reminds us of the poem's central order. It appears in the syntax, the way most rhetorical effects in the refined style do, more as a heightening of order than as a departure or wrenching from even tone and regular progression. The effect is one Donald Davie[13] designates as "action" and, again, calls "strength," a control that is felt at every point evenly in the poem; that "lives along the line," in Pope's phrase.

The refined style dominates epigram, elegy and pastoral, in Greek and Latin poetry alike. For epigram, and for elegy, two characteristic spheres of interest are love and death, spheres that for obvious reasons absorb lyric poetry also. But in epigram and elegy the interest is so delimited, the subject so fixed, that while we may unequivocally call the lyric poem (of Sappho, of Keats) personal and in a sense momentary, the categories subjective-objective or personal-impersonal will not serve as anything more than a loose taxonomic distinction between the personal Cynthia of Propertius and the impersonal Berenice of Callimachus. And of course Catullus, the most personal lyricist of all, remains epigrammatic and rhetorical in his address to the Lesbia whose real name never enters the poem. It is just Catullus, personal as he is, who translates Callimachus' *Berenice,* and literally.

All poetry, through the invincible abstractness of its rhythmic vehicle, through the coherence of its verbal surface, may be spoken of as impersonal. And yet epigram and elegy are more tightly so with their highly abstract rhythm, with their substantive generality of refined diction, with their constant rhetorical deployments of syntax.

So rational, so fixed, is the subject of a poem in the refined tradition that the fluidity of, say Emily Dickinson, the depth of Keats or Pindar, the brilliant mastery of paradox in Donne, must remain forever closed to so normative a style. The refined style, in turn, can attain to a clarity and generality that remain closed to the other sort of lyric poet.*

It is to this use that it puts figurative comparison and incident. In the third poem of the first book, for example, Propertius centers on

---

* Of course these categories are not so rigid as to be mutually exclusive, and we cannot say that Catullus lacks the excellence of either Keats or Callimachus.

the most casual and trivial of incidents: he has stayed out late to drink; later even than he might have, for fear of Cynthia's reproofs. Finding her sleeping, he caresses her inert body. The moonlight wakes her and she upbraids him, but not quite the way he expected. The poem begins with the ironic overelaboration (a form of hyperbole) of three similes. (This is the same passage I used above to demonstrate the rhythmic and metrical precision of the style):

> *Qualis Thesea iacuit cedente carina*
> *languida desertis Gnosia litoribus;*
> *qualis et accubuit primo Cepheia somno*
> *libera iam duris cotibus Andromede;*
> *nec minus assiduis Edonis fessa choreis*
> *qualis in herboso concidit Apidano:*
> *talis visa mihi mollem spirare quietem*
> *Cynthia non certis nixa caput manibus,*
> *ebria cum multo traherem vestigia Baccho,*
> *et quaterent sera nocte facem pueri.*

> The way the girl of Cnossos stretched languidly
> On deserted shores, while Theseus' keel withdrew;
> The way Andromeda, Cepheus' daughter, lay
> In first sleep, free at last from the rough crags;
> As no less tired for the persistent dances,
> The Edonian girl sat by grassy Epidanus:
> That was the way Cynthia struck me, breathing
> A soft quiet, propping head on uncertain hands,
> When I dragged in footsteps drunk with much wine,
> And boys were shaking the torch for the late night.
> (I, 3:1-10)

Cynthia is like Ariadne, like Andromeda, and also like a maenad. These comparisons, again, do not primarily identify a richness of association with the mythological names. They are tropes for general statements about Cynthia: she is as though abandoned by a lover (Ariadne), and this makes her languid enough to drop off; but she is also as though freed of a monster (Andromeda) and so breathes easily enough to fall asleep (*libera*). Further, she is like a dancer who drops of her own accord (*maenad*), tired enough (*fessa*) to sleep. The myths serve mainly as compressed analyses of complex intellectual relations: it takes three of them to begin to explain the ramifications of this emotional relation. It is not till the last lines of the poem that the fitness or unfitness of the similes, the truth or figment of the poet's fear, is worked out. Cynthia says she feared and bemoaned his infidelity (as he has just feared she is dreaming of the act with another). After diverting herself with embroidery and the song of Orpheus' lyre, tired (*fessa,* but not, as it turns out, from the maenad's "dancing") she went to sleep; and her last thought was of the poet:

> *dum me iucundis lapsam sopor impulit alis.*
> *illa fuit lacrimis ultima cura meis.*

> Till sleep drove me with wings of joy where I fell.
> That was the final care for my tears.

Cynthia speaks of sleep in an antithesis so closely related to the first three similes that one may call the structure of this elegy almost that of an expanded epigram. His fear was justified: she does complain to him. And it was also unjustified: she was fearful of herself. She was indeed like Ariadne: despair at a departing lover wore her out and into slumber; but she is unlike Ariadne in that her lover returns, and so unlike Andromeda (if he is in some sense an unwitting monster to have abandoned her so long) in that she has not been freed of him. Of course she does not seem to want to have been freed of him, and so her sleep is not like Andromeda's. He is therefore the more like the monster, for having hurt her without knowing it. She was not like the maenad under the insistent (*assiduis*) dancing rites of spring; yet as she wakes up out of her sleep, she becomes like the maenad in, as it were, resuming those rites. Here was a fourth state, unlike the three states blocked in by the similes. The sudden presence of the lover vivifies and redefines those three states.

To call the last couplet either antithesis or iteration, then, would be to oversimplify; yet the richness of the myth remains one of intellectual association, not of the archetypal resonance that lyric poetry sets in motion by using the intellectual structure as a sounding board.

The love relation is generalized into an extensive and complex pattern of human relations, but a rational one, as the style asserts with every word.

To the subject of love, and also to that of death, this elegiac tradition comes with a restricted sharpness of focus which can generalize the personal because of the scale its constrictions* imply: the personal moment becomes generalized—becomes in a sense impersonal too—within a frame small enough to keep the generality more like the argument of a special case than the enunciation of a universal maxim.

Within their restrictive diction and tightness of metre, within the delicate superstructure of syntax, each of these refined poems attains a sort of fixity—so much so that it seems fitting for the epigram to have begun as an epitaph, a last word in which the personal must by the nature of the utterance be fully incorporated into the summary, and graven on stone. Nor is it surprising that a whole book of *The Greek Anthology* consists of poems about statues: the stone fixity of the subject occasioning the small, fixed poem.

How light and artful, not to say artificial, the refined style is, even in Catullus and Propertius, may be seen by contrasting with their poems the deadly serious emotion, and highly ambitious sweep of the *De Rerum Natura,* specifically in its handling of love and of death.

Lucretius, in that other post-Homeric vein of philosophic poetry,

---

* In the poem (III, 1) where Propertius addresses the "shades of Callimachus" and eschews epic, he speaks of his personal subject matter as a literary choice that allows him to enter the "grove" (*nemus*) of the Alexandrian poets. He can be tightly exact (*exactus*) with fine polish (*tenui pumice*) because he has not given his phrases "free rein," and has kept from the broad roads (*lata via*).

somehow shows in the very violence of his rhythmic intensity that he is falling short of the epic scope, of that serenity attained by Homer. Lucretius strains after a glimpse of the epic serenity:

Suave, mari magno turbantibus aequora ventis . . .

But the *suave* cannot come about in this diction, rhythm, and fable: he is caught in the turbulent atomic winds, in the rough-hewn generalities of a total, but merely abstract, outlook. His insights must be mediated through his private terminology in order to attain wholeness.

Lucretius cannot incorporate the implied aesthetic distance of refinement; he is deadly serious. Refinement, though, is artificial, and preens in its artifice, with a delight in make-believe that would never submit to Lucretius' urgent claim for truth. How artificial it can become is exemplified in that Alexandrian tradition which can bemoan a death or lament a love in the same pattern, and can also at the same time praise the particularity of nature and discourse on kinds of order, including the order of its own song: the Theocritan pastoral.

Theocritus counterpoints his voices: his form is so closed as to seem a sort of super-epigram, or epigram for more than one voice. Drama? But nothing really happens; the idyll is sub-dramatic. It is not an alternative for Menander, but, so to speak, a refinement beyond Menander. Theocritus performs more lucidly what Menander merely intimates, because he has defined how to be himself, and Menander, standing weakly at the end of a tradition more "tragic" in feeling than comic, can no longer be Sophocles.

The pastoral structure is an artifice in its initial conception. A poet is a shepherd; a shepherd is a poet. This is not a metaphor, in grammatical structure at least: there is never one main term to which others are subsidiary, an ordinary condition of metaphor. A poet is to song (verse) as a shepherd is to song (piping); and then a poet is natural like a shepherd (spontaneous, dutiful, sociable, etc.) There is no main term, and no subsidiary. Metaphor also implies likenesses

among differences, and the totality of the pastoral conception offers
no criterion for discriminating differences from likenesses: it offers
instead a wholly coherent system which assigns primacy neither to
the shepherd, nor to the poet; the poet has primacy in Renaissance
pastoral, but we cannot read Spenser's metaphor back into Theocritus.

Analogy insists on likenesses, and the pastoral structure is, in a
sense, an analogy. But it is only a fictive analogy: a shepherd never
really partakes of what a poet does, or the other way around; only
within the poem. The fictive orders the real by insisting on its own
fictiveness: artifice contents itself with limits by glorying in its consistency within those limits, as the refined style asserts them at every
moment.

Theocritus insists on the fictiveness of his analogy in its very conception. Dante, on the other hand, insists on the reality of his analogy. The light in the *Inferno* is feeble because it really does partake
less of the divine light. But the urbane citizen of Alexandria is never
really thought of, even by analogy, as involved in activities like
those of a shepherd on Sicily or Cos.

Theocritus sustains the artifice of his analogy between shepherd
and poet, goats and emotions, nature and poetry, natural open air
love and civilized urban love, with a peerless lightness that no
Renaissance pastoralist attains. In Fletcher, in Tasso, poetry and
love are primary, the shepherd and his landscape but a vehicle.
There we do have a pastoral metaphor. In Theocritus' work, a balance is maintained so perfectly between each term of his underlying
analogy that we are unable to say either is primary: that poetry is
mainly an attunement to the real nature in which shepherds tend
flocks; that shepherds are mainly dimmer servants of the order and
grace which poetry serves. Nature, praised, is abstracted because the
artifice holds in suspension the possibility that all references are to
the sort of ideal harmony the poem explains and exemplifies.

In this ideal state of refinement, the limited world of the poem is so
ordered as to seem suspended in its identities. So perfect a balance in

the central conception allows its diction to range, to particularize somewhat more freely than usual in the refined style. Theocritus is at once lighter in artifice and freer in particularity of diction than are Bion and Moschus.

And so a blunt-nosed bee, a nanny goat, figs from an Attic deme —these touch lightly, not merely through categories of diction but through the central artifice, on the harmony of a world where poets sing and flocks equally graze. In the diction of Eclogue X, for example, we get an interplay between general substances (pipes, rose-bud, apple) or words on Wimsatt's second level; and such particu-larities on his third level as knuckle-bones, lettered hyacinth, shoes from Amyclae, and moon-clover. The frequency of the interplay keeps suggesting the fictive lightness of the analogy between har-vesters and poets, poets and lovers, lovers and harvesters:

Μοῖσαι Πιερίδες, συναείσατε τὰν ῥαδινάν μοι
παῖδ'· ὧν γάρ χ' ἅψησθε, θεαί, καλὰ πάντα ποείτε.

Βομβύκα χαρίεσσα, Σύραν καλέοντί τυ πάντες,
ἰσχνάν, ἁλιόκαυστον, ἐγὼ δὲ μόνος μελίχλωρον.

καὶ τὸ ἴον μέλαν ἐστί, καὶ ἁ γραπτὰ ὑάκινθος·
ἀλλ' ἔμπας ἐν τοῖς στεφάνοις τὰ πρᾶτα λέγονται.

ἁ αἲξ τὰν κύτισον, ὁ λύκος τὰν αἶγα διώκει,
ἁ γέρανος τὤροτρον· ἐγὼ δ' ἐπὶ τὶν μεμάνημαι·

αἴθε μοι ἦς ὅσσα Κροῖσόν ποκα φαντὶ πεπᾶσθαι·
χρύσεοι ἀμφότεροί κ' ἀνεκείμεθα τᾷ Ἀφροδίτᾳ,

τὼς αὐλὼς μὲν ἔχοισα καὶ ἢ ῥόδον ἢ τύγε μᾶλον,
σχῆμα δ' ἐγὼ καὶ καινὰς ἐπ' ἀμφοτέροισιν ἀμύκλας·

Βομβύκα χαρίεσσ', οἱ μὲν πόδες ἀστράγαλοί τευς,
ἁ φωνὰ δὲ τρύχνος· τὸν μὰν τρόπον οὐκ ἔχω εἰπεῖν.

Pierian Muses, sing me the slender girl;
For, goddesses, you make lovely whatever you touch.
Delightful Bombyca, all call you the Syrian,
Scrawny and sun-scorched; I alone call you honey-green.
The violet is black and the written-on hyacinth,
And always for garlands these are gathered the first.
Goat chases moon-clover, wolf chases goat,
Crane chases plow, and I am mad for you.

Would I had as much as they say Croesus once got!
Then we should both lie golden, offered to Love:
You would have pipes and a rose, or else a fruit,
And I a suit and new shoes on both my feet.
Delightful Bombyca, your feet are knuckle-bones
Your voice is nightshade—I don't have the way to say.

(X, 24-36)

Bucalus here ends his part of the amoebic song by saying he cannot describe the girl's beauty. This kind of statement Dante makes again and again in the *Paradiso:* the reality of the mystic vision is said to exceed any possible poetry, and memory as well. But Theocritus balances the statement with its contrary, his initial invocation to the Muses here, that *poetry* confers the beauty. Artifice reaches out and then reaches back, more beautiful than its object, and less beautiful. And since he who speaks is himself an artificial character, we are unable to set the analogy on any firm designative frame.

When the diction is particular, it lists, as here, individual instances of beauty. But the listing is artificial, for the comparison itself occurs as a set virtuoso piece of rhetorical argument. Darkness in women is beautiful because it is so in such dark flowers as hyacinth, violet, and moon-clover. The rhetorical argument happens to be explicit here, but it is always implicit. The artifice contains all particularities, whose beauties it itemizes through a form that is still too rhetorical, for all its evocativeness, to be described mainly in the terms we use to describe Keats.

The metre too, is an abstract vehicle, a sheer Mozartian artifice of melody. When the amoebic singers carry on a contest, they delight in paralleling each other's syllables and statements in words whose difference of identity to create a sameness of reference and music is a rhetorical triumph similar to that of a whole poem:[14]

ἄγκεα καὶ ποταμοί, θεῖον γένος, αἴ τι Μενάλκας

Valleys and rivers, race divine, if ever Menalcas . . .

κρᾶναι καὶ βοτάναι, γλυκερὸν φυτόν, αἴπερ ὁμοῖον

Springs and pastures, herbage sweet, if Daphnis indeed
Makes a like music . . .   (VIII, 33, 37)

The metre, too, is made to improvise the artifice it glories in. The
subject is self-contained, and the music exults sheerly in the fact of
its own building exactness. The ancients made a distinction between
rhythm and metre, as we do.[15] In the mellifluousness of Theocritus
the metre and the rhythm chime almost exactly: the rhythm is the
abstract vehicle of the metre itself. Concordantly, the pastoral conception is so identified with its own artifice that the reference to
reality is resubjected, and artifice interchanges with reality.

Theocritus provides a vanishing point for the refined style. His
extreme exemplum proves, as Vergil was to learn from him, that
the larger subject—even if only somewhat larger, *paulo maiora*
(*Ecl.* 4)—, while it demanded the refined style, demanded something
over and above it as well.

CHAPTER FIVE

The Ivory Gate

*. . . Als blickte er mit zugleich trostlosem und gefasstem
Blicke in das Innere derjenigen, denen er nichts Neues an
Handlung und Vorgang, nichts an Charakteren und Situa-
tionen zu bringen hätte, sondern nur die Seelenmusik einer
kontemplativen Begleitung zu allen diesen Geschicken . . .*

R. BORCHARDT, *Reden*[1]

AS a normative style that aims for generality and not for special,
brilliant effects, the refined style is well suited to the directness and composed generality of epic verse. But its precisions work
most obviously for a delimited subject, for exclusive poetry and not
for the inclusive poetry that epic must be. Consequently, the most
successful writers in the refined style abandoned epic, some of them
explicitly. A big book is a big evil, Callimachus said; and rightly,
given his circumstances. His longer poems delimit their mythical
subject matter by focussing on a single myth, and on its cause: they
are *Aitia*, aetiological poems. The *Metamorphoses,* too, for all its
length, is one long series of aetiological set-pieces, composed on the
exclusive subject of myths in which some metamorphosis occurs.
Ovid's virtuosity at sustaining and varying this artifice is so striking
that it has led some modern critics to exercise their ingenuity at
seeing in metamorphosis a universal creative principle comparable

to the ones of Empedocles and Lucretius. There is nothing in the *Metamorphoses* itself, however, which lends support to this sort of reading for depth. Ovid's poetry lies all in its refined surface. Linear in extensive construction, it can be read piecemeal; he could have concluded it at any point and nothing would be felt to be missing. Ovid effectually eschewed heroic verse as summarily as Propertius did, though he does not devote a poem, as Propertius does, to telling us why.

It was Vergil who made the refined style serve an epic purpose, but of course not at once, and not easily. Perhaps driven obscurely by this purpose, he never attained the precise fictive balance of Theocritus, unless he abandoned it so early that nothing of his in that phase survives.

It is possible that like Valéry he knew how to manage his silences, and perhaps he was troubled by them, for the *Eclogues* demonstrably strain their conception; and we have no felicitious triumphs of epigram by Vergil's hand such as we have from Theocritus'. Moreover, if he had felt comfortable in merely exercising his style, his poems were so quickly celebrated by his contemporaries that if shorter pieces by his hand existed, we should probably have them, along with the oddities of the Vergilian appendix.

This is conjecture. We do have the *Eclogues,* however. From their very commencement they resist the sheer equipoise of the Theocritan fiction. The balance of artifice has been tipped: the analogy no longer fully holds between shepherd and poet. The First Eclogue speaks of a poet who owns a farm, for whom the pastoral name is understood to be a pseudonym, and merely that. There is nothing in him of the fully ambiguous Theocritan shepherd. We understand poetry to be the main reference from the very first lines:

> *Tityre, tu patulae recubans sub tegmine fagi*
> *silvestrem tenui musam meditaris avena:*

Tityrus reclines under the spreading beech and meditates the sylvan muse: he is a poet living in the country, not a "sensitive shepherd."

The pastoral designations reveal their merely formal character in the very next phrase:

> *nos patriae finis et dulcia linquimus arva.*

No real shepherd, no Theocritan shepherd, leaves his native boundaries and ancestral acres.

Tityrus also sings of a beloved who serves him only as a subject for song: the poem does not center on the beloved, or take her as more than an occasion:

> *tu, Tityre, lentus in umbra*
> *formosam resonare doces Amaryllida silvas.*

The *Eclogues* use the refined style, but they already manage special Vergilian effects. Theocritus, in the lightness of his fiction, lends a certain discreteness to his individual words. The profound tonal interpenetrations of words, the special stylistic mark of the *Aeneid,* come through in such a phrase as *lentus in umbra,* "relaxed" or "soft" or "gentle" in the shade. Such conjunctions, and such statements, bring something new to the refined style, something which forces the words to work harder because the fiction is looser. *Silvas:* the *Eclogues* will ring change after change from poem to poem on this key word, anticipating the key words of the *Aeneid*. But Theocritus leaves each poem self-enclosed in an identical fictive balance; he would not have permitted the verbal associations to drift from one poem to another, whereas Vergil struggles for just this effect.

Vergil attributes the poet's leisure to the offices of a real person:

> *O Meliboee, deus nobis haec otia fecit.*

The "god" is Augustus. He has not yet been declared officially *divus,* and so the word is a perhaps Homeric trope for a powerful man. Still, the real Augustus stands in Rome, and the word points at him, outside the poem; whereas the Theocritan fiction is always self-enclosed. The *Eclogues* present no Theocritan veil over a distant land, but an actual situation, heightened by poetry, in a present Italian countryside. The leisure, *otia,* is leisure to write poetry, and nothing else.

Poetry, love, the emperor, the restoration of a farm, respect for fellow poets, the wonders of Rome, the empire's span to Africa, Scythia and Britain—all these topics wander in and out of the First Eclogue, a poem only eighty-three lines long. We have come far from the delimited subject usual to the refined style. And all topics are given the heavier emotional weight which Vergil is already able to make the refined style carry. The pastoral fiction in this first poem serves mainly as a trope; but if it possessed the Theocritan delicacy, it would have to keep the subject more delimited, whereas Vergil is already straining for a scope the pastoral will not afford him. "Let us sing a little grander," *Paulo maiora canamus,* he will say in the Fourth Eclogue, and then attempt to compass millennia of social recurrences.

In this First Eclogue the attempt at some sort of fusion comes also in the obliquity of the last line, which takes on, as it announces the time of day by iterating the word *umbra,* the tremendous new task of rendering emotion in the landscape:

> *maioresque cadunt altis de montibus umbrae.*

> Longer are falling the shadows from the lofty mountains.

Standing for nothing, the shadows evoke much: metaphorless, they hold a charge which the looseness of this pastoral fiction permits them. Moreover, the understatement and disjunction of this line bring something new, syntactically as well as verbally, to the refined style. Theocritus could not conceivably end a poem on a line so little capping. To take just one example, the end of Theocritus' *Pharmaceutria* also mentions the time:

> Farewell other stars, followers of the wheel-rim of lovely night.

But this caps a number of farewells, and it also caps the enamored speaker's feeling, which is unswervingly singleminded. Vergil's falling shadows, by fitting the speaker only loosely, can more fully suggest the world beyond the speaker. We do not know quite how to take them: the fiction is not firm enough to tell us. And this very confusion serves to increase the emotional resonance. The poem does not close rhetorically; and so it leaves a sort of open silence after the *umbrae*.

Lacking the Theocritan precision, Vergil can change his fiction, as he does, practically from eclogue to eclogue. In the Second, he suddenly adopts the Theocritan fiction fully: poet equals shepherd equals lover. Still, in surveying his own fields, the Corydon of this eclogue is, again, more inclusive than the Cyclops of Theocritus' Eleventh Eclogue: he speaks of the gods, the seasons, the nature of property, and also the nature of love, the recurrent but not the fully dominant theme of all the Eclogues. The poem's coda rises to a statement midway between proverb and philosophical generalization: *trahit sua quemque voluptas.* "Every man's pleasure draws him."

The maxim resembles in form the ones in Theocritus' Tenth—"goat chases moon-clover, wolf chases goat," etc.—but Vergil is in full earnest, and that tips the Theocritan balance. Love, as the Eighth Eclogue tells us, may make its own dreams:

> *credimus? an, qui amant, ipsi sibi somnia fingunt?* (109)

The fictions of the *Eclogues* move more or less at random from the Theocritan to the messianic to the merely personal, and back again to the Theocritan. Love may—*credimus? an*—make its own dreams; the word for these fictions is still the simple one, *somnia,* and not the obscure *insomnia,* of the ivory gate in *Aeneid VI.*

Omnia vincit Amor, the Tenth Eclogue at last tells us. The statement made in these terms is unconvincing, because *amor* has not even conquered the particulars of the Eclogues themselves. What does love have to do with serving Augustus? Nothing, unless that too is a *voluptas,* and the poetry cannot yet convince us so.

These woods of the *Eclogues* are too thin to harbor so many beasts. Surely not the apocalyptic ones of the Fourth Eclogue. The poem's opening argument, that pastoral poetry is a fit instrument for such a burden, does not come off, because it has not been thought through yet in conception, let alone in style:

> *silvae sint consule dignae.*

The woods may be worthy of a consul.

Silvae and *dignae,* these are the general words of the refined style. But *consule* is the label of an office, and no Catullan sureness of fictionalized conception can pull *consule* together with *silvae,* any more than such a statement can make pastoral poetry political. This statement fails on the level of diction. And it also fails on the level of conception: *silvae* is too uncertain in fictive reference, *consule* too devoid of all fiction in its dead seriousness.

The Fourth Eclogue gathers power as it goes on, but gathers power to the degree that it forgets pastoral altogether. The apocalyptic-political is a convention we know from the sibylline books. Vergil, whatever in the world he may be prophesying here—it is hard for the Christian to deny inklings of the Nativity—foreshadows, with respect to his own writing, the *Aeneid's* fusion of the national with the spiritual. But he does not yet know what he is doing, because he has not yet struck the tuning fork of the mode he will want to compose in, a mode much more than *paulo maiora.* Right up through the Tenth Eclogue he cannot make the changes of *silvae* bear his chosen diversities harmoniously. He cannot keep free of the imperial, even in a culminating poem, the Tenth, where his main subject is love. *Trahit sua quemque voluptas.*

The woods are said to echo all things:

> *respondent omnia silvae.* (x, 8)

But this declaration cannot bring off so difficult an imaginative act. The lover pretends to give up song for love, which the woods suddenly no longer echo: *ipsae rursus concedite silvae.* "Woods go away again!"

And the poet, pretending to end on uncertainty about the power of poetry, exemplifies that uncertainty in the last three lines, heaping up *umbra* thrice without getting anything like the force from the repetition that an Alexandrian would. And he dismisses his goats at evenfall with a disjunct statement that bears little of the poetic weight residing in the final line of the First Eclogue, the sureness of *maioresque cadunt altis de montibus umbrae.* He ends, that is, by repeating unsuccessfully two tricks that had worked elsewhere in the *Eclogues:*

> *surgamus: solet esse gravis cantantibus umbra,*
> *iuniperi gravis umbra; nocent et frugibus umbrae.*
> *ite domum saturae, venit Hesperus, ite capellae.*

2

I emphasize Vergil's hesitations and partial failures, passing over his marvelous virtuosity at extending the refined style. I do so because it is in the hesitation of the earlier work, and not in the success, that his impulse to extend the refined style appears. One can still trace that impulse, and further hesitations too, in the *Georgics.* For his next work Vergil chose not the refinement of pastoral but a genre that from Empedocles through Aratus, from Hesiod through Nicander, had proved resistant in its factual seriousness to the delicate poetic effects of the refined style.

In the *Georgics,* of course, Vergil does not seriously intend to fulfill Hesiod's function. The prose of Cato and Varro serves that purpose. For the Greece of his time, Hesiod's verse manual must do the job of Cato and Varro, as well as of Vergil, because there is no prose. The existence of prose manuals on agriculture relieves Vergil of the necessity for Hesiodic seriousness.

Still, in the *Georgics* his fiction has changed into an anti-fiction. The hands that once held the flute in the shade are horny with planting trees, or said to be so. The *silvae* are broken up into their component species, and the roots and branches are inspected in the hard light of what will really make trees grow.

Love makes no more fictions; *labor* makes reality—*labor,* the key word of this sequence. The first line of the last Eclogue had spoken of *labor:*

> *Extremum hunc, Arethusa, mihi concede laborem:*

> Grant me this last labor, Arethusa.

But the labor is a trope for writing poetry, and it is to be granted by a fountain's nymph. The *labor* of the *Georgics* is real, work on the land. It is a labor both base and indomitable (*improbus*), on a par with a leanness in hard things (*duris . . . in rebus egestas*). In the *Georgics* labor conquers all, as love is said to do in the *Eclogues:*

> labor omnia vicit
> *improbus et duris urgens in rebus egestas.*
>
> > (*Geo.* I, 145-6)

This *labor* extends all the way back to the Golden Age, since when things are said to have been hard and difficult, *durus* (another key word).

Love in the *Georgics* is an almost Lucretian physical force, the same for all creatures (*amor omnibus idem,* III, 244). It, too, is hard (*durus amor,* III, 259).

Vergil strives as Lucretius did, at times echoing Lucretius, to master in verse the external world without filtering it through the pastoral fiction. It is a world merely external, though, and the words do not yet embody the depth of internalized struggle that is got into *labor* in the *Aeneid:*

quae regio in terris nostri non plena laboris?

(*Aen.* I, 460)

What region in the lands is not full of our labor?

Here *labor* is passive, and abstract; it is the deeper for being both, than the active and concrete *labor* of the *Georgics.*

Vergil emulates Lucretius, and yet he does not intend a philosophic system. He falls short of Lucretius, and also of the farmer, for he does not intend to farm. He gives *labor* a cyclic recurrence:

redit agricolis labor actus in orbem, (II, 401).

This recurrence is not compassed within an overall explanatory scheme, Lucretian or Homeric. Hence, as he says he could not choose to include everything, even if he had a hundred mouths and a voice of iron:

non ego cuncta meis amplecti versibus opto,
non, mihi si linguae centum sint oraque centum,
ferrea vox.   (II, 42-44)

The poet is not able to till the land either. So for the time being he falls short of what he calls the felicity of Lucretius; and also of the felicity of the farmer:

felix qui potuit rerum cognoscere causas,
atque metus omnis et inexorabile fatum
subiecit pedibus strepitumque Acherontis avari.
fortunatus et ille deos qui novit agrestis
Panaque Silvanumque senem Nymphasque sorores.

Happy he who could know the causes of things,
and who could put under his feet all measures,
inexorable fate, and the noise of greedy Acheron.
Fortunate also he who could know the rural gods,
Pan and old Silvanus and the sister nymphs.   (II, 490-4)

He goes on to say that the farmer is happy because he can forget Rome and kingdoms. Vergil himself, though, cannot forget the Empire; and so he is forced to circle the subject. Simply filling out the refined diction of the *Eclogues* with particulars, simply abandoning the pastoral fiction for a basic agriculture—these strategies cannot give him the innovation he seems to be striving for. Ovid, too, is sometimes too dead earnest about the gods (*Fasti*) and sometimes too little earnest (*Metamorphoses*) to carry off poetry which is more than pretty. But Ovid's poetry has its own limited perfection, while the artificial *Eclogues* and the earnest *Georgics* both strain with more than they can handle.

In the *Georgics* this strain appears in the composition. The sections digress uncontrollably, nor are the digressions wholly sanctioned by the "almanac" form. The strain appears, too, in Vergil's merely casual use of myth, especially in the Fourth Georgic, when the search for origins gets out of hand and breaks the frame of the subject (bee-keeping).

To explain the origin of bees, at the end of the last Georgic, the long aetiological myth of Aristaeus is suddenly introduced. Behind that myth stands Proteus. And Proteus speaks of still another standing behind himself, Orpheus, describing with grace note after grace note of refined verse the mourning and death of that poet (Proteus himself being a *vates*): Aristaeus has offended Eurydice, and as he propitiates her the bees come into life.

The interlocked and telescoping myths recede; the poem trails off abruptly with a praise of Augustus, a personal summary that Vergil ends by quoting the first line of the *Eclogues*. In this way he links his attempts at the inclusive and the real (*Georgics*) with his attempts at the exclusive and the fictive (*Eclogues*).

3

The sense of whole motivation in a person and a people presses upon the *Eclogues* and the *Georgics*. These poems can accommodate the Empire only by way of digression, and then in the extravagance of encomium or apocalypse, rather egocentrically and at the same time impersonally. Vergil, till he plunges with the *Aeneid* deep into the personal psyche, remains shy of people, curiously shy for a follower of Theocritus and Catullus, a contemporary of Horace and Propertius.

His remains a problem of inclusion: how does one get the Lucretian universality while holding back, as he does in the *Georgics,* from the full Lucretian sweep? And it is a problem of scope as well: of epic. But Vergil is a cautious poet, cautious enough to have wished the *Aeneid* destroyed by fire. As perhaps all poets must do, Vergil comes to epic late, and then with the prohibitions of Theocritus before him, who was willing to confine himself, as he says, to the smaller poem. And of Callimachus, too, who said it negatively, "a big book is a big evil."

Callimachus said this of Apollonius. And Vergil had before his eyes the failure of the *Argonautica,* that young man's over-ambitious pastiche of Homer which the justly scornful criticism of Callimachus has not been able to deflect from the too worshipful classicism of later times. With the patina of time upon it, even the sensitive Sainte-Beuve[2] felt that he must find something in the *Argonautica* to admire, the love episode of the third book, which he saw with anachronistic eyes.

That poem itself—and it is hard to imagine Vergil's not agreeing with Callimachus—is one long rhetorical exercise, occasional flights in the refined style interspersed by narratives which elaborate simple events in a style worthy almost of Lycophron, without according the events much poetic resonance (and without attaining Lycophron's eccentric grace). Vergil gives the Mediterranean in the *Aeneid* something of the wonder of the unknown, a wonder Homer got effortlessly, just by living at a time when the sea remained somewhat fabulous. Vergil does return to the fabulous time, but Apollonius goes back even farther, to Jason, still treating the sea as a known pond, an occasion for a geographical virtuosity of naming. His sea, through all the particulars of the voyage, remains somehow almost static and motionless, as idle as a painted ship upon a painted ocean.

Detail proliferates in the *Argonautica,* with no hint of coordination. There is a perverse attempt to gain scope by the recapitulation of myth: the Argo passes Philyra, and so Cronos' seduction must be mentioned (II, 1234-64); it proceeds to the Caucasus, and Prometheus is viewed. The muscle-bound diction resembles the muscle-bound athletes of late Hellenistic times, trapped perversely in an excess of mere exercise.

Homer himself, in his tact, in his instinct for proportion, is far more literary—more civilized, actually—than the jejune Apollonius. Vergil must have seen this, and in his few echoes of Apollonius, for example in the passage on sleep,[3] he may be seen to have used the refined style with far more resonance, and also with far more relevance.

Ennius, of course, had tried to write a national epic, but on the blunt and simple plan of following Rome's development chronologically, an *Annales.* The fragments that remain from this poem possess a kind of rugged force. One of its chief devices is the interesting conclusion of an end-stopped line on a simple monosyllable, *fors, dis, est,* and others. But the movement is stiff—primitive in fact—and the refined style is even more remote from this poet than is the simpler Homeric grace:

> *Incedunt arbusta per alta, securibus caedunt,*
> *Percellunt magnas quercus, exciditur ilex,*
> *Fraxinus frangitur atque abies consternitur alti.*
>
> (FRAGMENT 187, VAHLEN)

To get epic meaning into the mold of the refined style without breaking the mold was the task Vergil set himself in the *Aeneid.* The undertaking ignored the sternest prescripts of his masters, the Alexandrians. It braved the failure of Apollonius. It had to avoid at once the rusticity of Ennius and the philosophical technicality of Lucretius.

A return to Homer seemed an obvious recourse, or seems so after the fact. But, again, this is precisely where Apollonius had failed;

it is precisely what the Alexandrians avoided. Homer is not in the refined style, and that style was their voice.

The refined style manages, and demands, a multiplicity of references from word to word within a line, in which each syllable is assigned a precise rhythmical function. As an instrument it allows a sharp focus for a small scope. Homer, by choosing and managing his fable, was able to give a simple sweep to his line, a sweep the more compelling because individual words bore little extra-colloquial weight the poems themselves did not give them.

The scope was large and the focus still sharp: the Homeric line acted as a sort of telescope. One could then call the refined style a sort of microscope, defining with proportional clarity a limited field. Apollonius might well have realized this; but when he threw away his microscope, and put the telescope to his eye, nothing but a thin aetiological landscape appeared in the glass. He borrows the Homeric diction, imitates the Homeric particularity, and tries at the same time to eschew the refined semi-generality of the Alexandrians. But words had changed since Homer's day, and to wish them to be as they had been was, then as always, more an archaizing than a literary enterprise.

Vergil realized that the microscope—to alter the metaphor—was a sort of undetachable contact lens, fixed to his verbal eyes for good or ill. The refined style had become the language of poetry, and if he wished to widen its focus, he would have to do so not by abandoning it but by transmuting it.

Homer's fable and his management of it were still viable models: words change but stories do not. To borrow from Homer—how to borrow from Homer—this was a perilous choice, as the example of Apollonius showed. Vergil chose to return to Homer, and yet he chose not to borrow his style, though at times he might imitate this or that casual effect. He chose instead to borrow the Homeric conception, and not superficially by choosing some other voyage than the *Odyssey*'s as Apollonius had done, or some other war than the *Iliad*'s, as Statius and Lucan were to do. Instead, with the instinct of his own poetic insight, he went back, we may suppose, to his own original conception, compared it with Homer's, and rethought it on the same primary basis that Homer had done with the materials provided for him by the traditions of Troy.

The solution Vergil arrived at is so bold as to be obvious only in retrospect. He fused the *Iliad* with the *Odyssey:* a warrior voyages to a new conquest. This fusion he announces in the very first words of his poem, *arma virumque cano: arma,* the subject of the *Iliad; virumque,* the subject, and also the first word, of the *Odyssey.*

For the rest, he felt free to borrow, to conflate, from the Alexandrians, whom otherwise he does not imitate. This he does with an admirable selectivity, as Heinze[4] has demonstrated. Of course the poet masters his borrowings enough to depart from them wholly on key occasions, to invent entirely such episodes as the death of Priam[5] or the love of Dido[6].

A range of human action, involving a whole life and the possibility of death, must be embodied by the epic poet in the figure of his central hero. Vergil had not only to deepen the refined style, but also to face getting a unified fullness of humanity into his hero, when he himself lived in a society of cosmopolitan diversity. For centuries the poet had managed this diversity by excluding large sections of it from poetic treatment: by setting just the high cosmopolitan society in his poems, as Catullus did, or inventing rural elegances, like Theocritus, or retiring to a farm, like Horace, or refusing to write of more than a personal love, like Propertius: these are literary, and of course also personal, self-limitations.

Vergil, to begin with, had been shy of people before the *Aeneid;* and this, in a sense, was an advantage: how else in fact are we to reckon it in the face of the poem's undeniable success? The nation was the prototype of whole humanity, but the nation was external to the woods of the *Eclogues* and the labors of the *Georgics,* even when the future of the nation was supposed to bear the whole apocalypse of the Platonic Great Year.

Vergil, finally, internalized the nation within his hero by choosing a hero who existed before the essential ideal of the nation did. For Aeneas the nation is nothing but a memory of *labores* on the one hand and a dim sense, more sorrowful than hope and less established than conviction, that *fatum* will bring Rome about, that the race—after a great epic effort—will be founded.

> *tantae molis erat Romanam condere gentem.*
>
> so great an effort it was to found the Roman race. (I, 33)

The man internalizes the destiny of the people: the destiny of the people serves for the destiny of the man. The moral life and the emotional are fused. Correspondingly, death can enter the picture only through the past, not through the mortality of the actual hero. Mortality inheres in the whole world; *sunt lacrimae rerum*. But the whole sense of mortality rises in the hero's breast. His sense thereof, it may be observed, permeates the whole world in the poem. For Carthage shares the Roman quality of resurgent hope:

> *o fortunati, quorum iam moenia surgunt!*
>
> Happy those whose walls are already rising. (I, 437)

And Carthage also shares human sorrow: the sadness of the Trojan War is painted on the walls of the circular temple built in the sacred grove at the very heart of Dido's city. And what is true of Carthage would be true of anywhere on earth:

> *quae regio in terris nostri non plena laboris?*
>
> what region in the lands is not full of our labor? (I, 460)

In this poem of destiny, Italy stands for something requiring sight and endurance. It lies under the great human ignorance—and confidence—about the future. Aeneas does not know except by hidden signs got through consulting the mighty dead just what Italy is, even when he sees it, though it must be visible to become embodied.

He does not know how long he must endure. The prowess of Achilles, the sleights of Odysseus—these would be of little service in gaining the fulfillment this hero seeks. A wholeness is intimated, plumbed in a deep sense of time which Homer had not envisaged. Homer's Trojan towers in the black night are innocent of the internalized and upwelling Vergilian maturity.

This is Vergil's fable, which Homer could not have allowed: the myth of the continuity between the leader's private psyche and the very success of public events. The sense of total destiny occupies and expands the emotions of Aeneas, as the tone of the verse renders them. The Homeric "objectivity" has been turned into something vastly internal. Or as Heinze again puts it, Vergil differs from Homer in that he has *Stimmung* or mood. There is a response to all outward actualities, and everything bears on the psychological world where its meaning acquires a depth this poem renders: *Sunt lacrimae rerum et mentem mortalia tangunt.* Between man and fate, Theodor Haecker[7] says, lies a sea of tears.

The very body throughout responds to these assailing emotions. "I recognize the traces of the ancient flame," Dido says of love; and of love's effect on her stricken body, *"agnosco veteris vestigia flammae."* (IV, 23) Aeneas says a cold sweat flowed over his whole body as he heard the Penates speaking:

> *tum gelidus toto manabat corpore sudor*   (III, 175)

These bodily effects are marked, almost as much as they are in Dante, who may well have got the idea of them from his *duca* in the first place.

Death lies in the past, not in the future; and the future itself forms a pageant in the land of the dead. At a key point Aeneas consults the dead. But his own death remains silent in the life of the hero whose sense of mortality it permeates. The death dominant in the epic vision here appears under the aspect of time, not as the transience of the *Odyssey,* but as a sensual permanence. Past, present, and future are felt as one destiny for the hero, and past differs from future more in mood than in time; the future is already embodied in the hero's heavily sensed purpose and in what he actually sees underground. The joyful (future) is set in opposition to the sorrowful (past): what is *labor* for the past and *spes* for the future remains a sense of *fatum* in the present. What the gods have uttered (*farefatum*) in the past, and what is held for an unconfirmable destiny in the present, will become a visible city and nation in the future.

Fate is whole, in the mind of the hero; it connects with the smallest event:

> et, si fata deum, si mens non laeva fuisset,
> impulerat ferro Argolicas foedare latebras,
> Troiaque nunc staret, Priamique arx alta maneres.

> And if the fates of the gods, if mind had not been wrong,
> he would have driven to desecrate the Argive flanks with iron;
> Troy would now stand, you remain, high citadel of Priam.

(II, 54-6)

This means not that Aeneas can really conceive of the action as happening otherwise—is it not his *fatum* to go on to Rome?—but that he is here ravaged by the sense of how the smallest events of the past *fatum* all hang together.

Achilles must learn *aidos* toward the laws of society, and toward his subservience to something beyond the society, the perennial limit of his self, for which Priam stands. The *pietas* of Aeneas is based on the society, and yet its laws do not exist outside himself: he carries them in his own breast. *Pietas* senses *fatum*, embracing the Rome to come as well as the Troy of the past.

Aeneas has already gone through the utmost that can happen to a Homeric hero in this world: utter defeat. In Homer, the victorious hero alone can measure the fullness of humanity: it is the bitter fact of human destiny that the defeated are already half slaves, that the fullness even of sensitivity is open to the Achaians, to Achilles, and not to the Trojans, to Hector. But Aeneas, a hero who will found a society, goes beyond Achilles, in the framework of Vergil's poem, to do what only a defeated hero could do, sail off into the future to make a society that as yet does not exist. He carries his fate on his shoulders.

Like Hector he has measured the fullness of human sorrow. The saddest (*maestissimus*) Hector stands weeping at his bedstead, while Troy falls, to tell Aeneas he is the hope of Troy. Unlike his kinsman, Aeneas will remain a warrior, glorious in defeat, where Hector, as Vergil describes him, is gory and unkempt, sadly changed from the fighter who came home clad in the armor of Achilles.

Hector's whole being is expressed by sorrow; he is *maestissimus*. Aeneas, in the very discovery that the sadness exceeds telling, finds himself transported beyond sadness into his destiny:

> *quis funera fando*
> *explicet aut possit lacrimis aequare labores?*

> who might unfold
> the deaths by speaking, or could equal the labors with tears?

> (II, 361-2)

But the labors that cannot be equalled with tears can be exceeded by more labors. And these will serve to bring about a new society. —Even when the queen of the gods opposes. And Juno is uncompromising beyond any Homeric deity:

> *flectere si nequeo superos, Acheronta movebo.*

> If I cannot bend the gods above, I shall move Acheron.

> (VII, 312)

So she speaks, in determination against Aeneas. The will that stands up to her bears a fullness of destiny beyond that known to a Homeric hero; it is the fullness of a whole society which the hero impels himself towards.

In this, Aeneas is so much more ambitious than Odysseus as to differ from him essentially. Odysseus returns to the known Ithaca, the beloved Penelope. But for Aeneas Troy is destroyed and Creusa dead. He must sense his way to a new city in the heart of a wilderness. He must understand who is to be the new queen. And on his way to this understanding he must meet the test of overpowering physical and emotional sympathy in the person of Dido. To think of Aeneas as slighting Dido is to undervalue the power of her impact on his spirit.

His experiences are internalized, and oriented in time. Achilles sings of the glories of men on a lyre captured in the sack of Andromache's father's city, while he has the cosmos blazoned on his shield. In the *Aeneid* it is the song of the Carthaginian bard Iarbas which praises the cosmos. On the shield of Aeneas is blazoned his own future, destined scenes from the history of the Rome to come. The culminating scene on Aeneas' shield is a representation of Actium, an event still reflecting the devotion to Dido that Aeneas rejects. Had he been an Antony, Rome would never have existed. He subordinates the Antony within himself to the Augustus who can then become his descendant.

Aeneas does not, like Antony, sacrifice with Dido his renown to his fate; instead he masters both his fate and a renown among his future descendants. He carries them in the shield his shoulder sustains, though he is ignorant of them and wonders at them. And he also delights in the image. All of this we are told in the last two lines of the book where he receives the shield:

> *miratur rerumque ignarus imagine gaudet*
> *attollens umero famamque et fata nepotum.*

(VIII, 730-1)

Aeneas includes all of Rome, and Rome all of destiny in Vergil's eyes. So the *Aeneid* can be read as a history of the soul: its literary achievement lends itself with formal ease to the Christian purpose.

4

The diction of the *Aeneid* holds the weight of the hero's emotion, a weight that the burden of the fable makes it bear. The myth Vergil

has invented forces these words beyond the impersonal generality of
Alexandrian diction, beyond the soft diction of the *Eclogues* and the
hard diction of the *Georgics*. Many key words are repeated, *durus*
and *labor, gens* and *fas:* but their definitions carry, in addition to
the weight of the lexicon, a special Vergilian weight. A *labor* is now
a tear-charged experience because the word presents such experience.
Saevus describes opposition to someone undergoing a *labor*—it is an
active word because always used in an active context. *Gens* does not
have the semi-abstract neutrality of Callimachus or even Horace: it
is a word that fuses the most primitive meanings of Clan with the
most sophisticated meanings of Nation, a word whose intellectual
weight is to be sought in the emotions, the sense of *fatum,* within
Aeneas' heart.

By dint of many repetitions, by dint of the consonance of terms in
the similes and figurative expressions, by dint of their relation to the
fable, such words in the *Aeneid—fortunatus, cor, metum, cura,
surgere, altus,* and many more—receive a special charge above and
beyond the generality of their refined style, which of course they also
share by their mere existence in the lexicon of Vergil's time.

The very adverbs—such as *quondam, tandem, iam pridem, iam,
tantum*—are heavy with the sense of destiny. An emotional statement funds its depth in these heavy words:

> *mene efferre pedem, genitor, te posse relicto
> sperasti tantumque nefas patrio excidit ore?*

> Do you hope, parent, I could move a step when I had
>   abandoned you,
> And has such an impiety fallen from a father's mouth?

> (II, 657-8)

Aeneas is addressing the Anchises who has just proposed that his
son leave him behind to die in Troy. The words transmit the emotion because each of them bears the largeness of the hero's destiny.
What does *genitor* mean but one who has physically sown the seed
of a line of responsible emperors? The hope in *sperasti* refers not

only to Anchises' momentary conviction; it groans with its weight, from repetitions elsewhere in the poem, of the impossibility of this notion as against the only true hope for a pious man, for a man subservient to the rights of the gods, to *fas*. This idea is *nefas*, the magnitude of which—the *tantum*—is measured against the poem's whole myth of *fas*. (*Tantae molis erat Romanam condere gentem*.) Aeneas is bound by that *fas*, which determines *posse* for him; possibility is defined, again, not as a neutral class word of active modality, but as an emotionally weighted assessment of the breadth and limits of a destined hero. Surrounded by so much weight, even the ordinary words—*effere, excidit*, even *pedem*—are charged with the sense of subjective tears in objective facts, *lacrimae rerum*.

Even the words of physical description bear this emotion to such a degree that Pöschl[8] can assert them (falsely modernizing, I believe) to be "symbols" of Aeneas' feelings:

> *hinc atque hinc vastae rupes geminique minantur*
> *in caelum scopuli, quorum sub vertice late*
> *aequora tuta silent; tum silvis scaena coruscis*
> *desuper, horrentique atrum nemus imminet umbra;*

> here and there vast cliffs and twin crags
> threaten into the sky, under whose peak widely
> safe seas are silent; then a stage with flashing woods
> above, and a dusky grove threatens with bristling shade

> (I, 162-5)

vastae, silent, tuta, atrum, the verbs *imminet* and *minantur*—these are heavy with an emotion which is Aeneas' only because he embraces the whole myth of the poem. They do not *stand for* that emotion. Such analogies remain for Dante to invent. But they do partake of that emotion: Vergil has stretched the refined style to allow it the burden that in the *Eclogues* and *Georgics* it would not bear for him, so much so that even the little spatial adverbs—*hinc atque hinc, desuper*—receive something of that color, in addition to their Callimachean abstractness and precision.

Vergil involves his very verb tenses in the emotional charging of past and future, more boldly than an Alexandrian poet would have dared to do:

> *forsan et haec olim meminisse iuvabit.*
>
> Perhaps it will help to remember these things another time.

(I, 203)

The perfect (in form) of *meminisse* is brought up against the future of *iuvabit,* and the two tenses render schematically all the interaction in Aeneas' spirit between the future which he can look forward to as having become past and the present whose meaning is found in striving toward a future already *fatum.*

Olim usually means "formerly" but here means "in the future sometime." Moreover, the perfect form of the verb *meminisse,* coming directly after *olim,* leads us to expect the meaning "formerly." That meaning is not ruled out until we reach the last word of the line *"iuvabit,"* which surges the more powerfully with its futurity because it caps, includes, and alters the two past-seeming words just before it. The meaning "formerly" lingers as a disappointed expectation—we had thought *"olim"* to mean "formerly" all through the line until we reached *"iuvabit."* Thus the future is rendered as tinged with the past in the poetic interaction of the words.

Vergil characteristically suspends the sense through the end of the line, as the purpose is suspended in Aeneas' mind till Turnus dies in the last line of the poem. This suspension—a syntactical miming of action—exceeds the common suspension of the verb in the Latin sentence, because it often involves creating false expectations in the line, as with *olim.* Or take this line:

> *Forsitan et Priami fuerint quae fata requiras.*
>
> Perhaps you may ask what were the fates of Priam too.

(II, 506)

Priami hangs waiting—as for his execution—till we go three words further, almost to the end of the line, for *fata.* As we meet *fuerint* it has not been introduced by any of the relative pronouns or conjunctions which might announce the perfect subjunctive, and we therefore take it for the future perfect indicative, which in form the word could also be. *Quae* immediately opens the possibility of the subjunctive, but that becomes a certainty only with the last word of the line, *requiras*. All through the line we suspend a likelihood that *fuerint* is future perfect: alas! it is not, and Priam's fate is even more firmly a past than the tension of the line had at first led us to suppose. The expectation, and the disappointment, are conveyed not only "objectively" in the line, but dramatically, charging again with the sense of destiny this question which Aeneas imagines Dido to wish to ask him: the sense moves as certitude in his mind; as wonderment, he supposes, in hers.

Just as Vergil charges the refined diction and syntax to carry a burden heavier than a lyric one, so he stretches his rhythmic uses in such a way that the hexameter can render effects of a greater complexity and range than those accessible to the calibrated rhythms of his predecessors.

An epic usage, in any case, seems to call for some overriding rhythmic principle to convey the flight of the verse, some mark of a classic line. Given a meter like the hexameter, there are three ways in which pause, or accent, or variation between dactyl and spondee can be managed in the verse. First, these extra features may be ignored, and the meter felt as a loose sweep. This is the practise of ballad writers and of earlier epic poets; Homer, the poets of *Beowulf*, the *Cid*, *Roland*. Second, the extra features may be tightly calibrated into the rhetorical pattern: and this we find in the refined style. But this second practise will not suffice for epic. Therefore, Vergil had to evolve some third principle such as—to anticipate the matter of coming chapters—Milton's sustained sequence of uniform major accents, Dante's elaborately dovetailing rhyme scheme.

This overriding principle for Vergil would seem to be the one which W. F. Jackson Knight[9] discovered in him, and in him alone among the Latin poets: the calculatedly varied counterpoint of the stress accent of the word in Latin (which must come on the penult when it is long, or on the antepenult if the penult is short), and the quantitative length of the dactylic foot (which, wherever the words fall, must of course come always on the first syllable of a foot, and in a spondee on the second syllable too). Knight's whole book, *Accentual Symmetry in Vergil,* is taken up with analyzing the effects to be derived from having stress coincide with ictus (an effect Knight calls "homodyne"), or from having stress and ictus not coincide (heterodyne). Vergil, then, harnesses stress for special effects, as the Alexandrians do not; as well as ictus, which they harness but Homer does not. The doubleness of effect complicates the rhythm, endowing every line with the sense that it must be dwelt on for full sound. Every line bears a double charge, and thereby the progression of words is heard to undergo intensification.

Otherwise the charged diction would strain against inadequate rhythms, and we would have something like the *De Rerum Natura,* where the ruggedness of the poet's voice breaks again and again with an excitement that falls breathlessly short of the rhythmic capacities necessary for the poetic task he has set himself.

But for Vergil the rhetoric of diction and syntax and the counterpoint of rhythm work together from the outset of the *Aeneid*:

> *Arma virumque cano,/ Troiae qui primus ab oris*
> *Italiam/ fato profugus/ Lavinaque venit*
> *litora—multum ille et/ terris iactatus et alto*
> *vi superum,/ saevae memorem/ Iunonis ob iram,*
> *multa quoque et bello/ passus, dum conderet urbem*
> *inferretque deos/ Latio—genus unde Latinum*
> *Albanique patres/ atque altae moenia Romae.*

As Knight points out,[10] for the fourth foot in every one of the first six lines, stress and ictus diverge. Only in the seventh line—with the characteristic effect which he calls "Released Movement"—does the stress of the fourth foot coincide with the ictus, building up "the

high walls of Rome" so to speak, when at last the struggles of
Aeneas are spoken of as ending.

"*Altae,*" then, is the first of seven words in the fourth-foot position
to get the full coincidence of ictus and stress. It receives a rhythmical
charge, in addition to its semantic charge of association with both
height and depth. Here of course it means height: walls are not
deep. But the association of depth is brought closer by the proximity
of *alto* in line 3, where the word means primarily "deep." There,
too, stress and ictus coincide, but more forcedly, because *alto* comes
at the one point in the line, the sixth foot, where a disyllabic word
not only may but must have stress and ictus in the same place.

Another word full of the Vergilian destiny is the word that almost
rhymes with *altus: multus,* a word that occurs adverbially as a
singular in line 3, *multum* (interechoing with *alto*), and multiplies
into a plural of sufferings in line 5, *multa.* The first time its stress
and ictus coincide, except that it also elides—as though the verse
could not quite bear saying it fully out and so must run it faintly
on together with the pronoun of Aeneas, *ille.* The second time, too,
its stress and ictus act together, and in the firm position of the very
first foot; an effect, as again Knight says, with which Vergil characteristically begins long clauses.

The suspension of the syntax also, as it were, imitates Aeneas'
movement through the poem. Clause is added to clause. We are
given the long parenthesis, the pitch at *unde,* and yet are held up
till the final resolution.

Working with all these effects refinedly are the caesurae which I
have marked but not analyzed in the passage. An elaborate but supple rhythmic structure builds over a long cadence, and on a small
scale, too, from foot to foot.

These effects without the epic burden would seem trivial: Ovidian;
the burden without the effects would seem rough-hewn: Lucretian.
Vergil's very originality, in rhythm as in diction, consists in his
having been able to adapt lyric procedures in such a complex way as
to make them fit for epic uses. Here, as in other respects, he is a

"father of the Western World," and the only epic poet in our tradition who bequeathed a usable technique to his successors: both Dante and Milton are Vergilian in certain (quite different) stylistic respects; but no one else succeeds in being really Dantesque or Miltonic.

5

Vergil's concentration of effects in language and rhythm amounts to a foreshortening of detail in the moving story: every event slows down to receive an almost sculpturesque treatment. Between event and event we find little continuity: we go from the storm to Carthage, from Laocoon to Troy's nocturnal carnage, from the games to the concern of the gods, to the death of Palinurus. Each event appears in the poetry as rounded and sculpturesque as on a frieze, and each stands to each as one frieze to another in a sequence.

A sequence absorbs and impels the mind of one man, Aeneas, whose *pietas* towards his own *fatum* is tested and deepened by each event. The events themselves proceed in a sequence not of narrative so much as of mood. For it is mood, not narrative, that would cause us to dwell far longer on an encounter with Andromache than on the actual death of Anchises, that would make the love of Dido occupy a poetic space smaller than that given to her frustration and death.

The scenes are set in montage; they are selected for their congruence with the unfolding will of the singleminded hero. Odysseus, above all, encompassed variety: pleasure and pain, monsters and maidens, sophisticates and naifs. The generality of Aeneas involves little variety but much unity; it resides only in his depth, and toward this depth the events appear in a montage of similar emotions. *Sunt lacrimae rerum*. Each is a *labor*. "Vergil shows us his Man," Heinze says again, "wholly preponderant in a state of emotion; he spares himself nothing for the high points of the portrayal, but, aside from a few pauses for rest, sets the emotional scenes in uninterrupted order one after another."[11]

Feeling determines the temper of events, their selection, and also their order. The punishments come last in the *Odyssey*'s presentation of the underworld; for Odysseus they press less on his consciousness than do the meetings with Tiresias, with his mother, with his fellow warriors. They are varied experiences, deferred in the narrative because he did not get to them till he had attended to more important matters. In *Aeneid VI* the punishments come first; they constitute the first in an ascending series of fates which will culminate with the cyclic mystery of Rome's future glory.

So in the montage of Troy's fall, we do not hear much about Aeneas' role till the very end of the events he tells to Dido, though he says at the outset he had a great share in them, or more precisely was a great part of them (*pars magna fui*).

Through this montage, through the others, the public becomes the private in the epic unity of Aeneas' feelings. Homer's Odysseus, when he tells the Phaeacians of his travels, touches on events that interest him and engage him personally. Aeneas' innermost private life is the public *fatum* he carries, and so Troy is at once a past truly felt and the model for a future truly to be realized. (A number of false realizations are possible: Andromache and Helenus have constructed a replica of the old Troy; Dido's offer is another.)

Troy becomes his past: much of the book about the fall of Troy takes place in a flaming night. Where there is no fire, there are Greeks: *tenent Danai qua deficit ignes* (II, 505). And it is men of the past, old men, who fall. Only Laocoon remains undeceived by the wooden horse, and he and his progeny are strangled by prodigious serpents from the sea. The old man writhes in defeat, for his very prophecy. Then comes the montage of Priam's death, which taken by itself would exhibit an odd Euripidean despair. Taken together with the fortunes of two other old men, the strangled Laocoon before and the wearied Anchises after, it portrays the overwhelming sorrow which inheres for Aeneas in a vanished Troy.

Book III is a montage of the horrors attendant on too facile a choice of destiny. Aeneas must be active; he learns as much in the brooding passivity of each person he meets during this phase. Polydorus' host has broken every pious rule (*fas omne,* III, 55), and the man himself becomes a tree whose broken branches drip blood. Aeneas and his followers sit back in passivity while the clanging harpies devour their plates. Achaemenides is reduced to being an unkempt scavenger on Sicily. Andromache is a compact image of what a false institution of New Troy would be: she weeps perpetually beside a false Simois. Her marriage with Helenus exudes a sad hopelessness, and her greatest joy can only be to send Aeneas auspiciously off.

Women are traditional vessels of emotion, and Andromache stands in a montage of other women. A woman goddess pursues Aeneas from the outset with a fury that seems excessive even for the celestial spirits (*tantaene animis caelestibus irae?*). Venus protects her son; and she at first approaches him in a disguise that suffuses her person with the appearance of her opposite, Diana. In Book II Helen is shamed by Aeneas, and Creusa frees him: Andromache, the stricken survivor, shares the emotion of both, but more deeply than either.

These women are lovers, not rulers or warriors. Dido is not only a lover but a ruler who rides armed to the hunt (while the disguised Venus had walked lightly dressed). And later, Camilla, no lover, will fight as an all but invincible warrior, an expansion of the Amazon Penthesilea mentioned in Book II. Only for a balance to the montage of other women can we justify as more than an eccentric digression the prolonged attention given to Camilla, particularly in Book XI.

We would expect Lavinia to overbalance her; and we should: for Vergil, as critics have long pointed out, succeeds only intermittently and dimly in the last six books. He is too much the slave of Homer to realize the scenes of his frieze in complete consonance with the necessity of his poem's life feeling. Once again we have the epic marvel, unexampled in lyric, of the partial success glimmering through even the unsuccessful portions. Vergil's language has been forged into such a powerful instrument that it carries the feeling even when it is describing events that cannot in themselves be read for more than superficial machinery.

Dido is herself the most charged of the false fates. Venus and Juno, for once, combine to urge the alliance; Venus is for once taken in, on the grounds that the Rome to come will assume the form of an amorous union between the Trojans and the Carthaginians. Dido has her own sorrowful Phoenician past, her own projected future of a Carthage whose walls are already rising. And it is by arguing the political advisability of the union, the congruence with destiny, that Anna gives the culminating blow to her sister's *pudor;* the sexual reticence is overmastered by the political aspiration.

The private and the public, love and the state, all emerge as emotions in this poem; and so all easily become one, for Aeneas as for Dido. The falsehood, though, is immediately apparent; the walls stop rising at once while Dido pursues love. And the greater part, just in the bulk of the poetry, is taken up with the sorrow of sundering this false union. Aeneas, too, feels the troubles of it to the depths of his great heart (*magno persentit pectore curas,* IV, 448). But he sets sail and takes himself away from what he cannot know, her death, recounted in the last line of the book.

He had transcended other deaths too. For from the second book on, every phase concludes with a death: Creusa's at the very end of Book II; Anchises' at the very end of Book III; Dido's in IV; Palinurus' at the end of Book V.

The epic hero comes up to the actual place of death in Book VI, deep with a knowledge of death. Palinurus' alone, the last one, has been deceptively calm. In Book VI Aeneas must understand the meaning of death before he can know what his future is to be. Between the deaths of voyage and the deaths of war comes the easy descent to Avernus, the hard *labor* of ascending from it.

The meaning of death and the meaning of the future: he must understand that the two are one. Death holds the meaning of the future, the millennial scions of future Rome parade past him in the

meadow: except that this is a fiction, which in turn must be understood, at least by the poetry . . .

The father, and the father alone, does Aeneas seek to see in the
underworld. The father will show him the future, and in the misty
(*aeris*) realms of death, *fatum* will wear the mask of past or of future
indifferently. Since the private is to become the public, since Rome
exists first and most necessarily as the *fatum* within the hero's
spirit, Aeneas in this poem will not finally black out, like the
Homeric hero. Nor will he sacrifice himself, heavy with age, in the
supernatural combat of a Beowulf. His own death will charge the
race he founds with a sense of *fatum*. Not only will his spirit live
on; but also, through an identification that cannot be pressed too
closely (if only because questions are circumscribed in the realm of
the shades), he himself will be his own descendant:

> *tu Marcellus eris . . .*
>
> Marcellus you will be . . .   (VI, 883)

This might be a metaphor, did Anchises not speak of something
like the transmigration of souls. The explanation he adumbrates for
the real presence of future heroes on his meadow lies somewhere
between the oriental doctrine of transmigration and the Lucretian
atomism. Yet his explanation, in turn, cannot be pressed.

In one sense the visit to the underworld is an expansion of Aeneas'
own consciousness; he tells the sibyl he has grasped and acted it all
out in his own soul beforehand:

> *omnia praecepi atque animo mecum ante peregi.*   (VI, 105)

Vergil divides his underworld between the fulfilled and such unfulfilled persons as infants, unmarried girls, frustrated lovers, Tanta-
lus, forcers of false destiny like Salmoneus. Aeneas is to be fulfilled. The last line of the entire poem seals the death of the last man
who stands in the way of the hero's fulfillment, that man himself
unfulfilled, and so given over to an almost Dantesque indignation:

> *vitaque cum gemitu fugit indignata sub umbras.*   (XII, 952)

ndignata means "unworthy" as well as "angered." The worthy, by
contrast implied in this identification, remain calm in their ful-
illment.

But we know Aeneas must die, and so the question of what his
visit to the underworld means, of what these "shades" in the last
word of the poem are, presses on the poem.

The question is answered cryptically, with an unexpected lightness:

> *Sunt geminae Somni portae, quarum altera fertur*
> *cornea, qua veris facilis datur exitus umbris,*
> *altera candenti perfecta nitens elephanto,*
> *sed falsa ad caelum mittunt insomnia manes.*
> *his ibi tum natum Anchises unaque Sibyllam*
> *prosequitur dictis portaque emittit eburna,*

> There are twin gates of Sleep, of which the one is made
> Of horn, through which easy exit is given true shades;
> The other shines perfect in glistening ivory,
> But the spectres send up false dreams to the sky.
> When this had been said there, Anchises attended his son
> And the Sibyl with him; and sent them out the ivory gate,
>
> > (VI, 893-8)

Aeneas goes out the ivory gate, and the Sibyl goes too.

We can carry the echoes of ivory and horn all the way back to
Homer, and beyond him to the remotest Mediterranean rituals.
Similarly we can find the structure of Daedalus' and the Sibyl's
palaces in Minoan Crete. But this is only to enrich the substances,
ivory and horn, with a weight of implication. Nowhere in the poem
is that weight explicit, and the farther we go, the more rarefied the
air of connotation we are scrutinizing; the farther below the surface
of denotation we have gone.

On that surface, the ivory gate produces *falsa insomnia,* whereas
the gate of horn gives exit to true (*verae*) . . . shadows (*umbrae*).
Falsa exactly contradicts *verae*. Yet how much more substantial *insomnia* are than *umbrae* depends on how much weight we give to

the connotation of *in* on the one hand: are "non-dreams" to out
weigh "shadows"? On the other hand, how concrete can *umbrae*
be? It cannot denote merely "ghosts" because the *manes* are respon
sible for what comes through the other gate. It cannot simply mean
"infernal" shades, as in the poem's final line, because the shades do
not take an exit through a gate. *Umbrae* hovers between "ghost" and
"shadow," and it will not come clear. It has to come clear, though
to help define its opposite, itself left somewhat in the air. We do
have *falsa* ascribed to *insomnia*. However, the plain fact of the poem
is that Rome's destiny, shown to Aeneas, is not *falsum*. It is true; i
is already history from the vantage of the actual Vergil.

Thus at its turning point the poem comes up to its own fiction
and fades in a sad, enigmatic echo. Homer need not provide a theory
for his fiction; he need only be consistent within the world he makes
for himself. Dante in his way, Milton in his, will provide elaborate
theoretical underpinning within their poems for the mode of their
own fictions. Vergil adumbrates this problem; he must do so as a
post-Alexandrian. But the emotional sense of destiny within him
cannot fully embrace its relation to the destiny of a real empire. Not
able to answer this question, he knows he cannot skirt it as Apol
lonius does by writing as though it did not exist; he cannot avoid it
as Callimachus does by eschewing epic. And so he broaches it lightly
with the image of the ivory gate. In what sense is Aeneas real? In
what sense does Vergil really believe in Juno and Venus? In what
sense do souls really transmigrate? These questions disappear
through the ivory gate. In Homer we can provide an answer. Milton
and Dante provide answers for us. Vergil leaves the question hanging in the air.

With unexpected lightness. For the sibyl had said that the return
from Avernus, like everything else in the poem, would be a soul-
searching *labor* that only the most virtuous souls could hope to
achieve:

> *Tros Anchisiade, facilis descensus Averno:*
> *noctes atque dies patet atri ianua Ditis;*
> *sed revocare gradum superasque evadere ad auras,*

hoc opus, hic labor est. pauci, quos aequus amavit
Iuppiter aut ardens evexit ad aethera virtus,
dis geniti potuere.

Trojan son of Anchises, the descent to Avernus is easy.
Night and day the door of dark Dis lies open.
But to recall that step and escape to the breezes above,
that is the task, that the labor. A few, whom impartial
Jupiter has loved, or burning virtue raised to the upper air,
sons of the gods, have been able to do it.   (VI, 126-31)

And yet they go out very easily through the ivory gate, by no *labor.*
Not a word is said about the contradiction.

The entry had been with the golden bough. What does the gold
mean to Vergil? Not, following Frazer's title, a submission to the
sad ritualistic progression of the seasons, to the magic that will make
boughs bear successful fruit: this is a gold bough, not a green:
Aeneas' destiny somehow transcends that anthropological world . . .
though to ask how is to evoke, again, the ivory gate.

Gold hints at the golden age, a time free of our *lacrimae rerum.*
We need not go back to the beginning of the *Georgics* for this evoca-
tion; Anchises speaks of it later in the same book, the *aurea saecula*
Augustus will found (792-3).

Gold leads to the underworld; the rare plant stands to be plucked
in the very thick of the forest; *tenent media omnia silvae* are the
sibyl's very next words, filling out the last of the lines quoted above:
woods hold all the middle regions. The *silvae* of the *Eclogues,* the
separate trees of the *Georgics,* hold deep within themselves the
growth of a miraculous bough, of gold.

Gold is royal, and ritualistic. Daedalus' roofs are of gold (*aurea
tecta,* VI, 13). A little later we are told he has wished to depict
Icarus' fall in gold, but that the father's hands fell down twice (32-
33)—(marvelous touch!).

Three times in two lines the word gold is used of Dido's dress as
she goes out to the hunt:

cui pharetra ex auro, crines nodantur in aurum,
aures purpuream subnectit fibula vestem.   (IV, 138-9)

But the use of the golden bough is by far the fullest. It would be idle to try to make the millennial and palatial, the opulent and beautiful uses of gold comment on the bough: it comments on them.

Aeneas, like the poem that charges him with the mysterious transcendence of his own destiny, does not go in through the ivory gate, but by help of the golden bough. He comes out through the ivory gate.

CHAPTER SIX

The Bread of Angels

IN THE *Divine Comedy* the significances of a fourfold allegory converge in a verse whose refined style exhibits the completeness of the convergence by a remarkable simplicity of surface. A central fiction has been achieved which allows for a very high order, an order Dante defines as composed by the music, a *fictio rhetorica musica composita*.

To achieve this balance, higher than Vergil's, was more difficult than for Vergil, because for "the chief imagination of Christendom," poetry could not be paramount in its own right. For a soul aware of grace it could not be of utmost moment to be led by a sibyl through the ivory gate. The poem, to be neither scripture nor theology, would have to refer to them both as well as remain a poem. Dante's earlier work splits into pure poems of troubador refinement and prose discussions of the ideas in the poetry; a way had to be found to reconcile and fuse the poetic fiction and the scriptural truth. And as E. R. Curtius[1] points out, Dante finally describes his poem to Can Grande in terms drawn equally from theology and from rhetoric. The epic hero, ultimately, became the poet himself, someone who was neither Vergil's protagonist nor a figure in the scriptures. And Dante near the beginning defines himself as neither of these, neither Aeneas nor St. Paul:

Io non Enea, io non Paolo sono: (*Inf.* II, 32)

For the complete action (*actio completa, De Vulgari Eloquentia,* II, 8, 50) of his poem, Dante could not leave poetry separate from the theologian's reasoning, as in his prose treatises of explication, nor could he refine theology out of the poetry,* as in his earlier lyrics themselves. Though the "ten terms" by which he defines the *Comedy* combine the rhetorical (and poetical) rather casually with the theological, the poem could not be casual in its combination: it had to be *transumptivus:* to combine theological extrapolation with poetic intrapolation in such a way as not to be simply a fable (*Enea*), and also not to set forth scriptural truth baldly (*Paolo*), or even miscellaneous facts, as does the *Tesoro* of Brunetto Latini. The problem as implicitly set by these two seemingly conflicting demands, evoked a solution which had to bring all its meanings together into no less a convergence than the high simplicity of the *Comedy* exhibits at every point.

Vergil himself could handle philosophy with eclectic casualness, the more readily for being free of Lucretius' compulsions. The comprehensiveness of squaring fiction with Christian truth, on the other hand, obliged Dante to reason out the scheme of existence before he could poeticize it. Hence the drive towards the large theme appears not in Dante's earlier verse itself, as it does in Vergil's. It appears in the philosophizing prose of the *Vita Nuova* and the *Convivio*. His lyrics there, and elsewhere, harmonize a contentment of utter troubador refinement, and embarrassing questions do not perturb or purge their ideality of love. Reasoning is left to the prose. The notion of a *fictio rhetorica* does not dominate the definition of this kind of complete poetic action, but just the music:

> *cantio nil aliud esse videtur quam actio completa dictantis verba modulationi armonizata.*

* As E. R. Curtius points out, the Middle Ages had no one word for "poetry," used the word *"theologus"* in a more general sense than "theologian," and allowed for a much greater overlap between the modes of prose and verse than we do. All this, of course, does not mean that we must restrict ourselves to medieval uses when discussing medieval literature.

The song seems to be nothing else than the words of a speaker
harmonized by modulation.   (*D.V.E.,* II, 8, 50-2)

Yet the food of the *Convivio's* banquet, Dante says, is to be the
same he later ascribes to the *Paradiso,* the bread of angels. The subject was an imaginative one, and Dante had encouraging license in
the *Benjamin Minor*[2] of Richard of St. Victor for thinking that some
modes of mystical imagination were accessible to the natural reason.
Yet the prose work is offered to those who have before "eaten
acorns," the high verse to those whom years have accustomed to the
celestial diet. For the time being, that bread could only be described
in prose. A strain toward the higher theme of epic shows not in the
conception of those prose works themselves so much as in the very
fact that he abandoned both treatises before finishing them.

In the earlier work philosophizing was divorced from poetry. And
no style of poetry in the "vulgar speech" lay at hand that could
offer more than the triumph of lyric grace that Dante had already
demonstrated. All styles in the desired vernacular left to one side for
expression the coordinated meaning of the very love experience he
was praising.

The love of the troubadors could not bear the full burden of epic
knowledge. And not for the theological reasons that made the cen-
sorious post-Tridentine editors tamper with the *Vita Nuova,* but for
reasons essentially literary.

The love for Beatrice, even if it be pressed, as with Charles Williams,[3] to make her an analogy of John the Baptist, or God himself
through the divine likeness in all men, was still too restricted in
the poetic vocabulary that could be applied to it. Within the traditions of the troubadors, style, diction, rhythm, and subject matter,
all met too simple an allegory. A larger fiction was necessary, and a
more neutral scheme, one that would, while remaining neutral,
allow Dante to put everything into verse instead of displacing his
ideas into prose. And also without displacing Dante from the center
of his own poem: otherwise he would have another *Tesoro* of Bru-

netto Latini, a casually encyclopedic poem. Brunetto taught him
come uom s'etterna. But Vergil is his *duca,* his *maestro,* his *autore*
It is the *breadth* of Vergil's utterance that Dante names first in his
surprised recognition:

> *Or se' tu quel Vergilio, e quella fonte*
> *Che spandi di parlar si largo fiume?*

> Ah, are you that Vergil and that fountain
> Which poured so broad a river of utterance?

> (*Inf.* I, 79-80)

In literary terms, the *exemplum* of the *Aeneid* allowed Dante to
conceive the *Divine Comedy.* Vergil, however, stands only for a
technique, and a limited perception, that must in turn be invoked
by higher powers, and by the love which retains a supremacy:* Beatrice and the Virgin sent Lucia (Grace) as a messenger to Vergil,
to send him to Dante. He had to get the Vergilian ring into vernacular verse, and get the Thomistic generality over into it at the same
time.

The internalized pathos, the difficult aspiration—these the *Aeneid*
has, and these Vergil offers Dante: he can guide him up to *Purga-*
tory, and to just short of its perfection. But the style of pathos and
aspiration cannot indulge itself; the Vergilian modulations become
more severe, the Vergilian polyphony is muted to a different order,
as Vergil leads Dante not through his own underworld but the
Christian inferno he could not have known till he died. To order
the fourfold significances Dante can begin, but only begin, with
Vergil.

2

The method Dante worked out as a solution for his epic task was
one which he himself, of course, calls allegorical. His description of
it in the letter to Can Grande comes back again and again to the
question not only of the fourfold senses, but more notably to that of

* Already indicated in the *Ego Dominus Tuus* of the *Vita Nuova.*

the modality of relations among them: he speaks of *relatio*, again of *polysemos*, then of the presumably Aristotelian end or goal (*finis*) as being *multiplex*. He invokes several sets of rhetorical categories, and in his most summary statement, on which Curtius and Auerbach among others dwell, he mixes rhetorical categories indiscriminately with theological: *Forma sive modus tractandi est poeticus, fictivus, descriptivus, digressivus, transumptivus; et cum hoc definitivus, divisivus, probativus, improbativus, et exemplorum positivus.* (*Epistulae* X, 9) These ten terms themselves, as Blackmur[4] shows in his essay on them, can be made to bear many, if not all, of the abstract transformations possible to literature (and so to criticism). And Dante has built his poem so firmly up on the fourfold "allegory," that one might, by way of exercise, work these terms out even more specifically with reference to the *Comedy*. Its system would surely sustain such a complexity of examination, so thoroughly is it conceived.

And so firmly is it based on the literal sense, in which, as Dante himself says, all meanings are funded. His mode of handling the literal tenor of his allegory, indeed, makes even his own use of that term misleading, and allows Coleridge to call it "quasi-allegorical",[5] while Auerbach[6] can consistently urge that the method is figural rather than allegorical, *figura* in his sense describing the dynamic interrelation of the literal with the other senses. Resting heavily as he does on the literal sense, Dante is able to make easy transitions from the literal to the allegorical and back again, especially at the beginning of the poem, as Singleton[7] demonstrates. Each of his persons, including himself, works as a *figura* in comprising at once the total literal existence of his life and another, "alle-gorical," set of senses transumptively included in it. Vergil is realized in the *Commedia* as a person who transcends the earthly poet and his earthly poem. He is a *figura* who compasses both his historical actuality and his allegorical significances without diminishing either.

Vergil reasons in the *Commedia*, but he is not Reason only: he is himself. Even for reason he falls short of the theologian, a point that a single example may illustrate. In spite of what some medieval-

ists tell us about the so-called Goddess Fortuna, we cannot imagine
Dante as following that popular tradition to present her personified
sway the way he has Vergil do; St. Thomas would not have done
so. Vergil gives a more limited view of Fortuna than a theologian
would, and this limit shows itself as his (*Inf.* VII, 69 ff). It is, he
says, *mia sentenza.*

Vergil remains a person, *literally* so. Within the fiction, he is the
actual dead poet whose voice rings with the range of all he literally
voiced in this life. *Allegorically,* perhaps, he is the guidance of a
natural reason he alone especially exemplified; and *morally* he is
unredeemed natural virtue. *Anagogically* he represents the capability of the unaided soul almost to attain grace, or at any rate to be
deprived of only the light of God:

> *Semo perduti, e sol di tanto offesi,*
> *Che senza speme vivemo in disio.*
>
> We are lost, and only hurt to the degree
> That without hope we live in desire.   (*Inf.* IV, 41-2)

Which returns us to his literal existence, and the mood of the *Aeneid*
that these lines evoke. And so to the immediate, personal interchanges with Dante himself.

The remarkable fact in Dante's fourfold figural significances lies
in this unfailing immediacy of his *literal* reference, an immediacy
that will bear large disquisitions on the multiplicity of senses.
Through the principle of its analogies, the fourfold senses become
one sense, and this sense inheres in the literal: Vergil, for all that he
may mean, remains Vergil, and if the Augustan poet fuses with
Dante's guide to the dead, it is only by way of his (imagined) existence in the eternal realm which the equally "literal" Dante himself visits.

Dante is at pains to build one meaning with exact modal propriety
into another:

> On the evidence of what is to be said, it ought to be known
> that the sense of this work is not simple, but rather it can be

called *polysemos;* that is, with a number of senses. The first
sense is the one that obtains for the letter, the other is that
which obtains through the things signified by the letter. And
the first is called literal, the second allegorical or moral or
anagogical. So that how this is handled may be more mani-
fest, consider these verses: "When Israel came out of Egypt,
and the house of Jacob from among the strange people, Judah
was his sanctuary and Israel his dominion." Now if we look
to the letter alone, the exodus of the children of Israel in the
time of Moses is signified to us; if to the allegory, there is signified to us our redemption made through Christ; if to the
moral sense, there is signified to us the conversion of the soul
from the grief and misery of sin to a state of grace; if to the
anagogical, there is signified the exodus of the holy soul from
the servitude of this corruption to the freedom of eternal glory.

(*Epist.* x, 7)

Dante goes on, after this, to insist once more that all the allegorical
senses may be taken together. And he says at the beginning here
that the allegorical is contained in what is signified by the literal.

If the highest or anagogical meaning is the deliverance of the soul
from this life into the freedom of eternal glory, then Dante achieves
the fusion of the most literal with the most allegorical by making
the literal fiction just this: the living soul on a literal earth imagined
as moving beyond earthly life, the Dante of the *Divine Comedy*
being its chief and central *figura.*

The central fiction of his poem permits the four senses to become
one sense: the poetry can be all-embracing and immediate at the
same time. Earlier in the *Convivio,*[8] when discussing the four senses,
he picked a passage from Ovid to illustrate the allegorical sense, a
passage from the Gospels for the moral, and this same Exodus psalm
for the anagogical. Now, once the *Divine Comedy* lies clearly conceived before him, he can bind all the senses up in a single illustration. One event gets many meanings, polysemously. Each meaning
is unspectacular, and not at all strained. All cohere layer by layer.

We can see how fully he brings these meanings into convergence by comparing his description with a more usual medieval theological allegory. Dante's poetic fusion is in contrast to the usual ingenious and disjunct allegorizings of the theologians, as for example Hugh of St. Victor's[9] summary of interpretations, on this same biblical event:

> And so Egypt is the saecular life, the desert the spiritual life, the promised land the celestial life, Pharaoh the devil, his princes demons, the mud luxury, the straw vainglory, gold philosophical wisdom, silver eloquence, brick hardness of heart, the river of Egypt the flux of the age, Moses preachers, the sons of Israel Christians . . . the Red Sea baptism, the people of the Amelekites carnal vices of perverse men, Og and the other kinds spiritual vices or demons, the possession of the promised land eternal blessedness . . .

The essentially disjunct character of this normal kind of allegorizing might be paralleled throughout this whole work, or in similar works like Richard of St. Victor's *Adnotationes Mysticae in Psalmos*,[10] (the very writer whose discussion of the powers of contemplation Dante recommends in the same letter).

By virtue of its convergence of all senses into the literal, the poem conveys a constant force of dense figural appositeness, while achieving an epic directness of unparalleled simplicity. To take the example he explains to Can Grande, when Dante has his souls sing this Psalm (114) as they sail towards Purgatory, he does not need to unfold the multiple senses of the *Exodus* explicitly, as he does in the letter. The verse moves in the full simplicity of its literal incandescence because the conception itself lies beneath the event to carry without rhetorical amplification the polysemous burden:

> *Da poppa stava il celestial nocchiero,*
> *Tal che parea beato per iscripto;*
> *E più di cento spirti entro sediero.*
> In Exitu Israel de Aegypto
> *Cantavan tutti insieme ad una voce,*
> *Con quanto di quel salmo è poscia scripto.*

At the poop was standing the celestial pilot,
Such that he appeared "blessed" by inscription;
And more than a hundred spirits were sitting within.
"When Israel came out of Egypt"
They were all singing together in one voice,
With as much of that psalm as is afterwards written.

(*Purg.* II, 43-48)

These words move in a simplicity beyond even Homer's, because all the poetic labor of funding the associations has been referred to the mere order of the poem, in which the significances cohere, detail by detail.

To be specific, the souls sing in a joy of morning, but not an ordinary morning. A morning in Purgatory is an evening in Jerusalem, the poem says earlier. And on this Jubilee Easter weekend, as soon as morning comes, Libra has risen over the Ganges. The whole astronomical structure of the world, in fact—the relative (imagined) literal positions and their various allegorical senses—has been given in the first six lines of this Canto, with verses equally simple in their actual movement and equally complex in the fullness of their epic reference. And the simplicity depends on the complexity: if it were less "polysemous," it would also be less direct in presentation.

One figural detail finds its ordered place by implied analogy to other figural details, the moving self of the poem providing a connection and a hierarchy from point to point. On this particular morning an angel pilots the boat and makes it move, by power of his own virtue: an act whose force of love stands in the poem's order as a contrast to Charon's creaky rowing. Dante has just come up from the Inferno in the fable of the poem, and his wonderment is measured still by the presence of Vergil.

Charon's boat moved by toilsome power; it was smaller; it took the souls singly; it took them as soon as they gathered, like fallen leaves on the shore; they cursed their parentage. In the simple dark, and not in the Purgatory's entire reversal of morning. The meaning of this voyage, with its more than hundred souls entering the boat only when ready, and singing in a unison, finds its figural density not in tropes of interpretation as they are presented, but in the ordered analogy, point for point, with the transport into the dark realm. And also with the ascent to Paradise. There, however, no corresponding details are given to compare as a third term with Charon's boat and the angel's. All detail is transcended in the simple soaring of the purified soul. That part of the poem, Dante tells of the *Paradiso* in writing to Can Grande, is *contractus,* contracted.

Charon's counterpart, however, is not only the angel in this section of the *Purgatorio,* but Cato: the analogy from part to part is never simple. The functions in Purgatory are more various because they are fuller. Not that Charon is more than the angel plus Cato. The realm of Purgatory is more; as its light, its beauty, and the very resurgence of the poetry from *"morta poesì"* (*Purg.,* I, 7), all proclaim. This angel bears a light on his face, of such a sort that "blessed" appears written on it by inscription, a more mysterious light than that in the canto before, on the face of Cato, *"freggiato di lume,"* friezed with the light of the four stars of the classical virtues.

More than a hundred spirits: they exceed, and are calm in, that biblical round number: this is a simple voyage and not the rose of the blessed; so the numbers do not become the mystical ones of *Revelation,* or even of Exodus Revealed: forty years, four and twenty elders, and the like. But the principle is that of *Revelation,* where figures are numbered, like these spirits, in multiples of ten, a multiple that in the Italian associations of "cento," as in the Latin of "centum," carries the suggestion of a cycle completed (the *Commedia* has an even hundred Cantos).

The poem binds into each of its simple high songs—its *cantos*—the fourfold significances. We come into these and fill each out in an intensified perception of the whole order. Here the psalm Dante interprets for Can Grande is laconically introduced, *In exitu Israel de Aegypto,* just a single line. The Church Latin stands out against the *dolce stil nuovo* of the vulgar tongue as a cryptic embodiment of the revealed.

Within the order of this single Canto we have another song, written not for the redeemed by David but for the earthly by Dante himself. It is sung to him by the Casella who waits on the bank till the pilot beckons:

Amor che nella mente mi ragiona,

Love that reasons in my mind   (112)

Rested souls sing the psalm across the water, and not the winded and waiting Casella who sings Dante's poem. And while the psalm, as scripture, is more anagogic than Dante's own lyric, yet this line, by virtue of deserving a presence in the same part of Purgatory, may itself be taken for a version of the psalm: the two come to the same thing ultimately: to enter Israel, to have love reason in the mind. And speak in the mind: the two meanings of *ragionare* will converge, but not quite yet. The lyric sounds most like the language of the *Paradiso,* where such a line might occur. But Dante has not yet arrived there, nor has Casella. Hence, as we know by invoking the later part analogically, to sing this song on this shore is an indulgence, more precisely a laziness or slackness: they are *spirti lenti,* as Cato rebukes them for being (II, 120). Literally Casella sings to Dante. Allegorically this is such a foretaste of the divine love as the troubador love of the poems would be. But morally it is an indulgence and a slothfulness to be satisfied tasting the foretaste, and anagogically it delays purgation (which—the unspoken fear—will be very painful for these waiting souls). So they dutifully give up the lovely song, "like doves come together at feeding, flying away from something that frightens them—" itself a detail susceptible of the fourfold interpretation, and of contrast with the bird similes of *Inferno* and also *Paradiso.*

3

Angels do not need words, Dante tells us in the *De Vulgari Eloquentia,* because they communicate divine knowledge directly, and beasts do not need them because they have no such knowledge. Men do need them, though, to express what the angels know directly, in order to "unhusk a concept to others" (*enucleare aliis Conceptum*, I, II, 12-13). What is unfolded, enucleated, really is one in the mind of God, and a ladder of analogy exists in the created world, and in the structure of man's spirit (which St. Bonaventure and others compare to the relations among the persons of the Trinity). Revealed truth lies also in the Bible, and in the Church.

These analogies lay at hand. For Dante they were real, not fictive. Of such a reality the epic poet Vergil, for example, may have been uncertain, and the shadow behind the ivory gate may express his uncertainty: did Aeneas *really* found Rome, is Augustus *really* his descendant, do souls *really* transmigrate in a vast circular order? We are never certain of Vergil's certitude. But Christ, for Dante, really did redeem man. The Bible is really the Word of God. The Spirit really seeks to know the Good of God. The Church is really a channel of Divine Grace.

Though Apollo is a fiction for Dante in the *Paradiso*, the shadow he speaks of when invoking him is a shadow of something real, the kingdom of the blessed, an afterlife about which Dante's *ombra* was a form of certitude (as faith is the substance of things hoped for), and lay under none of the obscurity embodied in the *umbrae* who flit through Vergil's ivory gate:

> *O divina virtù, se mi ti presti*
> *Tanto che l'ombra del beato regno*
> *Segnata nel mio capo io manifesti,*
>
> O divine virtue, if you lend you to me
> as much as the shadow of the blessed kingdom
> signed in my head, I manifest.   (*Par.* I, 22-4)

The shadow itself, in his mind, was a kind of Bonaventuran analogy. To use these analogies poetically was another matter, and learning to do it took Dante much of his poetic life. The analogies fell into place only when he had invented his consistent and inclusive

THE BREAD OF ANGELS 223

epic conception, and this demanded a treatment of figural modes rather different from the method offered by the rhetorical device of metaphor.

A metaphor compares two different things with regard to their likeness in some one respect. Hence, the differences in other respects must be calibrated in the poetry. Homer's similes use the differences (those accruing above and beyond the point of likeness in his metaphors) for contrast and expanded reference. Vergil's harness the differences for a more involved likeness. Milton invents an interlocking order for his similes, wishing his poetry to strain in that Vergilian polyphony which Dante had left alone.

Dante need attend to no differences, because his poem is based not on metaphor, but on quasi-allegorical or figural analogy. Physical light is analogous to spiritual light in all respects—though the two are not the same—because both attest to the same Creator. Wisdom is like the sun in all respects because Wisdom is an attribute of Him who created the sun.

Analogy is based structurally on an assumption of an all-inclusive likeness, rather than on the partial likeness of metaphor. Once he has found a conception that may by its very order expand the analogy through mere implications, Dante's verse need not strain with tropes and special effects. It can move calmly at its own dead center without strain, oblivious of differences. The similes fall simply into place. The angel with the shining face, the hundred singing spirits, the psalm they sing, the resigned spirits on the shore, are sometimes explained to Dante by themselves; or by Vergil or Cato or Beatrice or St. Bernard. The verse can still rest in the intense immediacy of their analogic conception.

The principle of analogy which Dante follows, insofar as it is based on a theological idea, resembles that of the "allegory of the theologians." It differs not only in the superior compactness of its applications, but in the constant poetic inventiveness of that application. Hugh of Saint Victor and others simply translate a biblical reference into a moral abstraction, an allegorical significance. Dante, who may or may not get a given fact from the Bible, does not translate his poetic figure until he has digested it in a direct and sensual, a "literal" apprehension become figural in the fiction of the poem. Brunetto Latini's face is *cotta,* baked, and that visual apprehension *becomes* sodomy, as the burning soles of legs protruding from a hole in the plain *become* simony. The moon has spots which the eye can see: such a visual effect, adapting this popular or that theological commonplace, is spoken of in the *Inferno* as Cain with his bundle of thorns. In the *Purgatorio* it is thought a rabbit, and in the *Paradiso* as merely the unequal layers of love. Each phrasing accords with what is being phrased, not only literally, but allegorically. Through the principle of analogy the allegorical and the literal are one. What fuses them is not only the principle, but the wide application of Dante's potent visualizations.

The remarkable range and accuracy of Dante's visual imagination, which evoked the prolonged praise of a great art critic, Ruskin,[11] scarcely appears at all in his earlier poetry. That literalness, in all the apt concreteness of its presentation, resides in the analogic fiction of the final poem where alone Dante was able to render it. "Not to speak of Paradise," says Croce,[12] "It is impossible to draw artistically a rose or a cloud if imagination does not first transform sentiment into either rose or cloud." And this transformation, on the negative evidence of the earlier poems, depended crucially on the figural matrix, without which we would not have even the literal detail that enters into polysemous, but convergent, signification.

Lust is a wind, and what this means abstractly cannot be separated from what it means concretely. The two are one because the power of Dante's imagination has made them so by reading the spiritual into the visual as intensely as Baudelaire does, and more widely.

Furthermore, whatever anyone literally says depicts the character of his allegorical state; the brusque *chi fuor li maggior tui* (*Inf.* X, 42) of Farinata reveals not only a personal brusqueness but the unwarranted shortcutting of heresy; heresy distorts theological truth by oversimplifying it, and so is a sin linked, in the presentation, with pride. Brunetto's personal courtesy becomes that of sodomy, whose devotees have a courtesy that derives from the amorous attachment of their failing. The hopelessness of their sin inheres in the marvelous drift of the flakes of fire down upon them, like snow in alps *without wind*. (So, indeed, their lust may tend to vanish.) The illusion of justification which the sodomites permit themselves is got by Dante into the very bearing of Brunetto as he departs—so often sentimentalized that we tend to forget his continuance in the procession of the damned. He *looks like* one who wins in the race at Verona for the green cloth. So he, so the sodomite, bears himself; and yet he can win no race. He cannot partake in the innocent festival of using the body gratuitously as in a running race, because he has forever misused his body. For him the imagined *drappo verde* is as valueless as the banner run after by the lukewarm damned of the *Antinferno*. The green, the color of hope, concretizes an image here ironical. *Verde,* the last word in the Canto, leaves Dante in a silent hopefulness of rich response to his old master; and yet the "I" of the poem moves on, no more justified in the sentiment of response than he was justified at falling like a dead body after hearing Francesca or at lingering in mysterious fascination with the schismatic Bertram de Born. All these reactions themselves figure the states to which the central figure responds as he moves—and moves by responding.

So Dante exhibits a total congruence of the imagined physical and dramatic reality of his scene with its spiritual meaning. Through this visual consistency, his similes, as I try to show when I compare them with Homer's similes in an earlier chapter, gain a full application of their subsidiary correspondences between the things compared, the vehicle, and the poem's reference, the tenor. Vergil similarly gains such fullness of correspondence in his similes, as when he compares the busy Phoenicians to bees, and one may say that they are not only noisy and swarming but also making the "honey" of imperial success. And when he compares Aeneas under Dido's blast to a great oak in the storm, one may even read the ritual uses of the oak into the comparison. But this involves a certain strain, a dazzle, in Vergil's verse. With Dante there is neither strain nor dazzle; all statements move at the dead center of analogy in the calm adaptive order of the cosmically progressing poem. Every visual and dramatic moment stands by itself, in the end-stopped simplicity of line, in the high generality of diction. And each moment also acts as a coordinate *esperienza* for the moving self of the poem. By virtue of this analogic identity, every image can effortlessly exhibit a visual precision. There is no need for the vague grandeur of Vergil or Milton, the clean distinctness of Homer.

The convergence of the four senses, as Dante modally presents them, gives his frequent similes a character which partakes of the same analogic function as the statements he makes without the mediation of simile. When, for example, Dante climbs, from the cliff edge of those who repented on their deathbed, up to the souls of the indolent; he goes through a small opening in the rock, twisting up. The opening through which he and Vergil climb is compared to the break in a hedge:

> *Maggiore aperta molte volte impruna*
> *Con una forcatella di sue spine*
> *L'uom della villa, quando l'uva imbruna,*
> *Che non era la calle, onde saline*
> *Lo Duca mio ed io appresso soli,*

> A greater opening, many times, does there hedge up
> With a forkful of his thorns
> A man of the farm, when the grape is darkening,
> Than was the path by which we rose,
> My leader, and I afterwards, alone.   (*Purg.* IV, 19-24)

The visual experience of this world, as it is drawn on for this simile, aids one to see the precise physical size of the opening on the spiritual (physical) mountain. The hole is a certain size, smaller than one a farm hand might fill up with thorns. But Dante says "greater than," putting it in such a way that the constant increase in *Purga-*

tory gets into the language, even when he wants to say that the Purgatorial aperture is smaller than the earthly.

The farm hand hedges it up to keep out thieves from stealing the grapes. And he puts up thorns. Here in Purgatory there can be no thorns. And here a hole, rather than a tangled barrier like that of the earthly farm simile, keeps out sin, because there can be no thieving in Purgatory. The opening was small, so small that the two went up alone; Dante is momentarily isolated from all that his leader figures at the point where he is passing from one view of indolence to another.

All terms of the comparison may be read. The simile is chosen as of a time close to harvest, because Purgatory is a fruitful mountain, with a miraculous garden at the top. Even thorns are spoken of here as having a function: they guard. They were useless as they grew sterilely and painfully in the wood of the violent suicides.

And the transumptive thoroughness of this analogy permits us, in the effortless visualness of the principle that creation resembles Creator, to read the comparison both ways. For grapes to ripen, for farmers to do their job, may also resemble the purgatorial ascent to God—may, that is, within the poem and for this passage. Dante need not labor, as Milton does, to work his comparisons both ways. The richness of association holds completely for the ascending Dante, but for the farmer only if he performs his naturally good tasks in a prayerful spirit—as Dante's poem need not tell us, because its moral categories in themselves do the telling. Other dramatic experiences may be brought to bear spiritually on the farmer; and so, when he enters the comparison, he exists simply, the designations about him taking the shape governed by the moment of the poem and not by his implicitly analogous activity.

Every moment in the poem, whether of imagined scene or of the simile, possesses its own clarity in itself, fourfold and single. And it also, singly and quadruply, represents a stage in the moral life. This provident employee of a *villa* who dutifully pitchforks thorns into hedge openings when the grapes ripen—he stands for an earlier stage of Purgatory, though he merely exists in a simile, than does the voyager whose desire turns and heart grows tender in the simile that introduces the first evening in Purgatory (VIII). Dante's desire is already turning. He is closer—the voyager images the fact of being closer—to a spiritual ascent than the man with the pitchfork, whose mere providence is seen as less full of the inspiring love than the voyager's turning desire and tender-growing heart. Both in turn, though, are Purgatorial. Their fine shades of difference are measured against each other, but their sameness of spiritual intimation is measured against such metaphors as that of the old tailor squinting into the needle's eye (*Inf.* XV, 21) to which the look of the sodomites toward Dante is compared, "as one tends to look at another in the evening under a new moon" (18-19). The Purgatorial images, too, are seen by double contrast: with the Infernal, and with such Paradisal ones as the "full bins" that the "husbandmen" of good souls "store" in the eighth heaven:

> *Oh quanta è l'ubertà che si soffolce*
> *In quell' arche ricchissime, che foro*
> *A seminar quag giù buone bobolce!*

> Oh how great is the abundance that is stored
> In those richest bins, that they were
> Good husbandmen to sow down there!   (*Par.* XXIII, 130-2)

The order, being progressive, implies such a structure of comparison —only thus could such progress be measured.

4

The multiplex schemata of this poem, as they are brought through the progressing intellect of the central figure, converge in a language that can be at once general enough to cover all the poet wants to say and common enough to move out of and up to the direct simplicity of speech. Though it is difficult for the vernacular to imitate Latin models (and Dante in *De Vulgari Eloquentia* stresses both this difficulty and the desirability of staying close to Vergil), the common tongue offers the possibility of combining a technical generality (the maximum delimitation of the refined style) with a colloquial suggestibility. As R. P. Blackmur[13] well says, the common tongue is "a language where learning and secrecy lived *in* or *under* the words, and which made not a pretense but an ensampling of universal language."

The Latinity could not be abandoned; it was from Vergil, and Vergil *alone,* not the troubadors, to take him at his own word, that Dante learned his refined style, one that was "sweet" like Vergil's but "new," and so different from Vergil's, a *"dolce stil nuovo":*

> *Tu se' solo colui, da cui io tolsi*
> *Lo bello stile che m'ha fatto onore.*   (*Inf.* I, 86-7)

Through the figural fullness of his literal sense, Dante can make his terms bear the schematic weight they would carry in a scholastic treatise without having them lose their common character. His penchant for substantives which he carries to the point of inventing new ones, as Luigi Malagoli[14] remarks, stretches but does not distort the limits of his common voice. Dante's style remains faithful to his intention of voicing a *commedia* in the sense that its speech sounds unrestrained and humble (*ad modum loquendi, remissus est modus et humilis, quia loquutio vulgaris, in qua et mulierculae communicant. Et sic patet quare Comoedia dicitur. Epist. X, 10, 222-26*).

Language, he says in the *De Vulgari Eloquentia* (I, III, 12-15) is a sign both rational and sensual, *rationale signum et sensuale.* Where Vergil charges the sensual by repetitions and syntactic dexterities till it bears a rational weight large enough for epic, Dante identifies the rational and the sensual, again, by locating them in a framework large enough and unified enough to keep every statement utterly simple for the moment, and fully profound for the poem. The refined style, in Vergil and others, aims for a sort of generic normalcy. Dante, schooled in the universals of scholastic diction, creates an

even greater generality for his words by breaking through the refined style. Not that he mixes the levels of diction (the view, mis-
taken I believe, of Auerbach). He simply speaks, in one tone and
on one level, in a conversational voice whose range covers universals
by virtue of the order it speaks in and towards. He himself, again,
stresses the generic and normative character of language, when he
says (*De Vulg. Eloq.* I, XVI) that it is the common *mensura* for
various *species,* as one for number, white for color, etc.

Even when Dante refers to a specific event in history, he does so
in terms which remain scrupulously general enough to cover the
whole theological situation at the point of his poem:

> *Vidi e conobbi l'ombra di colui*
> *Che fece per viltà lo gran rifiuto.*
>
> I saw and knew the shadow of him
> Who made through vileness the great refusal.
>
> (*Inf.* III, 59-60)

Is this Celestine V or Pontius Pilate? On so little specific evidence
we can never know. For the poem, however, it is enough that the
self of the poem "saw and knew" him, knew him as the shadow of
the man who made a refusal that was a great one, and made it
through vileness. What is an *ombra?* Popular speech can tell us,
but it takes theology for an adequate explanation. And the same can
be said for *viltà, refiuto,* and even *fece* (what does it mean to act?).
How great is *gran* in a great refusal? The greatness is defined by
all that is refused, a personal calling, a duty to the visible Church
and to God and to the souls of one's fellow men—*gran* carries a
literal, colloquial force, and also the several polysemous senses, the
allegorical, the moral, the anagogical. Which returns us to the literal,
the one that the voice had never left. The sentence remains one in-
candescent unit. It does not even elevate itself. The poem is not
defective, nor are we, to fail to identify the great refuser. The self of
the poem knew him, and phrases the encounter in terms unfailingly
general.

Or again, Trajan is imagined saying of himself as a statue cut in the rock:

> *Giustizia vuole, e pietà mi ritiene.*
>
> Justice wished and pity held me back. (*Purg.* X, 93)

The charity of such a remark falls into allegorical relief against everything said by any ruler in the *Inferno;* the damnation of each infernal ruler involves his not being able to speak with such simple frankness. *Pietà* is a colloquial word, and a Christian one; but in the mouth of a Roman emperor it is also a Vergilian one, and Vergil is one of the auditors. In the *Aeneid's* own grand utterance, a word like *pietas* stands lofty in its associations, redolent of *fatum,* of the inner life and the Rome to come. In the *Comedy,* as always, the universalizing conception of the poem takes the word's Vergilian echoes, its Christian correlatives, and also its refined generality of emotion, and funds them into the simple language of the vulgar tongue, just as Trajan's act initially contains a simple human emotion—"pity held me back." This simple emotion, by and with the word, is placed in the figural, theological order. Dante's terms are immediately far simpler and crisper than Vergil's, and also more universal: they are more objective. Vergil's *pietas* always reverberates with the internal sorrowing and willing of the hero. But in the *Comedy* no emotion is just savored for its overtones; even if Dante stops to do so, the guide prods him on. So much time, so many lines of verse more or less, are allotted to every level of moral and anagogical existence: Dante himself is a live experiencer, not a dead expiator. Each word retains its place in the divine song, and in a pure note; each word voices the common tongue in its hard incandescence.

This simplicity, rooted in the diction, is, as Eliot declares,[15] Dante's most remarkable stylistic trait. It is the more remarkable when coupled with, and ordered into, the most elaborate verse form any epic poet has ever managed. Rhyme is a bondage, to use Milton's word, when the theme attains epic grandeur. And normally such a pattern as the *terza rima,* to judge by the comparable stanzas of Tasso and Ariosto, of Spenser, would be too cumulative to be adaptive.

For Dante this bondage is a freedom because the mind bound in its orders is a growing mind. The cumulative can at the same time be adaptive, in the rhythmic order of the *Comedy.* Gradually, over the round number of the hundred cantos, the reason of the poem builds up more and more and more into the reasonable joy that every tercet links, ahead and backwards, a sober and profound music simple in the given line but polyphonic in the given canto.

The song, as in Homer, does not attend to special precisions of effect, at least not to my ear. (None, that is, beyond the onomatopoetic ones that Dante himself, to be sure, speaks of as desirable.) The hendecasyllables may mix in an extra syllable; or they may come down heavy now and then with *rime sdrucciole;* in either case the extra syllables get pulled up in the overall line. The song overpowers them: Vergil's rhythmic bas-reliefs come to life in Dante's verse and become a company of the blest. Technically the line retains its identity, and links elaborately with its choiring fellows, because of the *terza rima.* The rhyme makes the terminal echo more important than any echoes within the line, and the line predominates so much that no Vergilian grouping of rhetorical coruscations can stand out, as they may in an unrhymed line.

The song does the poetic work of binding the ideas. In such a pattern, the words can carry their full scholastic weight while remaining colloquial. It is just the rhythmic scheme that helps them to be simple, performing a work that Dante could not get either the prose or the verse of the *Convivio* and the *Vita Nuova* to do. Song is the binder, he says in the *De Vulgari Eloquentia* (II, VIII, 8-9): *Fascis . . . cantio est.*

Reinforcing the strength the *rime* give to each verse is Dante's pronounced tendency to end-stop his lines, to give each single line a syntactic as well as a rhythmic identity.

These lines, from Francesca's speech, carry their strong simplicity in the end-stopped rhythms of each, as well as in the direct words of each:

> *"Amor, che al cor gentil/ ratto s'apprende,*
> *Prese costui/ della bella persona*
> *Che mi fu tolta/ e il modo ancor m'offende.*
>
> *Amor, che a nullo amato/ amar perdona,*
> *Mi prese del costui/ piacer si forte,*
> *Che, come vedi,/ ancor non mi abbandona.*
>
> *Amor condusse noi/ ad una morte:*
> *Caina attende/ chi vita ci spense."*
> *Queste parole da lor/ ci fur porte.*   (*Inf.*, V, 100-108)

Each line here, by being end-stopped, stands in a defining simplicity. The rhyme that each line pairs with, and the rhyme that waits to triple with them, stand both at the distance of an intervening line. In such a regular progression, even enjambments or near enjambments, like that of *"forte"* in the fifth of these lines, pause for definition. By rhythmic position in an end-stopped series—rhythm is always defined by position—one pauses in spite of the enjambment still more than the end of the line usually leads one to pause. The other end-stopped lines strengthen the separate identity of an enjambed line.

The next rhythmic unit larger than the line is not so large as to predominate over the lines that make it up: the tercet. And each tercet is bound by only a single rhyming pair, the outer two, while the middle line, for the tercet, suspends its echo till the next tercet. And then it moves outside to become the rhyming pair. *Apprende* here rhymes with *offende,* holding *persona* between them; and then, for the next tercet, *perdona* rhymes with *abbandona, forte* held between them.

The pronounced and dominant unit in this simple interlacing remains still the individual line. And Dante keeps this so by tending to round out or end-stop his tercets too, just as he does his individual lines. He avoids the effect many poets seek with rhyme, of counter-pointing the rhymes against the sentences in such a way that a new rhyme is made part of an old sentence, an effect Yeats often gets, as here:

The Leaders of the Crowd*

They must to keep their certainty/ accuse
All that are different of a base intent;
Pull down established honour; hawk for news
Whatever their loose fantasy/ invent
And murmur it with bated breath,/ as though
The abounding gutter had been Helicon
Or calumny a song. How can they know
Truth flourishes where the student's lamp has shone,
And there alone, that have no solitude?
So the crowd come they care not what may come.
They have loud music, hope every day renewed
And heartier loves;/ that lamp is from the tomb.

This poem consists of three quatrains (abab, cdcd, efef). At the end of each quatrain one might normally expect a stopped ending. But this is just what Yeats makes a point of not giving us. At both the quatrain endings where he can—on *invent* and also on *shone*—he enjambs. The effect is further heightened by the question on *solitude,* the internal rhyme on *alone,* the semi-enjambment on *renewed,* the strong caesura after *loves;* the last provides for the final line, instead of a full ringing cadence, an abrupt, capitulating half-line.

Such are the counterpointing procedures by which a poet may vary a regular rhyme scheme. Dante never, or almost never, uses them; though every single tercet offers him as much opportunity to do so as each quatrain does Yeats. He buoys the tercets up in their individuality, itself a metrical feat comparable in difficulty to that of using *terza rima* to begin with.

In the lines quoted above he further isolates the tercets, and further intensifies their cumulative effect, by beginning each with *Amor*. Again, we find him keeping such rhetorical turns working with the tercets and not against them. It would be quite out of tune with the rhythm of the *Commedia,* for example, to have the repeating *Amor* take up one of the three-line sequences that by themselves did not rhyme, as for example in the sequence of endings *offende, perdona, forte,* here. And of course this other counterpointing effect is technically possible once every three lines, fully half as often as his actual effect of regularity.

Within the line, too, there is none of the tense modulation and elaborately interlinked grouping to be found in the Vergilian hexameter (though Italian admitted of them; the sixteenth century poets tried for just this effect of Vergilian *asprezza*[16]). Instead, each line balances simply, the smaller half against the larger (hendecasyllables necessarily have unequal halves). And this is a balance Dante sought deliberately, as we know from his discussion in *De Vulgari Eloquentia* of effects to be sought within the line.*

In the lines quoted above, each side of the line across the caesura contains a syntactic unit of nearly equal importance with the other half of the line:

> *"Amor, che al cor gentil/ ratto s'apprende . . .*
> *Amor, che a nullo amato/ amar perdona . . .*

This adapts the Vergilian word-by-word suspension to a balance within the halves (or thirds sometimes) of a line. If the syntax

---

* There, after dividing the whole art of "singing" into its constituencies of rhythmical units, from the poem down to the syllables within the line (II, IX, 24-28), he proceeds to examine (II, XI-XII) the different effects one can get by balancing syllables across the caesura; but always they must balance over and above the individual feet. The effect of "construction" which he calls *"excellentissimus"* as being both *"sapidus"* and *"venustus"* is one illustrated by, among others, his own line *"Amor, che nella mente, / mi ragiona."*

tipped that balance, the line could not retain its strength: if, for example, we had

>   *Ch'ancor non m'abbandona,/ come vedi*

instead of

>   *Che, come vedi,/ ancor non mi abbandona*

or even

>   *Amor ch'amar perdona/ a nullo amato*

instead of what we do have.

Dante avoids such imbalances, though to allow them would widen his range of potential metrical effects. Yeats, for example, often uses extreme imbalances, and if the reader will look back he will see that in the lines with marked caesurae in Yeats's poem the "short" half of each of these four lines weighs so little, not in number of syllables but in syntactic strength, against the "long" half, that we might confidently say we could not parallel them in Dante. But the other eight lines, in their balance, may be seen, through that balance, to have just the "Dantesque" ring that the marked lines lack. Each of Dante's half lines must hold to its identity, like each of his whole lines, his tercets, his cantos, in the ordered rhythm of his poem's rational order.

5

Death in an epic poem lies at the verge of the world. Roland and Beowulf in their endeavors risk it and go out to meet it, the one trammelled mortally in honor, the other burdened with extreme age. In the *Iliad* mortality becomes the bond of society, under the figure of fighting: the hero's mind grasps his mortal connection with the world. For Aeneas, the world that holds full meaning must come into being through something after his own death. That his

mind at once wills and senses: Rome is the *fatum* he carries deep
within himself, and death is felt in the sad foretaste of inevitable
transcience and loss, *lacrimae rerum*. The actual place of death lies
back through the ambiguous gates of ivory and horn. It is shadowy,
indefinite, and sorrowful; so much so that the "life" of Turnus, in
the last line of the *Aeneid,* wails as it flees down among the shades.

For Dante the Christian death is not a bitter end, or need not be.
It is not an ivory gate, but a gate of heaven. It leads to something
real, all that is permanently real. Hence the other world is not a
metaphor of this life, with differences to be accounted for, but a
full analogy of what in this life is a spiritual perception of ultimates,
of what this life ultimately means. As Charles Williams[17] puts it

> . . . the whole of hell is hidden though exposed: we see
> through a glass darkly. It may be said that Dante thought of a
> physical hell, and no doubt that is so, but he also thought of a
> spiritual. The corporal vitality of the diagram, on his own
> showing, is not yet here, and the spiritual reality is a fixed
> truth, yet infinitely recessive to the understanding.

The understanding moves towards the spiritual states, those easiest
to hand being the worst. Once understanding has been cleansed,
though, remoteness, in the paradise, will have become a function of
ease.*

For the Christian, the ultimate summation of any man's life in this
world, and the only final reality, lies in what Judgment will reveal
him to have made of his soul. Death, far from being shadowy, sets
the end of reality "face to face" that in this world must be seen
"through a glass darkly." To know even the world, the Christian
would have to know the divine disposition of people in the world.
For the intellect of his central figure, then, Dante invents just this
fiction, that the live poet strays from the center of the way of this

---

* For *Paradise,* the part he explains to Can Grande, as for the whole, the end
could be multiplex in being both near and remote: *Finis totius et partis esse
posset multiplex, scilicet propinquus et remotus.* (*Epist.* X, 15)

life, *nel mezzo del cammin di nostra vita,* into the structured kingdoms of the dead. The literal impossibility of the fiction is matched
by the transcendent reality of what it figures, and a make-believe
progress through something unknown but most real becomes a real
imaginative aid for spiritual progress towards that reality.

Dante moves like Aeneas, toward the unknown, down, and then
up with pained difficulty, and then aloft. But traversing the unknown works toward salvation. He even moves like the Ulysses of
Inferno XXVI towards *esperienza.* Ulysses, however, wrecked at the
foot of Purgatory; he did not wish to internalize the experience
morally, and so he is a mere painful voice, enveloped in a huge
tongue of fire.

Just as Aeneas visits the underworld to prepare himself for the
future and to learn about Rome, so the "I" of the *Commedia* proceeds in order to prepare his own salvation. The conquest, com-
passing the world, is to be of the self: salvation will come when his
own imagined death becomes real, when he no longer throws a
shadow among the surprised shades.

He internalizes the sense of death, as Aeneas does. But the sense
plumbs far deeper, because its converse is far higher. Aeneas, like
the poet whose voice presents him, knows only desire, sad or felicitous. Vergil in limbo lives in mere desire, *senza spema noi vivemo
in disio.* The Christian poet knows hope, and so he knows its converse, despair. As the "I" gets lost from confusion of the way, *via
smarrita,* the sight of the wood, "savage" beyond any Vergilian
silvae, strikes him with a fear that, like the *lacrimae rerum,* tastes
death internally, but far more bitterly. So bitterly that death itself
is little more, *Tant' è amara che poco è più morte (Inf.,* 1, 7).

The central act of movement, for the experiencing self in the
poem, remains intellectual by virtue of being a fiction. It is so make-
believe that while it massively orders history, it cannot pretend to
have its center touch history at all; as Aeneas does, and Roland, and
the Cid, and even (or especially) Milton's Adam. Dante remains

alive, and his movement when he dies cannot by definition be known while he is alive, or the poem's particular movement be permitted.

Dante is not an epic hero of action. The politics of his time in which he took part enter the poem not through his acts but in the categorizing statements—and the ascending emotions—of the poet who meets his countrymen in the country beyond. The intellection of virtue is dramatized, but not its action: he is not a saint, though he comes on saints in Paradise.

> *Io non Enea, io non Paolo sono.*   (*Inf.*, II, 32)

His final guide is not Beatrice but a theologian of love, St. Bernard. It is his mind that undergoes experiences, under the figure of his body. But if Aeneas, he says to Vergil at the outset, deserved to go to the other world while yet alive, it does not appear unworthy to "a man of *intellect:*"

> *Non pare indegno ad uomo d'intelletto.*   (*Inf.*, II, 19)

It is the good of the intellect that the damned have lost:

> *Ch'hanno perduto il ben dell' intelletto.*   (*Inf.*, III, 18)

The mind or intellect goes down into the other life; the principle of order in the poem seen as a fixed diagram is built into the progress of the poem seen as an unfolding journey.

However, the fixed diagram is only revealed as the journey unfolds. Consequently, within each canto, and also within the *"prima divisio"* of the "form of the treatise" (*forma tractatus, Epist.* X, 9), all senses converge, and every definition holds, at once for the point of the diagram schematically and for the stage of the journey progressively. For example, in the accurate visual presentation of the poem, illumination plays a major role, and every point has its appropriate degree of brightness. At the same time, all the various infernal darknesses, measured against each other, are also measured generally against the heightened natural lights and complex astronomical bearings of Purgatory. These natural lights are in turn measured by their actual analogues and sources, the progressively increasing spiritual lights of the *Paradiso*.

The character of the diagram within one large section is only revealed when the corresponding point of the next section is reached. The change brought about by the poet's progress reveals still another aspect of what had seemed to be totally defined. Gluttony stands next to the top of Purgatory, and so is met late; in the *Inferno* it is met early, near the entrance. There is no gluttony in the *Paradiso*, but the second sphere upwards is that of Mercury, the sphere of the souls who were good out of love for earth rather than for God. So they may be said to correspond to both kinds of gluttons, as excessively devoted to a temporal good. Moreover, gluttons speak of politics to Dante, in both *Inferno* and *Purgatorio*; and the sphere of Mercury is filled with political figures.

Justinian speaks for this whole sphere (*Par.* VII). He summarizes the sweep of history in the Roman empire, filling out the whole canto with his song. In the Inferno of the Gluttons (VI), not a famed emperor but a personal friend, Ciacco, addresses a saddened Dante, telling him of the coming bloody feuds of Whites and Blacks. Ciacco stops abruptly and looks asquint, then drops asleep. The deprivation of this interview may be measured against the satisfaction of the one with Justinian, as well as in its own rhetorical and dramatic progression. It may also be measured against the interview with the purgatorial glutton, also a close friend of Dante's, Forese Donati. Forese is so meagre and scaly, so shrunken from fasting, that Dante does not recognize him till he speaks. Then, though, the interchange is joyful. The subject, again, is Florentine affairs. But this time it is the degenerate immodesty of Florentine women. The purgatorial glutton has the right to excoriate the gluttonous side of the next sin, lust, which in the next sphere he may well (so Dante wrote of Forese elsewhere) have in turn himself to purge. The excoriation is a kind of spiritual movement towards that purging, as is the concern for the commonweal, a proper temporal good.

We take Forese's measure by Ciacco's on the one hand, by Justinian's on the other. All three, in turn, may be compared, in their spiritual bearing, their position, their motion of mind, their attitude toward self and visitor, to the many others in the *Comedy*.

Each interview in the *Comedy* contains its own allegory, for itself and by contrast with others. And each interview is unique. No one interview follows exactly the pattern of approach, withdrawal, question and answer, internal coherence, that any other does. Each is experienced for itself and ordered, through the matrix of analogy, in a progression for the ascending mind of the self at the center of the poem.

The literal identity of the poet with the protagonist carries its own figural allegory. The active ethics of his willed ascent converges with the contemplative theology of his ascending mind.

Dante speaks of *amor, salus* and *virtus* as comprising the subjects of poetry (*D.V.E.,* II, 2). One may bring love, salvation, and virtue together schematically and identify them as the three non-literal senses of the whole poem: its allegorical meaning is *salus,* its moral meaning *virtus,* its anagogical meaning *amor.* Looking at the central figure progressively, one may say that in watching the categories of the *Inferno* he contemplates *virtus.* In the *Purgatorio* he becomes more active, cleansing the sins from his brow; there he is earning *salus.* At the very end of Purgatory he has become *puro e disposto a salire a le stelle,* pure and disposed to ascend to the stars. And so he rises in the *Paradiso* by a progresive reflection through Beatrice's love to *amor.*

At last he moves no longer, but is moved equally. The schema and the progression utterly converge. His desire and his will become one, in the poem's last lines, through the love that moves the sun and the other stars:

> *Ma già volgeva il mio disiro e il velle,*
> *Sì come rota ch'egualmente è mossa,*
> *L'amor che move il sole e l'altre stelle.*

(Par. XXXIII, 143-5)

The self, at rest in utter motion through its progressive movement, becomes like the circle whose center is everywhere and circumference nowhere.

Corresponding to the three stages of Dante's ascent, are the three different kinds of souls to be found in each section. In the *Inferno* a life is totally defined, and thrown into shadowed relief, by the one sin that sums it up, the lowest sin that dominated it. Did the fraudulent Ugolino know gluttony (he gnaws in hell), or moments of familial fondness? Was Bertram de Born, being a troubador, lustful as well as schismatic? These questions are lost in the fixed and simplified identity of the soul damned by its gravest sin. The tail of Minos silently encircles his body a given number of times, and everything else falls away for the judged soul but the single dimension of his worst fault. He is fixed in it; and if he struggles to transcend it, he only exemplifies it: a pattern to which the (for us) moving courtesy of Brunetto adheres no less than the unflinching pride of Capaneus. The principle Vergil brings to bear on Capaneus —that the pride is his worst punishment—may be brought to bear equally on Brunetto's courtesy, that touching characteristic of the invert. Brunetto's diplomatic knowledge that he cannot lag behind without being penalized by a hundred years' defencelessness against the falling flakes of fire, his tenderness towards Dante, his modest apology for the clerks and great men of letters damned with him— these sensitive responses are all recognizable as typifying the male homosexual. They present Brunetto's sodomy figurally, the sad single dimension of his damnation.

The souls in Purgatory are already fuller: they move from level to level, with decreasing guilt and increasing love, a love each shares for the others by rejoicing when one of the number suddenly soars to the next level.

The souls in Paradise are completely full: their whole lives cohere in an instantaneous and eternal peace. They are the very life of the person, the ultimate essence:

> *Io son la vita di Bonaventura*   (*Par.* XII, 127)

In being so full, these souls, who define their own ultimate reality, and by contrast that of others, exist, beyond human memory or human speech, our double limitation. We must experience this life sequentially in memory; we can only define it in speech. Since in this life we exist within these limitations, our memory and our language must speak of those in Paradise, who transcend such limitations, as remembered in (at least) double existence: fictively each stands in his own temporal sphere, but "really" in the eternal great rose.

Dante, by joining them, imagines himself as transcending his humanity, *trasumanar,* a transcendence which by definition cannot be signified in the limits of human speech:

> *Trasumanar significar* per verba
> *Non si poria;*   (*Par.* I, 70-71)

In that *intimus (dentro)* which Richard of St. Victor[18] identifies with the *summum* (*De Contemplatione* IV, 23) he makes himself —the way Glaucus, at the taste of the herb was made—a consort of the gods of the sea:

> *Nel suo aspetto tal dentro mi fei,*
> *Qual si fe' Glauco nel gustar dell'erba,*
> *Che il fe' consorte in mar degli altri Dei.*   (*Par.* I, 67-69)

The whole final section of Dante's poem—and the whole poem, since this section defines the others—lies under what Curtius[19] calls the "inexpressibility trope," the statement, variously repeated in the *Paradiso,* that human speech cannot express what is (here imagined as) happening. The ultimate convergence of the literal senses with the others, and the ultimate state of the mind knowing God, passes beyond and through the instrumentality of that state. The mind, consequently, was wholly suspended as it marvelled at the paradoxal divine circle, fixed, immobile, and attentive:

> *Cosi la mente mia, tutta sospesa,*
> *Mirava fissa immobile ed attenta,*   (*Par.* XXXIII, 97-98)

Dante's own expanded figural mind in the poem comes to resemble the figure of God as a circle whose center is his circumference, each infinitely large and infinitely small: an infinitely large circumference because the poem is an all-embracing epic; an infinitely small one because it is only a fiction beside the reality of God. It is an infinitely large center because the central mind takes in all of history; and an infinitely small one because his language is limited to a vanishing point. He imagines himself as taking in the whole of his own life, widened by the history of all the souls known to it, which would be all of history seen, in the classical perspective, as beginning with Jason's first sail on the open sea:

> *Un punto solo m' è maggior letargo,*
> *Che venticinque secoli alla impresa,*
> *Che fè Nettuno ammirar l'ombra d'Argo.*
>
> A sole point is a greater lethargy to me
> Than twenty-five centuries to the undertaking
> That made Neptune wonder at the Argo's shadow.
>
>   (*Par.* XXXIII, 94-97)

One point, God, is greater than all secular history. One point is greater in the sight, and the words, of the poet; greater, though, as a stupor or lethargy, *letargo.** This lethargy of perception gives the

---

* Rhetorically, in a simplicity and balance worthy of Callimachus' epigrams (to compare greater with lesser), this line proclaims its heritage, through Vergil, in

limit to a finite poetry as it tries to compass the infinite. Here it is presented in terms of a mental response that is also bodily, a *letargo*. Earlier the same limit had been implied when he asked Apollo, who is no more real to him than Neptune (so the poetry, but of the *Paradiso* only, quietly admits its fictiveness), to enter his breast and breathe—as he had when he flayed Marsyas (*Par.* I, 19-21). His person being really alive cannot stand what it must stand: in the same sphere, the fourth, where he learned from Solomon about the Incarnation, he learns also, from the remote ancestor—his *bisavo* Cacciaguida—what he must suffer in his exile. And this is significantly the sphere of Justice.

All is finally a lethargy. We cannot go beyond the lethargy to expound it, in Dante's terms, in St. Thomas', in any others. We can, the term itself claims, only see it as a lethargy. Human language, its own or any other, can do no more than admit that sleep in the very act of proclaiming a comprehensive and epic vigilance.

---

the refined style. And not only because, as always, the words, each and all, control a degree of generality:

> *Un punto solo m'è maggior letargo.*

For one thing, the nouns and adjectives are in the simplest possible chiasmus. Moreover, *"maggior"* is an oxymoron: a "single point" is the smallest geometric figure; it cannot be "greater than" anything since it is smaller than anything. *"Letargo,"* too, is a sort of second oxymoron with *"punto"* in that if a point is something we expect it to be something acute, not something sleepy.

Letargo, then, exists in oxymoron with *punto.* It stands, further, in a kind of implied metonymy with what we would normally expect. A straight oxymoron, which that between *"solo"* and *"maggior"* leads one to anticipate, would suggest something like "dull" (opposite of "sharp"), as a straight oxymoron for *point,* instead of *letargo.* Through the oxymoron and through the metonymy, the *letargo* doubly evades a schematic relationship with the word *punto,* a relationship that the direct schematism of this simple declarative predication states: a point *is* a lethargy. Just so does the rhetoric of the entire poem at once evade and state its verbal cognition of God; that it knows what it cannot know (the oxymoron) and that even this paradox evades the terms that phrase it because in some sense the phraser drowses in a lethargy (the metonymy).

CHAPTER SEVEN

No Middle Flight

MILTON in *Paradise Lost* does not follow the universal epic precedent of taking a hero forward through a series of events, either an ideal person or himself. Instead of moving on towards God, as the Dante of the *Comedy* does, he looks back, himself fallen, to the unfallen state of general man. The central event has already happened, as he announces the subject of his poem. Homer does so summarize in his invocation; but Milton reverts continually, in various details of his verse, to the actual present of the speaking poet. In this way, as in others, he offers "Things unattempted yet in Prose or Rime."

His own mind, unlike Dante's, does not stand simply at the center of the poem though the structure of his own invocations keeps him present. Nor is he at the circumference. The poet's kind of identification with Adam (general Man, in the Hebrew meaning Milton well knew) remains problematic, and holds the fiction of the poem in the same state. Like Adam, Milton (and the reader) is fallen. Unlike Adam he has not been literally in the garden. To conjure up the garden is to try to reenter a prelapsarian state known, but in some senses unimaginable, "things invisible to mortal sight" (*mortal* sight; but not prelapsarian: it was Adam who "Brought *death* into the world").

When he finally chose his subject for an epic poem, then, he did not follow Dante. Milton, who cites Dante in his commonplace book, might well have chosen Dante as the starting-point for the conception of the Christian epic he early intended. And he might have found available to him in the live poetry of his time many of Dante's strengths already got into English—Dante's loaded dramatic interchange in the playwrights, his expanded allegory in Spenser, his spare but packed logic in Donne, the *dolce stil nuovo's* simple rhetoric in the refined style of the sonneteers and Jonson. At the same time it would be harder to compile a more exhaustive list than this Dantesque one of the qualities which Milton did not possess. And he did try to make every one of them his own. He wrote an undramatic drama, he tried his hand at allegory in exercises and in the beginning of *L'Allegro* and *Il Penseroso*. He also tried the metaphysical style in Donne's vein of obsequy; and, again, in *L'Allegro* and *Il Penseroso* he adopted a quasi-Jonsonian lightness and simplicity, as well as a measure often used by Jonson.

Dante's figural scheme of allegory was not available to Milton, whose unitary view of the human situation could not lend itself to the rational extensions of a poet content with scholasticism. Milton early declares, in *Areopagitica,* that he thinks Spenser a "better moral teacher than Aquinas." Nor was Spenser's own allegory unitary enough either, for all of its proposed identifications of the twelve Virtues within the single figure of Arthur. Milton began by assuming, for many of the years when he was "long choosing and beginning late," that his own epic would have the same central figure as Spenser's, Arthur. But Arthur could evidently not accommodate the Adamic unities, and he might also have seemed too fictive, especially when his historicity was powerfully challenged, for the first time, during Milton's own lifetime.

Milton, like Dante or any epic poet, had to find a fictive balance, and the powerful central presence of an acknowledged Truth in his world rendered fiction difficult for this Christian as for the medieval one—more difficult, if we are to credit Basil Willey's[1] assumption of the encroachment of science on the poet's sense of his own relevance. Milton solved this problem of fictive balance by basing himself on revealed Truth directly: by giving his poem the form of a commentary on the most revered part of the Holy Writ, the beginning of *Genesis*. When he first did so, though, he imagined he would be writing a drama, an allegorical one. And allegory remains at the base of his assumption through all four drafts of the Trinity Manuscript.

Finally, allegory is dropped, Spenser's kind, and also Dante's, which from the beginning would have been impossible for Adam. Adam, by virtue of his role in Scripture, is already fully figural for any person in humankind. In Dante's cosmos Adam's "contracted" life can figure alongside those of historical figures like Justinian and St. Francis. Put at the center of a poem, he becomes unexpandable, but problematical. And what Milton found he needed was precisely a problem: "To justify the ways of God to man," a dynamic "justification," instead of Dante's abstract *giustizia*.

Dante understands sins by hierarchizing them in embodied figuration. For Milton, Sin, while allegorical, remains a single figure of problematical power and plastic appearance, who occupies a space indeterminate enough not to lend priority to either the literalness of the physical or the spirituality of the symbolic; where in Dante, the literal stood always first, and last. For Milton there are no fourfold senses to converge, but only a single sense understandable to a *Reason* as comprehensive as the Thomistic *ratio*. His Reason, again, is far more unitary than the *intelletto* of Dante; Adam's failure of Reason really, and not fictively, affects his spatial position, which is also his spiritual condition, in this physical world. For Dante within his poem the meaning of the visual is clear and distinct. Milton's spiritual world takes the visual as problematic: he is rendering "things invisible to mortal sight." Instead of Dante's analogies, whose theology of identification leaves clear both the things identified and the structure of their interconnection, we are given a problematical presentation of the unfallen by the fallen, an attempt to embody things "spiritual" in things "corporal,"—and after their amount of interfusion has become subjected to the divisive dynamism of the Fall, when even before it the analogy was already necessary to mediate between angelic speech and human, as Raphael says to Adam:

> and what surmounts the reach
> Of human sense, I shall delineate so,
> By lik'ning spiritual to corporal forms,
> As may express them best, though what if Earth
> Be but the shaddow of Heav'n, and things therein
> Each to other like, more then on earth is thought?
> (P.L., v, 571-6)

But the mediation remains problematical; angelic stands close to human at least in so far as Milton's angels speak, while Dante's only shine.

Raphael's question is doubly problematical: as of the "shaddow" (Dante's *ombra*) for the Edenic earth; and as of the shadow for our postlapsarian earth, inexpressibly and incalculably but certainly different. In *Paradise Lost* this question must be left, as it is, hanging in the air, when for Dante it would have been a rhetorical question pure and simple: the whole figural structure of the *Comedy* answers the question, as does the Platonizing theology of his time. There was, of course, a Platonizing theology about "shaddows" in Milton's time too, at Milton's own university, and in the classical tradition which Milton had so thoroughly assimilated. But we can never get from the problematic Milton to the certitudes of some Platonism (nor can we get away from them). The one certitude of his poem inheres in the dynamism of what for the Christian is the integral situation in this world, where we are at once fallen and redeemed; but redeemed enough thereby to visualize the unfallen.*

---

* But not to be glad of the Fall. The notion of the *Felix culpa*, comes at just one point (and can come at only one point) of the Christian year: in the unparalleled exuberances of the Easter Even liturgy which, in joy for the Redemption, jubilates over everything in creation, even the Fall. It comes at just one point of Milton's poem too, and a similar point; it is also the only response strong enough for Adam to make when he first hears of the Redemption. *Felix culpa* is as marginal to *Paradise Lost* as to the Faith; to make more of it than Milton did is to distort the paradox-generating dynamism of his poem into the schema of a single, rather sensational, paradox.

Dante moves his poem to the limit of the "inexpressibility trope." Inexpressibility resides in the very Word of God for Milton, who elsewhere stresses the uncertainties of scriptural interpretation. Where Dante proceeds to a light he cannot express, Milton through the Fall can do no more than invoke the Light of a *deus abscondi-tus*, "No man hath seen the Father at any time." This light is obscure even to the Angels in *Paradise Lost*, as they say when they praise the Father:

> Fountain of Light, thy self invisible
> Amidst the glorious brightness where thou sit'st
> Thron'd inaccessible . . .
> Dark with excessive bright thy skirts appeer,
>
> (III, 375-80)

When Milton invokes the Classical Muse—which is all his conception allows him to do in a fictive poem that cannot itself stand as the truth of Scripture—he is really invoking the Holy Spirit. "The Heav'nly Muse" problematically comprises something of both but all of neither. As he says of the signification of "Urania" as he invokes her, "The meaning, not the Name I call" (VII, 5).

By internalizing the drama in the human soul, Milton extends it to include the cosmos. The problematical status of the Fall and the dynamism of the fallen condition give him, as a central conception, the imaginative leverage to erect a poetic fiction upon the scriptural truth. The "things unattempted yet in Prose or Rime"—though the phrase itself is taken literally from Tasso—may be supposed to include also the prose of *Genesis*, because Scripture, in being unproblematically inspired by the Holy Ghost, does not have to work within the limit of a fallen imagination.

Milton expresses his problematic limit by doubling Urania, the Classical Muse, with the Holy Spirit, and by calling Moses a shepherd in the Theocritan as well as the New Testament sense; Moses is seen partly as such a shepherd, within the poem. Milton, in not being a writer of Scripture but a poet following the classical conventions, cannot help *as a poet* seeing the Holy Spirit through Urania; and must retain the perspective of stating problematically the likeness of the traditional author of the Pentateuch to himself.

Dante does not ask such questions. Their solution is implied in the poem's order. Milton, though, like a modern poet, makes the process of the poem do his solving of how fallen words can approach the Word. To comment on Scripture in a poem is a perilous act, and a difficult one. The poet makes us aware he is following the Revealed with the fallen Imagination and that therefore what he sees dazzles. The generality of light carries him over, and yet the generality is factitious; Adam imagined in a poem written by a postlapsarian poet can be Man by the same sort of supposition that Moses can be spoken of as like Theocritus.

Milton's own blindness, by a pressing of the paradox in which fallen intellects are necessarily involved, is introduced to substantiate his request that he may understand the Edenic condition under the figure of light. Not to see natural substances in this world may invigorate his power to see supernatural ones; blindness helps approach more vividly in the imagination the time when natural and supernatural held together:

> But cloud in stead, and ever-during dark
> Surrounds me, from the chearful waies of men
> Cut off, and for the Book of knowledg fair
> Presented with a Universal blanc
> Of Natures works to mee expung'd and ras'd,
> And wisdome at one entrance quite shut out.
> So much the rather thou Celestial light
> Shine inward, and the mind through all her powers
> Irradiate, there plant eyes, all mist from thence
> Purge and disperse, that I may see and tell
> Of things invisible to mortal sight. (*P.L.*, III, 45-55)

What Milton sees is Adam, the Adam in himself, the Adam before the Fall; and all the spiritual beings, right up to the Trinity, who are involved in that cosmic event. Hence, while Dante moves the mind of the poet under the figure of the body through the world after death, Milton moves the generalized humanity of the poet, under the figure of the Primal Parent, in the world before the Fall. But Adam, while general, is unfallen: his generality rests—always problematically —on his prelapsarian condition. Where Dante moves from level to level in his cosmos, in *Paradise Lost* the whole cosmic order of spiritual forces—angels, devils, charity, wilfulness, reason, light—is felt to be brought to bear on every moment of the poem, rhythmically, syntactically, and structurally.

Hence dramatically. Dante's dramas are sequential, but Milton's are recapitulative; any moment is an aspect of, as well as a contrast to, the Universal Condition, which is possible for Dante's figures only in the *Paradiso,* and then after they have blissfully lost the embattled character that Milton's Adam never loses.

Adam's generality is insisted on, right from the very first noun of the poem, Man, a word generalized the more by virtue of being capitalized.* "Man" cannot be allegorical because the poet and all his readers are men. He cannot be other than literal because Scripture says Adam existed. His literalness differs from that of all other men in carrying an emblematic absoluteness: he is our Grand Parent, nameless until far into the poem, and all his features are the general ideal (a "Renaissance ideal," of course, only to us; not to Milton), as are all his gestures, until the Fall becomes actualized as the reality it has been from the first sentence of the poem. Even then, in his fallen gestures, Adam acts emblematically. Every man's natural reason is seen in the unfallen gestures of Adam and Eve; every man's ingrained propensity to sin finds its emblem in the pattern of their sin, and in their reaction to it. The reaction is not just

* The manuscript of Book I of *Paradise Lost* does not carry this capital, or many others that are found in the First and Second Editions. It seems more plausible that Milton would have instructed the printer to insert capitals at some stage between manuscript and edition, than that the printer would have been able—or wished—in both editions to impose so marked a feature of spelling on a Milton who, though blind, gives evidence of having attended meticulously to other details of spelling. There is some chance, I believe a good chance, that the capitals of the First Edition are Milton's own.

figural; the disobedience of eating followed by a new carnal greediness and self-awareness "means" here only itself, dynamically bringing a total consequence. No metaphoric structure can be erected on the sin of Adam and Eve, and theologizing about it attains a contingency, and remoteness, to the degree that it moves abstractly beyond the act—a theologizing that Dante's fourfold structure positively invites. Milton imbrues the senses of the act not into its separate gestures, but into the overall exemplary nature of the actors, from their very first appearance in the sight of Satan, to whom they are as new as they are to the reader:

> Two of far nobler shape erect and tall,
> Godlike erect, with Native Honour clad
> In naked Majestie seemd Lords of all,
> And worthie seemd, for in thir looks Divine
> The image of thir glorious Maker shon,
> Truth, Wisdome, Sanctitude severe and pure,
> Severe, but in true filial freedom plac't;
> Whence true autoritie in men;   (IV, 288-295)

The body remains the temple of the soul for fallen man too, but its perfection, its degree of likeness to the exemplary body of the primal parents, remains problematic. Lessons are constantly drawn, either implicitly, or as explicitly as in Milton's last phrase here. But the lesson when it becomes definite enough to be explicit, becomes thereby and therefore disjunct, an aside of the poet to the reader.

The supernatural beings are exemplary too: the Parliament in Pandemonium possesses the features of earthly assemblies in so far as they are bad. The fraudulent "smoke-filled room" tactics by which Satan puts Beelzebub up to introducing the capping proposal at a strategic point, like all these motions, carries extrapolatory suggestion. The Assembly in heaven exemplifies such bodies in so far as they are orderly. Satan's flattery of Eve is not Flattery, but an exemplary set of flattering gestures. And Raphael's courtesy sets out a pattern of courtesy without allegorizing it. The implicit lessons are not to be translated figurally, they are to be apprehended in the problematic dynamism of an action already fully defined before it begins, not only in Scripture, but in the unfolding of the poem: Christ has already stipulated the Redemption in Book III before Satan arrives in the garden.

We do not see Adam and Eve until he arrives. They are embattled from the outset of their presentation, and the real forces they strive with or towards are those supernatural beings "invisible to mortal sight," the good and bad angels. The cosmic battle is an emblematic and comprehensive one, and its problematic character is itself exemplary: "We wrestle not against flesh and blood but against principalities, against powers, against the rulers of the darkness of this world." Every man, in the Christian view, struggles against or toward those internal forces which in the garden, before the Fall, are external ones, under the prelapsarian world's problematic difference from our own of relation between physical and spiritual, internal and external.

The human beings in the heightened natural world of *Paradise Lost* possess heightened human generality, Adam and Eve. And so the achieved descriptions of the world they inhabit become generalized in the diction, through the felt strenuousness of rendering the unfallen in terms of the fallen. As the beings of the supernatural world are visible: devils and angels, their dramatic involvement with the natural world brings another "dubious battle" to bear on every moment of the action, every corner of the scene. Eden, Heaven, Hell, are never static, but the dynamic ground of the struggle on the part of the angels and God to keep man's will pure; on the part of the devil to corrupt it. Heaven meets in conclave to decide to defend him, and the beauties of heaven are wrought into harmonies and charities by the dramatic motive. Satan passes through Chaos at enormous expenditure of energy in order to arrive at the ground where he may pervert man; his intent serves to stir up and dramatize all the uglinesses of the indeterminate waste.

Since their spiritual forms are wholly visible, these Angels have become as they feel, by the law of their free spiritual creation. A few Angels, in military attitude, may constitute a "squadron" or a "phalanx," though only Gabriel, Ithuriel, Uzziel and Zephon are present. And their mere indignation, in the immediacy of a spiritual being's response, brings them by the fact itself into formation:

> While thus he spake, th'Angelic Squadron bright
> Turnd fierie red, sharpning in mooned hornes
> Thir Phalanx, and began to hemm him round
> With ported Spears, as thick as when a field
> Of *Ceres* ripe for harvest waving bends
> Her bearded Grove of ears, which way the wind
> Swayes them; the careful Plowman doubting stands
> Least on the threshing floore his hopeful sheaves
> Prove chaff. On th'other side *Satan* allarm'd
> Collecting all his might dilated stood,
> Like *Teneriff* or *Atlas* unremov'd:
> His stature reacht the Skie, and on his Crest
> Sat horror Plum'd; nor wanted in his graspe
> What seemd both Spear and Shield: (*P.L.*, IV, 977-990)

Satan's physical bearing so represents his spiritual existence that the classical trope of reversing noun and adjective—saying "horror Plum'd" instead of "a horrible feather"—creates identities beyond the verbal metaphor. The spiritual force of the supernatural creature leaves in generalized indeterminacy whether one has a feather with the quality of horror, or else the unallegorized (small letter) being of "horror" that seems to take the form of an allegorized (capital letter) Plume, through the past participle that emphasizes the transformation, "Plum'd". Similarly, Satan's weapon takes a form that is at once spear and shield.

Reading the other way, the appended Plowman, because of the Fall, must hover "doubtful" about his "hopeful" sheaves between angelic harvest and diabolical chaff; natural industry is good, but all crops do not ripen in a fallen world.

The devils *are* their feelings, the physical appearance of Satan mirrors his spiritual state dynamically; this can be concealed before Uriel only by a total hypocrisy, and only for a moment. Uriel sees him as he retreats. The dynamism of his acts and speeches exemplifies the motions of an absolute spiritual evil; and then, by a kind of unallegorical extrapolation, that evil as fallen men may embody it: a hypocrite acts and feels like Satan. The dynamism is built into the Vergilian ordonnance of the verse, wrought to a super-Vergilian pitch of refinement:

> O for that warning voice, which he who saw
> Th' *Apocalyps,* heard cry in Heaven aloud,
> Then when the Dragon, put to second rout,
> Came furious down to be reveng'd on men,
> *Wo to the inhabitants on Earth!* that now,
> While time was, our first Parents had bin warnd
> The coming of thir secret foe, and scap'd
> Haply so scap'd his mortal snare; for now
> *Satan,* now first inflam'd with rage, came down,
> The Tempter ere th'Accuser of man-kind,
> To wreck on innocent frail man his loss
> Of that first Battel, and his flight to Hell:
>
> > (*P.L.,* IV, 1-12)

An exclamatory main clause with a subordinate contrary-to-fact result is followed by another subordinate clause which moves for the first time in the "actual" past tense of narrated events, *"Satan . . . came."* (This shifts again; the next main verb is an historical present, "Begins.") The movement of tenses parallels the movement of references—from the scriptural Last Judgment, to the indefinite postlapsarian state ("men," "our"), to the actual situation. The cadenced movement of the syntax meets its greatest diapason, and its largest shift in pitch and stress, at the exclamation point of the quoted phrase which—in an Eternity here musically and syntactically suggested—applies the Last Judgment to every moment, and so includes secondarily Adam and Eve in the warning intended primarily for their descendants. But the poem presents primarily Adam and Eve, the descendants secondarily. And the poem strenuously adumbrates the problem of an imaginable state of spiritual affairs where primary and secondary would have no more meaning than present, past (*Genesis*), and future (*Apocalypse*): where in terms of language, as begins to happen here, denotation gets lost in connotation.

The possible (but unactualized) effort Adam and Eve might have put forth gets briefly mimed in the syntax around the repetition of *scap'd;* but this passage comes to a momentary resolution on three lines of simpler movement, direct theological reference, and straight narrative—straight, perhaps, all but for the problematic emotional reference in the double adjective and lower case designation in "innocent frail man," where the adjectives constitute a theological definition, while their repetition suggests a sigh of regret to trail off from the stronger *Wo* into which the fifth line suddenly breaks. The dynamism gets mimed all along, and can be traced at every point of the narrative; and of the speeches too, as in the very next one, Satan's invocation to the Sun. To mention only one detail, he brags of his insubordination in line 50: "I sdeind subjection," and the counter-compression of his effort enters dynamically into the contraction of the verb. It becomes hypostatized into an uncontracted noun by line 81, where he is easier with his feeling because he is expelled from the heaven where it evoked the dynamism of the pressure he no longer feels: it only keeps him from reentering heaven: "Disdain forbids me." Later, in the narrative, the full form is used as a verb to describe his choice of a concealed entrance into Eden: "Due entrance he disdained." (180).

In this Paradise the physical is not so much analogous to the spiritual as virtually equivalent to it. The good predominates as assimilable to any other good (wisdom to chastity to physical beauty), and the evil likewise (perverted intelligence to lust to physical ugliness). An inversion of good into evil is therefore total: and the first three books are very largely occupied with exploring the dynamism of that totality, the events which they present being fewer and simpler than in any comparable portion of an epic poem.

The abstractness of the refined style's diction is stretched by Milton to the point where the virtual equivalences become those of one word to another. The narrative carries the impression that its terms are expatiating on a unitary situation whose aspects can be brought endlessly, though for just a dynamic moment, into virtual equivalence:

> Him the Almighty Power
> Hurld headlong flaming from th'Ethereal Skie
> With hideous ruine and combustion down
> To bottomless perdition, there to dwell
> In Adamantine Chains and penal Fire
> Who durst defie th'Omnipotent to Arms.
> Nine times the Space that measures Day and Night
> To mortal man, he with his horrid crew
> Lay vanquisht, rowling in the fiery Gulfe
> Confounded though immortal.   (I, 44-53)

"Now the first thing to notice," B. Rajan[2] says of this passage, "is its preponderance of stock epithets. 'Hideous' does not limit the suggestions of 'ruine' and 'penal' does little to control our reaction to 'Fire.' Perdition has always been 'bottomless' and chains in poetry are usually 'Adamantine.' The associations of these words, moreover, are not developed but accumulated. 'Fire,' 'Combustion,' and 'flaming' all suggest much the same thing, and a similar grouping can be made of 'Ethereal,' 'down,' 'bottomless,' and 'headlong.' "

Rajan's point about Milton's diction, that its terms tend to interfuse, "hideous" tending to complement "ruine" rather than limiting it (the way modifiers usually work), sets the virtual equivalences out so that they become unidentifiable in their very physical intensity (is a "fiery Gulfe" made of water like fire, or fire like water"?) at times to the point where language breaks into oxymoron before paradoxical equivalents: "darkness visible."

Press the correspondences between physical and spiritual, and they become interchangeable: "and swims or sinks, or wades, or creeps, or flyes." The first two verbs of this line are mutually contradictory —you either sink or swim. The succeeding commas leave indeterminate, again, whether the verbs are on the one hand approximate, overly anthropomorphic, ways of describing the devil's motion— whether in short they all point at a single motion; or on the other hand are an attempt, slowed by earthly language (which cannot be any faster than these monosyllables), to approximate many rapid changes of motion.

A full thematic weight, then, may be seen to reside in the famous Miltonic vagueness, noted, perhaps first by Macaulay and berated by modern critics who value precision highly. Milton gives us not precision, but inter-echoing overtones, in which denotation and connotation get lost in each other ("fiery" denotes "hot" and connotes "flame-like"; or vice versa?). He does so because his poetic purposes are not those of precision—categorizing the attitudes of sin, repentance, and virtue—like Dante, organizing the gestures of virtue and vice—like Spenser. He aims, through his diction, at his own special kind of epic generality: "Man's First Disobedience and the Fruit/ Of that Forbidden Tree whose mortal tast/ Brought Death into the World and all our woe." Here such terms as "Man," "Fruit," "Tree," are given more generality even than allegory (though Milton allows himself to capitalize them for quasi-allegorical emphasis): allegory implies system, and system a specification of function, which Milton's whole poetic effort in *Paradise Lost* is to avoid.

If we introduce Valéry's idea, that a poet in some sense invents the meanings of the words he uses, then we may see that Milton's inventions are strengthened by the privacy of his diction. The word in a poem gets its particular newness, or at least its freshness, by appearing in vivid conjunction with other words. Milton's diction operates, we may say, only to free the words from a prose limitation, to allow them to assert their conjunction the more forcibly as a way of representing the plastic qualities of Man's theological experience. The limit of the refined style, which Dante expands by convergence of senses, Milton elevates by generalizing it so that it is made constantly to comprise the fallen yet redeemed human condition.

The tension of equivalence between physical and spiritual or natural and supernatural opens up actively in Milton's similes:

> Thir rising all at once was as the sound
> Of Thunder heard remote. (*P.L.* II, 476-7)

In an earthly parliament a similar sound results from the unanimous rising of the members; but that sound is muted. For spiritual beings, though, evil shows immediately in ugliness.

In this simile, the lightness of "as" makes the thunder of the devil's rising almost analogous to the effect in the natural world we know. The spiritual framework of the poem, in its generality, allows the likeness to be that of analogy too, the effect of Dante. And, as in Dante, one may then read the analogy both ways. Not only is the noise of devils like the thunder, but thunder is in some sense an infernal noise. One cannot, though, read this analogy, as one does in Dante, effortlessly and directly. Natural thunder can only be infernal if one remembers that inclement weather, including thunderstorms, results from the Fall, as Book XI tell us; and it is therefore one of the numerous, epically comprehensive, consequences of "Man's First Disobedience, and the Fruit/ Of that Forbidden Tree."

The difference between Milton's structure of signification, and Dante's, shows up most pronouncedly in his "epic" similes. Dante's similes rest in the simplicity of his architecture, whereas Milton perpetually builds his as he goes along. Or, to put it differently, Dante stands at a given point singly and universally in the stage the poem assigns; so he speaks, so he has the verse sing, in a simple clarity. Milton's "no middle flight" forces the mood of the poetry, the tensions of its syntax, at every point to do the work of universalizing the epic emotion.

This point may be illustrated by taking the two poets at the close range of their respective handlings of the same myth. When Dante compares Matelda in his Garden to Proserpina, he may do so quite simply: he merely states and categorizes the remembrance:

> *Tu mi fai rimembrar, dove e qual era*
> *Proserpina nel tempo che perdette*
> *La madre lei, ed ella primavera.*

> You make me remember where and what sort was
> Proserpina in the time when her mother
> Lost her, and she herself lost spring.

> (*Purg.,* XXVIII, 49-51)

Loss is named, and memory, place and kind, mother and spring, time itself.

The categorizations are external and literal. The poem's figural structure allows each of these words to carry its fourfold freight simply and directly. Milton internalizes loss and memory, place and kind, mother and spring, into cosmic echoes of the world before the Fall in the world after it. He does not name memory but, as Vergil might, he renders it in the *lacrimae rerum* of his verse; for instance in the four strong syllables before his enjambment: "Not that faire field":

> The Birds thir quire apply; aires, vernal aires,
> Breathing the smell of field and grove, attune
> The trembling leaves, while Universal *Pan*
> Knit with the *Graces* and the *Hours* in dance
> Led on th'Eternal Spring. Not that faire field
> Of *Enna,* where *Proserpin* gathring flours
> Her self a fairer Floure by gloomie *Dis*
> Was gatherd, which cost *Ceres* all that pain
> To seek her through the world; nor that sweet Grove
> Of *Daphne* by *Orontes,* and th'inspir'd
> *Castalian* Spring might with this Paradise
> Of *Eden* strive;   (*P.L.* IV, 264-75)

The relation of his Eden to the natural world of Sicily is declared in the very negation, the demonstrative pronoun insisting on Sicily's reality, the adjective on its shrunken similarity to Eden: "Not that faire field." Unless we also have the trope of preterition: to say the field is not so beautiful would be a way of hinting that in some sense it is. All this is given in a verse so sorrowing in its flight that by association (and not rhetorical structure) it causes us to think of Proserpina as like Eve, though the comparison is of difference between gardens, and only Proserpina is mentioned. Eve is a greater Proserpina, Proserpina a dim Eve; where Dante's Matelda shares certain qualities of Proserpina (beauty, existence in a garden, loss) because she is about to lead Dante into the transcendence of those qualities: Lethe for remembrance, gain for loss.

Milton's elaborate voice is at once building the general (but lost) original situation, and regretting the lost (but always present) primal condition. The world itself is seen as a transmuted Eden; poetic analogies from the fallen world are used to portray the unfallen. It is in the description of the Garden that this simile is introduced about Proserpina, with its implied comparison to Eve. And there is an abrupt shift in tense from the present of the first clause "attune" and the past of the second, "led": the garden is not permitted to hold the immediacy of a present tense. (This is prepared for, also, but the participial phrases, the present of "breathing" and the past of "knit.")*

Pan, then, in Adam's time and in the present of the poem is at once factitious, like the poem (Milton does not "believe in" the classical gods), and "Universal," this word being but an expansion of a reading of the Greek meaning of Pan.

In Milton's plastic world, Proserpina, a part of the simile's vehicle, moves to the center and assumes some of a tenor's freedom (the original comparison was of quality between a field and a grove). Proserpina's connection with Enna is rhythmically insisted on by the strong enjambment from the line before and by the major accent on each. She herself is compared to a flower with the same word—

* Lowry Nelson[3] finds this shift in tense characteristic of what he and others call "Baroque" verse.

"fair"—which had governed the initial comparison of one garden to another. The world of the simile is allowed to expand and include Ceres' search because the fictive conception of the poem will always suggest the poetic comparison actually made at the end of the passage, here that of the Castalian spring where the poet drank to be "inspired." We should note that this word is the first end word not a monosyllable since the low bass of Dis (or, if "flowrs" may seem monosyllabic by being printed so, since "Pan"); so that rhythmically we are made aware it is by such a poem that we can imaginatively transcend "all that pain," our own being like Ceres'. It is but another line to the ending assonance of "Paradise" (Greek *paradeisos,* pleasure-park), expanding into its Hebrew equivalent (Eden: Pleasant Garden) in the next half line. The loss implied (rhythmically, and also in sense, as Empson notes) by the word "all," is counterbalanced in the last half line, not so regretful as it would be if Milton had ended on "Paradise," with some such line as:

Castalian Spring might match this Paradise.

The whole passage—and the poem—is such a trope as we find in the word "inspired," applied by metonymy to the spring, when actually it is meant of the poet who drinks the spring. By a comparable shift Eden is actualized in the poem, a poem as lofty in its "no middle flight" as the Castalian spring is at "high" Delphi against the crags of Parnassus. Moses is "inspired" by the Holy Ghost and writes truth about Eden; Milton is "inspired" to a poetic fiction that offers what of Eden can be approached by a fallen imagination.

We may see Milton's strenuousness, too, in his sense of a verse line here. Where Dante end-stops and simplifies the line, Milton's line coils in charged groups of words, irregularly past the faint ending of the blank verse unit.

In the Miltonic simile characteristically, the hinge between tenor and vehicle is made to break. The metaphor will then expand to give the vehicle a life of its own (where it "ought" to be confined to illustrating the tenor). Or else one metaphor will be dropped and

another taken up; because the first, through the very lofty progress
of the verse and what it describes, will have been superseded. Both
these rhetorical presentations of extreme tension—the breaking of
the metaphorical frame, the shift from one elaborate simile to another—may be seen, appropriately, in the long description of Satan's
momentous first rise in Hell:

> He scarce had ceas't when the superiour Fiend
> Was moving toward the shore; his ponderous shield
> Ethereal temper, massy, large and round,
> Behind him cast; the broad circumference
> Hung on his shoulders like the Moon, whose Orb
> Through Optic Glass the *Tuscan* Artist views
> At Ev'ning from the top of Fesole,
> Or in *Valdarno,* to descry new Lands,
> Rivers or mountains in her spotty Globe.
> His spear, to equal which the tallest Pine
> Hewn on *Norwegian* hills, to be the Mast
> Of some great Ammiral, were but a wand,
> He walkt with, to support uneasie steps
> Over the burning Marle, not like those steps
> On Heavens Azure, and the torrid Clime
> Smote on him sore besides, vaulted with Fire;
> Nathless he so endur'd, till on the Beach
> Of that inflamed Sea, he stood and call'd
> His Legions, Angel Forms, who lay intrans't
> Thick as Autumnal Leaves that strow the Brooks
> In *Vallombrosa,* where th' *Etrurian* shades
> High overarch't imbowr; or scatter'd sedge
> Afloat, when with fierce Winds *Orion* arm'd
> Hath vext the Red-Sea Coast, whose waves orethrew
> *Busiris* and his *Memphian* Chivalrie . . .
>
> (*P.L.,* I, 283-308)

Satan's shield, (the tenor) is like the Moon (the vehicle) with respect
first to size ("large," "broad"). And even this is indeterminate. As
large as the moon actually is? No, as large as it is seen (though the

comma after Moon makes this ambiguous) in a telescope by Galileo. How large is that, we may ask, without ever getting an objective measurement; without,—the point is Macaulay's[4]—, getting the sort of measurement Dante gives us. Dante provides constant coordinates; and so he tells us exactly how wide the devil's wingspread is, how tall Nimrod is, and the like. Milton puts in a dramatic, a purely dramatic, context, the very size: the moon is larger than we habitually see it. Its physical size—in feet or miles—is obscured in our response to the physical size. Milton's perspective gives us not feet or miles—the exact power of the telescope, the distance of the moon—but the wonder and perhaps portent too, of discovery, of seeing something suddenly larger than it appears to the naked eye. The physical size of the shield comes through only in the drama of these psychological—and spiritual—effects, because the devil, as a spiritual being, identifies with those effects. He is as large as he seems to us, as he is able to be for us, and this constitutes a constant dramatic relationship with us, because of the Fall.

So portentous can this be that the metaphorical vehicle is broken, and as in Homer's similes, the Telescope, a mere part of the vehicle, a mere turn of phrase, comes into a referential life of its own, getting an evening, a mountaintop, two place-names, Galileo, and Galileo's intent, all appended to it. And we may read all these "digressions" and "tautologies", by analogy, the other way as well. Not only is Satan's shield like the Moon in the telescope; the Moon in the telescope is somewhat like Satan's shield, according to the principle Raphael tells Adam in Book VIII, that too much astronomical curiosity violates the limits of what man ought to know. Seeking such "forbidden knowledge," the "Tuscan Artist" is involved in a Satanic contrivance (so the etymology of *Art*ist implies). He goes to the top of a mountain, but he may be seen as in a *Valdarno,* a river valley, and the italicization of that name would seem, as here and there in the passage, to emphasize the involvement of earthly place-names in the Fall. (Before the Fall, there was only one place, Eden, and the very beauty of the earthly place-names—a valley of Arno is beautiful —arouses sorrow for the greater beauty that has been lost: "Not that faire Field/ of *Enna*"—the name italicized there too.)

The evening, the mountain, the place-names, Galileo, Galileo's intent, all press through to be compared to the shield, as the shield to it. The pressure mimes, in the structure of the metaphor, the constant tension between fallen world and unfallen Eden, between the flesh and blood of man and the Principalities and Powers against which he is, because of the Fall, perpetually struggling. Only by adducing the Fall can we press the comparison both ways. But the poem constantly adduces the Fall, here by breaking the frame of the metaphor.

The quality of feeling changes through the passage. The mood shifts from terror at height—the height of a flagship is as a wand, with all the implied analogies of magic—to the sadness of autumn leaves in *Vallombrosa,* shadowy valley: *Maioresque cadunt altis de montibus umbrae.* The Vergilian effect has been condensed and theologized. The Angel Forms are like this, as Vallombrosa is like the (fallen) Angel Forms—though not quite, because one cannot dwell on infernal sadness, and so not on earthly. (Eden is "able to drive/ All sadness but despair.") Hence an alternate metaphor is given, the scattering of sedge on the Red Sea; the sad leaves now are mere waste. And then they are like the terror—again breaking the frame of the metaphor—in the storm, in the whelming of the terrible Egyptian host. The terror of Pharaoh is swallowed by God's will in an impotence, as is the terror of the devils. Shortly Milton speaks of them, in the last line of this long sentence, as

> Under amazement of their hideous change.
>
> > (*P.L.,* I, 313)

The hideousness, the change, the amazement, have all been rendered in the tension, the excess, the pressed sequence, of the metaphors and their pitch of transformation, not only for the devils but for any earthly feelings that may be diabolical, reading the whole poem both ways.

2

Milton did not find his strenuous style in the verse of his time, and he did not find it in Dante. He had to shape it for himself, and the process by which he did so appears most notably in the rhythm of his verse. *Comus* looks much like *Paradise Lost* in diction and syntax. The difference between them, the special stylistic character of *Paradise Lost,* shows very notably in its verse rhythm, and it is on that essential feature of poetry that I should like to dwell.

Milton's style, from the start, strikingly adapts and adopts the Vergilian music, creating an abstract music of his own to resound with his all-embracing epic mood. As Vergil counterpoints stress and ictus in a unique way, Milton marshals the accents of his verses at a pitch that constantly strains the rhythms of speech.

In *Comus,* perhaps because it would be set to the music of his musician father's prominent friend, Milton found himself beginning to create his own abstract music:

> Hence had the huntress *Dian* her dred bow
> Fair silver-shafted Queen for ever chaste,
> Wherwith she tam'd the brinded lioness
> And spotted mountain pard, but set at naught
> The frivolous bolt of *Cupid,* gods and men
> Fear'd her stern frown, and she was queen oth' Woods.
>
> (440-5)

The chaste effect of such lines arises from the rhythm's confinement within a nearly syllabic norm (preserved by such contractions as the violent "oth' Woods"). This lies midway between the levelled accents of Spenser, which are all equivalent through the syllabic convention, and the rising accents of *Paradise Lost.* A broidery of near rhyme and assonance (lioness/men; chaste/nought/woods; dred/gods/

woods; huntress/lioness; feard/stern/frown) keeps a heightened
charm of echo smoothly associating the sounds. The music almost
seems to be lulling the sense asleep (an effect falsely attributed by
some to *Paradise Lost*)—so much so that the argument can allow
us the grace notes of "spotted" and "brinded," which are no part of
the Elder Brother's reasoning here, if not indeed contradictory to it.
And the very sound of "frivolous," almost thrills with a delight in
the very act of reproof, just as the argument of Comus himself
expands the beauties of the world in such a way as to allow them
some measure of good (though they come through as brutish, I feel,
in the rhythms of his speech). To this pure, abstract music, all things
can be pure, and it need not decide between syllable and accent any
more than it need reconcile classical gods with Christian.

In departing from the syllabic poetry of Spenser, Milton had to find
a way of managing the accents of his verse in harmony with the
classic requirements of a refined style, which neither the wrenching of Donne nor the lightly structured conversational flow of the
dramatists would serve.

A speaking voice, to begin with, gives varying emphasis to the
accents of verse, and any accomplished poet will orchestrate these
variations in some way:

> It is the cause, it is the cause, my soul;
> Let me not name it to you, you chaste stars!
> It is the cause. Yet I'll not shed her blood,
> Nor scar that whiter skin of hers than snow,
> And smooth as monumental alabaster.
> Yet she must die, else she'll betray more men;
> Put out the light, and then put out the light:

The second "cause" rising against Othello's attempt to stifle it by
logically needless repetition, will be emphasized over the first

"cause," as both over "soul," though these three accents stand out against (and gain firmness by contrast with) the indecision in the hovering accent on the first "it." "Name"—Othello's continuing endeavor in awed anguish to hush the unspeakable while voicing it—predominates over the spondaically frozen "chaste stars."

Changes in what presses for recognition in the obsessed mind of the soliloquizing speaker find their expression in the accent: "shed" gains over the previously dominant "cause" here; and also, in the third line, over "blood." By line four, the voice has moved so far into a dreamlike incantatory deliberateness that no triad of the five accents will press for extra prominence: "scar" is just whispered above the breathless wonderment of the other four accents. These stress, in their equality, the seeming chastity of Desdemona's beauty. "Scar" possesses still enough force to be felt as influencing position-ally (because coming in the same place) the main accent of the next line, "smooth."

Accentual contrast is restored as Othello gathers for his mad reso-lution to stress "die" in the next line, and to record his action of darkening the room in the next. The major accent, falling power-fully on the line's last syllable, the second "light," develops dramat-ically (as rhythmically) from the repetition of "cause," in lines one and three. This final line differs from the first in being more reso-lute: "put out" has lost the hovering accents of "it is"; and there is more reason for repeating "light," than "cause" offers, because the first time the light of the room is meant, the second time the light of the soul. If Othello implies some reference to a light of the tomb (repeating the snow and alabaster), then we may say he has not quite dared before this to give it the stress which his desperation here finally braves. At the same time the awe carries over from "scar" and "smooth" in the whisper with which the last emphases—perhaps the strongest in the whole sequence of lines to this point—must be spoken in order not to wake Desdemona.

The dramatic setting of this line, and the mastery of Shakespeare, enliven the play along these accents unusually beyond the pattern of the metre, in which all the accents are theoretically equivalent (or at least patterned more regularly than speech rhythms allow). Yet normally, in fact almost always, one can distinguish one major accent, and often three "more important" accents, in a line of verse:

//
Bare ruined choirs where late the sweet birds sang

(Possibly "bare" or "choirs," depending on interpretation)

//
Thoughts that do often lie too deep for tears

//
Or suck'd on country pleasures, childishly

//
Like a patient etherized upon a table

//
In the gloom the gold gathers the light against it

(Possibly "against," or even "gloom.")

It is a great mark of Milton's rhythm that, contrary to the practice of almost any other verse writers in English, including his own imitators in the eighteenth and nineteenth centuries, he carries his verse so far away from speech that one can seldom find in *Paradise Lost* a line where only three of the accents stand out over the other two. Never, I believe, does his epic verse give us a line in which we can distinguish a single accent alone.

// // //   //   //
Who first seduc'd them to that fowl revolt?
//   //   //   //
Th' infernal Serpent; he it was, whose guile
//   //   //   //
Stird up with Envy and Revenge, deceived
//   //   //   //
The Mother of Mankinde, what time his Pride
//   //   //   //   //
Had cast him out from Heav'n, with all his Host
//   //   //
Of Rebel Angels, by whose aid aspiring

To sét himsélf in Glory abóve his Péers,

He trústed to have equál'd the most Hígh,

If he oppós'd; and with ambítious aím

Against the Thróne and Mónarchy of Gód

Rais'd impious Wár in Heáv'n and Báttle proúd

With vain attémpt. Hím the Almíghty Pówer

Húrld héadlong fláming from th' Ethéreal Skíe

With hídeous ruíne and combústion dówn

To bóttomless perdítion, thére to dwéll

In Adamántine Cháins and penal Fíre

Who dúrst defíe th' Ómnipotent to Árms.   (I, 33-49)

Taking sense as necessarily the guide to the major accents, we cannot settle on a single word here as definitely more prominent in stress than the others. In more usual poems, even when we allow latitude of interpretation, we still assign primacy to a single accent at the expense of others: if it is claimed that the first "cause" receives most stress in the line from *Othello,* then the second will receive less: if it is claimed that they both received the same, a persuasive interpretation, this gives the line a strikingly abnormal reading; and it still puts "soul" into the background—unless it is assigned primacy. In any case all three cannot have equal value here—and this is precisely the way we must read the lines of *Paradise Lost.*

As we inspect the sense of the first line, "who" calls for stress because of the magnitude of the question; "first" because of the tremendous action initiated here, the subject of the poem, "Of Man's *first* disobedience"; "seduc'd" because of the fantastic treachery involved; "fowl" because of the enormity of the act; "revolt" because of the all-embracing nature of what the sin was directed against. The sense of the line seems simultaneously to concentrate in almost each accented word, as the abstractions of the refined style are stretched to virtual equivalence with the poem's theme. The equivalence of accents keeps running on this way through this quotation as I have marked it, and so on through the poem. This passage, in fact, illustrates rather more normal latitude of accent than is to be found in the prayers and invocations of the poem, which present nearly unbroken series of five major accents to the line. The voice to read this poetry must almost never flag in soaring, however much it modulates: a strong-ribbed structure of accents constantly buoys up line by line the mighty periods.

The rhythmic effect which Milton gains by assigning all his accents nearly equal value is unusually special, as compared, for example, with the syllabic verse of French. In that convention the accents have an equality not of prominence, as in Milton, but of uninsistence. While Milton achieves a strenuous personal rhythm which heightens each of the individual accented syllables over the unaccented, the French convention tends to level the differences between accented and unaccented syllables, giving the whole poem line by line a rhythm that subdues the sense to wear its convention like a uniform. A similar effect is to be found in syllabic Italian poetry, even that which Milton imitated, as F. T. Prince[5] points out, in seeking a Vergilian grandiosity and *asprezza*. Accents are levelled, too, not heightened, in the English verse of Chaucer, which echoes French conventions:

> Your . . yen two wol slee me sodenly;
> I may the beautee of hem nat sustene,
> So woundeth hit thourghout my herte kene.

Spenser, also, in his equality of accent, produces an Italian and French limpidity, and nothing like the Miltonic grandeur:

> A gentle knight was pricking on the plaine,
> Ycladd in mightie armes and silver shielde,
> Wherein old dints of deepe woundes did remaine,
> The cruell markes of many, a bloody fielde;

> Yet armes till that time did he never wield:
> His angry steede did chide his foming bitt,
> As much disdayning to the curbe to yielde:
> Full jolly knight he seemes, and faire did sitt,
> As one for knightly giusts and fierce encounters fitt.

No sooner have we stepped within the Faerie forest, than all designations exist on the same allegorical level; and as the concrete stands univalently for the abstract throughout, so Spenser's syllabic convention operates to keep each word of the sentence, and here each line of the stanza, too, patterned to an identical and formal emphasis. Even the rhythm has the two-dimensionality of the sort of medieval tapestry to which *The Faerie Queene* has often been compared.

Milton began with Spenser, and began by going beyond Spenser. We find an allegorical pattern in *L'Allegro* and *Il Penseroso* set at the beginning of each poem, and then violated by the main contrasts between light and dark almost as soon as the broken, tuning-up rhythm of each poem's introduction has been toned off to the prevailing tetrameter line.

Paradise Lost sets a poetic problem more simple in its generality than that of Spenser's epic, centering on Man instead of on twelve virtues. And the problem is more directly spiritual, involving angels and devils instead of maids, giants, and castles. The poem enunciates more thoroughly a literal but unknowable truth; given Spenser's conception, detail may be proliferated on a relatively simple principle, but Milton must at every point solve anew the problem of representing the unfallen Adam of *Genesis,* through a fallen imagination.

We get in *Paradise Lost,* as Eliot[6] says, "the peculiar feeling, almost a physical sensation of a breathless leap, communicated by Milton's long periods, and by his alone." This unique impression—the rhythmic side of Milton's "no middle flight"—derives from what it expresses, an imaginative conception which creates a dynamic equivalence among the verbal terms and their accents which the terms may not rest back on, as Spenser's are allowed to do by the syllabic norms and by his conception. In *Paradise Lost,* while every accented word stands out, when spoken, as the major one in the line, every one at the same time pulls against the rise of the accents, equally strong, which precede and follow. This creates a kind of tension analogous to the conflict of physical forces found in the structure of a Baroque dome, whose mathematics, Siegfried Giedion[7] tells us, introduces a new complexity of interrelated forces into architecture. Or, as Milton says in another connection:

> As in an Organ from one blast of wind
> To many a row of Pipes the sound-board breathes.
>
> (*P.L.* I, 708-9)

(We remember that the Baroque period is also the high point for that instrument in Church music.) The equivalence of accents gives Milton's verse a sound of rapt simultaneity. His rhythms, Arnold Stein[8] says, are "an integral part of the high, unwavering illusion of mystical motionlessness."

The rhythm helps perform the work of coordination which Dante assigned to the overall scheme of his poem. Through the rhythm every aspect of speech and idea gains paramount importance without suppressing the importance of another, just as angels gain rather than lose (which Satan wrongly thought) by the preeminence of the Son in Heaven. A rhythmic provisionality—the accent is major only while spoken—governs this mortal representation of "things invisible to mortal sight." And just so a rhythmic assertion—the accent is major while it occurs—governs the constantly reachieved equipoise of the poem's conjunctions.

Since the Renaissance, the comprehensiveness of the epic has been adapted for the fragmentary or lengthy lyric poem. One can trace, again initially in rhythmic terms, the beginnings of this development in Milton, the first epic poet to carry the epic style on further into works of a somewhat different formal character.

Paradise Lost was Milton's highest rhythmic achievement, but not his last. *Paradise Regained,* whose poetic excellence lies in an austerity barer even than that of the sonnets, proposes both a subject and a treatment more difficult than *Paradise Lost:* instead of Unfallen Man, the Man-God; and instead of a lofty treatment with an encyclopedic range of imagery, a nearly bare presentation, in which the most mysterious side of the poem, the fact that the Man is God, is not allowed to be seen from the heavenly viewpoint. It is deduced from His human actions alone, as the Christ of the poem is said to have deduced His Divinity from his natural human intelligence.

The Devil here is no longer the magnificent Father of Lies, but a shady old man with a bundle of sticks on his back. Here he operates under the severe limit of being able only to face the Truth with truth put in a falsifying light. He is denied, or denies himself, the gamut of false reasons, mendacities, contradictions, and perversions, with which his speeches in *Paradise Lost* always abound. The "darkness Visible" in this poem, and the light of heaven, are covered fires, fires which the rhythm, like the spareness of the diction, keeps covered:

> He added not; and Satan bowing low
> His gray dissimulation, disappear'd
> Into thin Air diffus'd: for now began
> Night with her sullen wing to double-shade
> The Desert, Fowls in thir clay nests were couch't;
> And now wild Beasts came forth the woods to roam.
>
> (*P.R.* I, 497-502)

One can say of the rhythm of this poem neither that there are special major accents in the line (as in Shakespeare and most poetry), nor that the major accents are levelled off in a syllabic pattern (as in Spenser or in French poetry, for instance), nor that each accent becomes successively major as pronounced (as in *Paradise Lost*). The directness, or near prosiness, of the refined style, which acts as a severe limit on paragraph-long flights (and on elaborate metaphors), is brought to bear on the rhythm in such a way that the syllabic pattern keeps the accents from being incantatory: very much as Christ is confined to His humanity, and is presented not in his positive glories (like God in *Paradise Lost*), but in his opposition to Satan. Just as Christ withstands temptation, the accents of the poetry that assert His steadfastness have a stark strength in their rugged, prosy resistance to absorption into the uniform syllabic norm of the poem. One could call it biblical rather than classical, as Christ in the poem rejects Pindar and all classical poetry for the Prophets.

The effect—of accents, and yet no one accent being major—is, we have been saying, almost peculiar to Milton; but here the rhythm is carried into a more extreme form than in *Paradise Lost*. There an equivalence of major accents kept the flight aloft. Here the syllabic pattern is brought to bear as a strenuous check, or mute, to keep any accent from being heard as major, but not to subdue the accents, as a syllabic norm works in all other syllabic poetry.

In *Samson Agonistes* we meet metrical practises so radical that they have puzzled generations of commentators; Hopkins recognized in the poem the kind of tension between underlying pattern and individual accent which he called "sprung rhythm," but actually the sound pattern of the choruses in *Samson* does not allow of quite so many accented syllables (or so many unaccented to the foot), nor is its underlying norm so ambiguously regular, as that in Hopkins' work. The blank verse of the speeches in *Samson* rather resembles that of *Paradise Lost,* a heightened formality of successively major accents, except where the rhythms of the chorus invade the blank verse, which they do mostly in easy transitions from blank verse into some choral rhythm, but occasionally in individual lines.

Samson is a kind of dramatic *tour de force* because the action of the drama—and action is central to a drama—turns on Samson's gradual attunement to the divine will. In this regard Samson is closer in conception to an epic hero than to a dramatic one. His decision to go with the Philistines, rather than to resist them, is both the Peripety and the Recognition in the play. Yet this central turn of the action is unprepared for, unmotivated, in the scenes with Manoah, Dalila, Harapha, and the officer. In fact, the effect of these dialogues is the opposite—to induce him to resist being taken to the festival of Dagon. The gradual stirring in *Samson* of the divine will is as inchoate and indeterminate, as secret, as Christ's realization of his own divinity and resistance to supreme temptation in *Paradise Regained*. Or as the purpose of the Cid and Beowulf, the slow decision of Achilles.

Milton represents this internal dramatic peripety not in the action, but in the poetry of the play, and particularly in the rhythm, a tremendous poetic feat. It is a feat in which an epic style and view have been brought into a more concentrated form than would have seemed possible before Milton. By this he anticipates the thematic pressures of modern verse; and this, along with the rhythm, may serve to explain some of the interest Hopkins found in the poem.

The rhythmic violence of Samson's despair is the beginning of his recognition:

> O dark, dark, dark, amid the blaze of noon,
> Irrecoverably dark, total Eclipse
> Without all hope of day! (*S.A.*, 80-2)

Here the strength of the equivalent major accents on each "dark" is matched by that of "blaze" and "noon"; but that strength is swallowed up in the long, liquid, hovering adverb "irrecoverably," in a line that has only four accents. Strength rounds out in the slow, measured, nearly spondaic third line.

We always recognize metre by position, and thus must always read both backwards and forwards. So this third line may be read, in conjunction with the second line, as a sprung rhythm four-beat line (like the second); or, in the blank verse, as a regular iambic half line, with the sadness of the half lines in Vergil, which it echoes; finally one may read it a third way, as the very first line in the poem looking ahead to the varying line lengths of the choruses.

Each of these three ways, the very fact that there are three, points to Samson's internal stirring toward his peripety. Reading it the first way, as a sprung, four-beat line, he is gathering his forces; the line is stronger than the dissolution of "irrecoverably" in the line before. Reading it the second way, as a Vergilian half-line, the silence at the end of the line points to the stillness of his own mind, that which he cannot voice because he is as yet unaware of it (the divine will which he will later recognize). Reading it the third way, as anticipating the choral measures; it echoes and sets the tone for the humility which characterizes the Chorus throughout. Finally, it suggests the triumph and joy of the choric passages which recount and formulate the sacrifice of Samson.

Milton has introduced a rhythmic indeterminacy, the sort of multiple possibility of reading which is functional, like the iambic-trochaic indeterminacy of *L'Allegro* and *Il Penseroso,* and like certain effects which Donne achieves. This indeterminacy is here also made to be dramatic; and further, it is made to carry the very burden of the drama. This burden is almost always carried by stage action, but Milton tells us that this poem—seemingly more dramatic than the performed *Comus*—"never was intended" for the stage.

We get this indeterminacy in the very first line spoken by the Chorus:

> SAMSON: Thir daily practice to afflict me more.
> CHORUS: This, this is he; softly a while,
>   Let us not break in upon him;
>   O change beyond report, thought, or belief!
>
> (115-17)

Their first line, read as echoing his last, would be a catalectic blank verse line read in sprung rhythm (with accents on "this," "this," "he," "soft" and "while"). So read, each accent—each one successively major—is like a plea to be quiet; the voice is raised in a whisper, out of consideration for Samson, as their second line tells us. It is a still small voice which asks not to be heard against the strong, resigned complaint of Samson's final line here. But we may also—

and simultaneously—read the line by referring it to the line ahead, in which case it follows not a blank verse pattern (only), but the pattern of their second line, a trochaic tetrameter line with reversal in the second foot. This reading, it might be said, emphasizes the dance, and thus the ritual function, of the chorus, because trochee is a singsongish dance measure. In this reading, the second "this" would go unaccented; as if, underlying the stark presence of Samson, requiring the astonishment of two "this"es, (accented with syncopation according to our first, blank verse reading), there were an image of Samson doubling his presence—an accented "this"— with something internal and hidden, all but silent—and a "this" slurred and unaccented.

The next line, too, their second, can be taken as iambic pentameter or trochaic tetrameter—but this time the rhythmic reference is altered, almost carried forward, by the fact that we read ahead, rather than backward, to get the iambic norm; and backward, rather than ahead, to pick up the trochaic.

The rhythm always opens out for an indeterminacy of purpose— which is a hope for Samson of internal and inspired change. It does so by presenting, often, rhythms not only modulated as in a Greek tragic chorus—*Apolelymenon* or "loosed" is the Greek term Milton cites in his preface—but themselves so indeterminate as to allow of two or more simultaneous readings. This very indeterminacy permits Samson, as we have said, to voice, in his last appearance, the sudden, and unmotivated, decision, quiet as none of his previous statements has been, to accompany the Philistine Officer, a decision he appropriately communicates to the Chorus rather than directly to the Officer himself:

> Be of good courage, I begin to feel
> Some rousing motions in me which dispose
> To something extraordinary my thoughts.   (1381-3)

Here the rhythm is kept ordinary, in the convention of *Paradise Lost,* so that the key word "extraordinary" may carry accentually, and rhythmically, the whole burden of a decision which even at this point remains an indeterminacy, for "extraordinary" is still only an adjective modifying "something."

Rhythmic indeterminacy, having gloriously expressed so secret and divine a calling, appropriately accompanies the joy of the Chorus at the end:

> CHORUS: Of dire necessity, whose law in death conjoin'd
> Thee with thy slaughter'd foes in number more
> Then all thy life had slain before.
> SEMICHORUS: While thir hearts were jocund and sublime,
> Drunk with Idolatry, drunk with Wine,
> And fat regorg'd of Bulls and Goats,
>
> (1666-71)

The first line of the Semichorus can be read as a blank verse line, and therefore as echoing most immediately the Messenger's narrative, detached and reflective. One can also read it for the more dance-like trochaic measure which is begun in the preceding line of the Chorus "Then all thy life had slain before" and carried forth, almost to a joyous tramp, in the unambiguous tetrameter—iambic (with some trochaic effect due to its position)—of "And fat regorged of Bulls and Goats." Taking this first line as trochaic, however, one is left with not only reversal, but an extra "sprung" syllable in "jocund and sublime."

And this extra syllable permits a third reading for this first line, an anapestic* one. Anapests are more strongly present in the next line "Drunk with Idolatry, drunk with Wine." The anapest is a dance measure like the trochee, but here, perhaps, more rollicking, a mockery of the jocundness of the Philistines, which the anapestic rhythm mimes in order to transcend, as the religious joy of the true God transcends the merely earthly, gross joy of Dagon's drunken festival. But the Chorus catches itself up into trochees again after

---

* The position, I believe, will not allow for reading this line as dactylic tetrameter catalectic. The strong accent at the beginning is not the first beat of a dactyl but the syncopation of an anapest.

only two feet—in "drunk with Wine." And this whole line, too, can also be read as a blank verse line. The rhythms look back to reflectiveness (iamb), ahead to controlled joy (trochee). Momentarily, without forgetting the other feelings present, they can rejoice in the very wildness of the enemy—but only with reference to the enemy's false devotion ("idolatry" is an anapest), not to the stimulant against which the Nazarite Samson has taken a lifelong vow ("Wine" is in trochee).

In some of these cases of indeterminacy, one carries two different readings ("This" in the previous quotation is unaccented by one reading, accented by another). In other cases, the accentual pattern is the same ("jocund and sublime") and the metre depends on whether the phrase is read back as trochee or ahead as anapest. This does affect the verse movement: if "and" here would be an extra sprung syllable, it shows a strength and assertiveness of its own; if it is read as the last of an anapestic series, it slurs onward the way the wildness of the anapests is here felt to slur.

For several accentual patterns to be present at once, and to be felt as coiling ahead and backwards, is Milton's achievement in *Samson,* an achievement new for him as it is for us. It is the last of his many versions of the Vergilian intensification, a high style which comes clearest when seen by comparison not with plays, Greek or other, but with epic poems, including Milton's own.

3

The refined style, in its tendency towards a semi-abstract and generic diction, resists the weighting of emotional resonances about concrete physical nature which Vergil succeeds in making it carry. Dante orders those emotional resonances schematically, capturing them, but never letting the poem pause to savor the sensuousness of a Vergilian shade, *lentus in umbra.* And the Renaissance poets before Milton, in their refinement, tend to structure if not nearly to allegorize, the sensual concreteness of nature. In their adaptation of the refined style's abstractness, lips are always red, trees green, and winds gentle. Whatever compositional problems Spenser may have had to face, he did not have to get behind his stock of adjectives for plants and streams, colors and sounds.

To do so was a poetic task Milton set himself from the beginning. He tried to get the Vergilian sensual shade in view long before he was able to make it convey Eden's coinherence of a physical world in a spiritual one. In this, as in other respects, his diction, like his syntax, works not through Dantesque order but through a Vergilian emotional leveling, as in the use of "all" into which Empson[9] reads almost purely emotive effects.

This concern, which becomes a pyrotechnic display in *L'Allegro*, begins to peek through in his earliest works, the translations he made at the age of fifteen from *Psalms:*

> The ruddy waves he cleft in twain
> Of the *Erythraean* main . . .
>
> The floods stood still like Walls of Glass . . .
>
> But full soon they did devour
> The Tawney King with all his power . . .

The underlined words and phrases exceed in sensual concreteness, I believe, anything or almost anything to be found in the lyric verse of the time (1623). For them the King James Bible itself has, respectively "Red Sea," nothing at all, and "Pharaoh;" and the Hebrew text has about the same—"yam-suph" (the regular word for the Red Sea), nothing at all, and "Par'oh."*

Milton consistently wants to get the tactile quality of the sensual detail into the open; at the same time, too, he will soon be trying to provide a structure large enough to include the tactile quality and its emotional resonances without allowing them a perilous sway. *L'Allegro-Il Penseroso* (best read as one poem, not two) manages

---

* "Pharaoh"[10] comes from Egyptian words meaning "great house" or "royal court"; and so not even etymology could have suggested "Tawney" to Milton.

this by giving each tactile sense as shaded by the other in an idealized but not allegorized alternation of moods (each poem begins
with an allegory which it drops). The light of gaiety is touched with
darkness:

> While the Cock with lively din,
> Scatters the rear of darkness thin . . .
>
> Whilst the Lantskip round it measures,
> Russet Lawns, and Fallows Gray . . .
>
> Dancing in the Chequer'd Shade . . .
>
> When in one night, ere glimps of morn,
> His shadowy Flale hath thresh'd the Corn

The varied lights shot with dark, in each of these quotations, is
savored each for its own tactile qualities; all are then referred to a
similar order, which is an order of mood. Similarly is the darkness
of *Il Penseroso* shot through with lights, all duskier, and each
individualized:

> To behold the wandring Moon,
> Riding neer her highest noon . . .
>
> Where glowing Embers through the room
> Teach light to counterfeit a gloom . . .
>
> To arched walks of twilight groves,
> And shadows brown that *Sylvan* loves. . .
>
> Casting a dimm religious light.

The natural is apprehended as an extension of feeling, and the
feeling defines all the human pursuits in which one senses its con-
cretions. The nuances of internal mood are savored while being
invested with meaning.

But this bothered Milton; and along with the breathtaking bravura
of concreteness, which makes *Comus* so masterful a poem, is the
uneasiness in the theme, and perhaps also the rhythms, of that poem,

as to how the natural world may be coordinated with the supernatural. There are, of course, theological answers here. Donne and
Spenser provide some, to say nothing of Dante, or the Aquinas
whom Milton says Spenser surpassed as a moral teacher. Milton,
though, seems to have wanted not theological answers, but a mastery
of feeling. The poet must be a sublime man, he says again and
again. Which is to say that he must internalize his doctrine, making
it accessible to (and in the poem an extension of) feeling, right
down to his physical universe.

   Comus does not yet resolve the feelings about nature. The "Hymn
on the Morning of Christ's Nativity" did so simply by having the
ministering angels chase away the demons of the merely natural
world, through images that assert the incredible power of poetry
—amounting to a magical control over the "speckled vanity" of a
nature that must be read as a physical one:

> For if such holy Song
> Enwrap our fancy long,
>   Time will run back and fetch the age of gold,
> And speckl'd vanity
> Will sicken soon and die,
>   And leprous sin will melt from earthly mould,
> And Hell itself will pass away,
> And leave her dolorous mansions to the peering day.

But Comus, in a song not quite "holy," extravagantly praises the
qualities of a nature that is apprehended in all rich immediacy. Still,
the Lady knows a higher virtue. The natural in *Comus* has not
found its easy place. So it is not possible, on the level of virtue, to say
either that Milton praises proper sexuality in the Lady's Chastity or
that he praises a simple Virginity. Nor is it possible to say that the
Lady has won entirely—Comus has somehow chained her up, though
the verse that tells the fact does not say he works his spell, or even
give him time to do so. His wand is not broken, nor is the natural
texture of the world brought fully into an order. At the end of that
poem, along with Cupid and Psyche, we are given, somewhat sur-

prisingly, Venus, and an Adonis who "reposes" on a dew-rainbowed bed of roses, on one with tactile properties the verse lingers over.

Lycidas displays a similar mastery at getting emotional resonance out of natural details, and a similar confusion at relating them to a spiritual order. On the one hand the Muse cannot save the bard "whom Universal nature did lament." ("Universal" significantly gets a capital in the 1645 edition, as if to insist on its comprehensiveness; "nature" significantly does not, as if to insist on its literal immediacy.) On the other hand, the flowers that existed in a "heavy change" respond mysteriously to the voice of Alpheus. Each lays its beauties, rendered in the verse with splendid tactile immediacy, "to strew the Laureat Herse where Lycid lies." He himself becomes a "Genius of the shore." Somehow since line 63, when nature was impotent to help Orpheus, she mysteriously gains that power, and no longer suffers the effects in lines 132 and thereon:

> Return *Alpheus,* the dread voice is past,
> That shrunk thy streams;

Of the many disjunctions in the poem, the one between the natural (pastoral) and the supernatural (Christian) orders might subsume them all, but only in *Paradise Lost* will the terms finally be found to do that, and then the terms will build the problematic tensions revealed in the earlier poems right into the general conception of the epic.

The last motion of the speaking poet in *Lycidas* renders precisely a physical gesture; his last rhyme gives the odd color of his mantle:

> At last he rose, and twitch'd his Mantle blew:
> To morrow to fresh Woods, and Pastures new.

As for Woods and Pastures—the capital indicates their importance— it would be decades before the shepherd could come to them. The Sonnets avoid woods and pastures for a stern rational structure; the cycle of Psalms translated in 1653 does not indulge in the sensual additions made by the youthful translator of thirty years before.

The new woods and pastures, at last, become those of a place where the natural somehow contained the supernatural and revealed it: Eden.

In *Paradise Lost,* in the natural garden of Eden, the sensual qualities are heightened because they are imagined as existing in their undimmed lustre, and their emotional resonances take on a spiritual ring over the loss of some spiritual inherence since the Fall. Fruits, for example, are a "vegetable gold," and though "vegetable" is probably an adjective, that grammatical reading does not allow us to say definitely that Milton means "vegetables of gold color," and not "gold that takes growing form." The Edenic generality fuses beyond the precision of postlapsarian language, and will not quite capture descriptively the fruit over whose loss the poet's verse sighs. Paradise can be known only in and through its loss, though in Paradise the natural creatures possess their tactile beauties in a way our world, and its verse, only echo:

> Groves whose rich Trees wept odorous Gumms and Balme,
> Others whose fruit burnisht with Golden Rinde
> Hung amiable, *Hesperian* Fables true,
> If true, here onely, and of delicious taste:
> Betwixt them Lawns, or level Downs, and Flocks
> Grasing the tender herb, were interpos'd,
> Or palmie hilloc, or the flourie lap
> Of som irriguous Valley spread her store . . .
>
> (*P.L.* IV, 248-256)

The very indefiniteness—"others," "som," "or,"——seems to enhance the sensual properties of Eden. Look closely, and here the fruits dissolve into odorous gum-tears, or into a scented liquid, "Balme." And the verse is so ambiguous as to prevent our deciding whether the "and" means *Gumms* to include or to exclude *Balme.* Other fruit is like untarnishable metal, as this fruit is like unsorrowing tears ("wept"). *Herbs, hillocs, valleys,* are of such exemplary nature that they may now be spoken of only with the generic adjectives of Spenser turned to other use than his—*tender, palmie, irriguous.*

The tensions of relationship between nature and grace that strain in *Comus* and *Lycidas* now coalesce in the central generalized tensions when a poet addressing a fallen humanity speaks of the garden of unfallen man. In Paradise nature and grace were one; Paradise is lost, and so nature and grace are at odds. The poetry, by dramatizing the moment of loss, forces the high language to present the lost but imaginable oneness.*

The animals leap forward at the Creation in a dramatic and theological fiction that allows the visual properties of their individuality to be rendered in dynamic action:

> The grassie Clods now Calv'd, now half appeer'd
> The Tawnie Lion, pawing to get free
> His hinder parts, then springs as broke from Bonds
> And Rampant shakes his Brinded main; the Ounce,
> The Libbard, and the Tyger, as the Moale
> Rising, the crumbl'd Earth above them threw
> In Hillocks; the swift Stag from under ground
> Bore up his branching head: (*P.L.*, VII, 463-470)

* In *Paradise Regained,* where Christ as the perfect man is thoroughly tempted, the natural world has been stripped to a desert that he makes once again a "pleasant garden,":

> And *Eden* rais'd in the wast Wilderness
>   (*P.R.* I, 7. Italics in text.)

The poem's designations of nature are simple but loaded:

> Night with her sullen wing to double-shade
> The Desert, Fowls in their clay nests were couch't;
> And now wild Beasts came forth the woods to roam.   (I, 499-502)

But the deprivation of nature can become an intensification of nature, religious but still subdued, in the quiet after the final night's storm:

> Thus pass'd the night so foul till morning fair
> Came forth with Pilgrim steps in amice gray . . .   (IV, 426-7)

> And now the Sun with more effectual beams
> Had cheer'd the face of Earth, and dry'd the wet
> From drooping plant, or dropping tree . . .   (IV, 432-4)

The near rhyme of the two adjectives in the last line has the effect of intensifying the sensual quality of the drenched vegetation, of bringing it into the focus of the dramatic situation for which it is thought, in the desert of the Holy Land, to be an appropriate setting.

In *Samson Agonistes* the spiritual victory, fully human, is the more fully inscrutable. The natural world appears almost wholly in its spiritualized effects of light and dark, for a protagonist who, like the poet of *Paradise Lost,* cannot see.

Here the violence of the initial near-metaphor exceeds visualization. Just how, in the imagining eyes, do Clods Calve? This violence prepares for the energy of the animals. They are seen not in heraldic pose or allegorical gesture but in the moment of muscular action, an action rendered generic because in the fiction of the poem this is spoken of as the very moment of their generation. They would be emblematic if fixed, but here they move, in the momentary texture of the verse, and also in their rhetorical and emotional function: Raphael in this long speech is trying to have his account tell on Adam so as to affect his mood and purpose.

The dynamic responsiveness of physical elements in Adam's world to the spiritual world they exemplify, comes through in an indeterminacy of those elements, a certain disposition to plasticity. The whole garden changes physically as a result of the spiritual Fall, and the plasticity which permits it to do so appears all through the poem. Spiritual creatures are plastic to begin with; they are visible or invisible at will. When an angel grows angry it shows through: he becomes red. Satan, in the indeterminate space of hell "lay floating many a rood." But when the devils pack together to enter Pandemonium, they become as small as pygmies.

Once inside, they are giants again, and the hall is mysteriously large. Now Satan appears sitting "High on a Throne of Royal State, which far/ Outshon the wealth of *Ormus* and of *Ind*"—a throne that seems to come out of nowhere as an excrescence out of his desire to rule.

Hell itself has already shown its plasticity. While the devils' initial fall has them "chained on the burning lake," once they rise to walk, that water, which is always also fire, mysteriously takes on the character of ground, as "burning marl." As in his "vegetable gold" descriptions of nature, Milton insists on this indeterminate plasticity of the physical world into which the devil moves:

> Forthwith upright he rears from off the Pool
> His mighty Stature; on each hand the flames

Drivn backward slope their pointing spires, & rowld
In billows, leave i' th' midst a horrid Vale.
Then with expanded wings he stears his flight
Aloft, incumbent on the dusky Air
That felt unusual weight, till on dry Land
He lights, if it were Land that ever burn'd
With solid, as the Lake with liquid fire;

(P.L. I, 221-229)

Water, earth, air, and fire, here merge indeterminately into each
other. It is deliberately left unclear whether it is the nature around
Satan that changes plastically or his own physical force that evokes
and responds to the changes. Do even "Air" and "dry Land" differ
as more than plastic aspects of one another, when the last two lines
explain that land in a sense is not land; when Satan, perhaps still in
the "Vale", is "incumbent" on the Air, an air itself also responsive,
"that felt unusual weight"?

This effect, as it gets into diction, is a Vergilian one. At the same
time Milton, in the duality of his conception, makes his words more
indeterminate—as his syntax is more amplified—than Vergil's. So
much so that a critic like Empson, with the refined Metaphysical
precision in mind, as much as a critic like Bentley writing under a
refined Augustan rationality, may object to Milton's usages by asking
the words to stay in place the way Dante, or Pope, or Donne, or any
poet in the refined style would keep them:

her Heav'nly forme
Angelic, but more soft and Feminine . . .

(P.L. IX, 457-8)

Angelic "So we must suppose, that she has Six Wings as Raphael
had . . ." *More soft.* "If Eve had been more soft . . . than such were,
she had been no fit mate for her Husband." So Empson[11] quotes
Bentley as censuring Milton; and he concurs. But *angelic* expresses
an emotional quality in Eve; it cannot be pressed, as it always may
in Dante, for theological definition; and the softness of angels (as in
I, 423, cited by Empson) is an aspect, not an attribute, because all

spiritual beings, in the plasticity of their supernatural manifestations, may equally appear, on an appropriate occasion, as hard.

So, too, *Bound with rigor and slime*, would be the contradiction both Empson and Bentley censure if Milton fixed the rigor, or melted the slime, beyond its aspect the word presents for the moment of description only. He does not mean *bound with slime*. Bound, in classical rhetoric, is a zeugma: one verb is used for two (Bound with rigor and melted with slime). Yet to name this effect as a classical figure does not explain the expression into denotative clarity, any more than we can, with Pearce, call "angelic" a metaphoric use. Milton pitches his modifier, his zeugma, in the tension of momentary plastic identifications; these contradictions are resolved in the whole plastic scheme, but not at any one point. One point can be inconsistent with another: rigor with slime, Eve's softness with the angels'.

Milton, even where he does not present a physical fact changing plastically before our eyes, does not set his universe up firmly on a structural principle. Rather, it is a unitary one, in which God himself, as Charles Williams[12] urges, is only the high point of heaven's bliss. Under these aspects it is possible to argue endlessly, with equal plausibility, that Milton remains semi-Arian in *Paradise Lost,* or else that he is Trinitarian there. The Son, seen in the aspect of subordination to the Father, looks less: semi-Arian. Seen as the creative Word, who performs the Creation (for God word is act), the Son is equal to the Father:

> And thou my Word, begotten Son, by thee
> This I perform, speak thou, and be it don.   (VII, 163-4)

> .   .   .   .

> Silence, ye troubl'd waves, and thou Deep, peace,
> Said then th'Omnific Word, your discord end;
>
> (VII, 216-7)

Here "Omnific" is an aspect of "Omnipotent," the Son of the Father. Since the Son always appears under one aspect or another, his existence in the unitary world of this poem does not rest on firm theological definition of a Dantesque sort. And his existence cannot be changed into theological attributions.

For the angels, too, Milton does not use the hierarchy of nine firm orders that Dante got from pseudo-Dionysius; though he does use the Dantean names. The angels are seen in aspects, not as orders. Now they are Powers, now Dominations; now Thrones, now Arch-Angels—a name Milton will give to some of the very highest angels, including Satan, who in another aspect uses the name of a higher Dantean order: "Fall'n Cherub . . ."

The same plasticity of aspects holds for the whole physical cosmos in *Paradise Lost.* It is vain to try to give it the kind of schematic diagram that fits the fixed cosmos of the *Divine Comedy.* Milton's universe, seen in its indefinite vastness, tends to be Copernican; seen in its nearly ordered cosmological description, it tends to be Ptolemaic. Actually it is neither, and not really a fusion of either. At one time, and in one spiritual aspect, the physical earth seems to exist at the center of a Ptolemaic universe. At another time it seems to be lost tinily in a vast Copernican spiritual cosmos: in the aspect, as it first appears to Satan, of standing physically (because, at that moment, spiritually) in the same view with the "Empyreal Heav'n:"

> Farr off th'Empyreal Heav'n, extended wide
> In circuit, undetermind square or round,
> With Opal Towers and Battlements adorn'd
> Of living Saphire, once his native Seat;
> And fast by hanging in a golden Chain
> This pendant world, in bigness as a Starr
> Of smallest Magnitude close by the Moon.
>
> (*P.L.* II, 1047-53)

"The Empyreal Heav'n," though, suggests a Ptolemaic structure because the term is Ptolemaic: it is impossible to present a fixed diagram for an earth whose distance from the Empyreal Heaven is represented by being "far off" from Satan, to whom earth is "fast by." The distance from Heaven to Eden is later (VIII, 113-4) called a "distance inexpressible/ By Numbers that have name." And how can one provide at the center of a Ptolemaic universe an earth "in bigness as a Starr/ Of smallest Magnitude?" One can do this no more than with the physical mathematics of a fallen world one could draw an "Empyreal Heav'n" which had solved the old paradox of earthly mathematics by embodying a squared circle: "undetermind square or round."

Eden has a similar plasticity of topography, appearing now like a plain, now like a high place faced by a cliff; now, to the approaching Satan, like a sort of insuperable elevation combining attributes of cliff and forest without being plateau:

> and to the border comes
> Of *Eden,* where delicious Paradise,
> Now nearer, Crowns with her enclosure green,
> As with a rural mound the champain head
> Of a steep wilderness, whose hairie sides
> With thicket overgrown, grottesque and wilde,
> Access deni'd; and over head up grew
> Insuperable highth of loftiest shade, . . .
> A Silvan Scene, and as the ranks ascend
> Shade above shade, a woodie Theatre
> Of stateliest view. Yet higher than thir tops
> The verdurous wall of Paradise up sprung: . . .
> And higher then that Wall a circling row
> Of goodliest Trees loaden with fairest Fruit, . . .
>
> (IV, 131-146)

Impenetrable thicket, above which stand insuperable trees, above which is a wall, above which are more trees. . . . Paradise never looked so to Adam, before or after the Fall. The aspect dissolves into the plasticity, as the physical appearance into the vision of the one, here Satan, to whom it appears to have loftiness after insurmountable loftiness.

4

The physical situation suggests its simultaneity with the spiritual by pressing its aspects to reveal what in a fixed scheme would constitute incongruity. The whole poem presents its own simultaneity, in the double time scheme of the present of the writing and the past of the Fall as the two conflate into the eternal situation of "Man's first Disobedience." The word "first" can be taken logically as well as temporally, since the poem gives us, as Charles Williams says, "not merely the conflict in heaven before creation but the conflict in the spirit after creation." "All the persons," he goes on to say, "also have this double state. It is not an allegory which we are studying, but an identity. But the identity is that of facts which belong to two categories—historical and contemporary, angelic and mortal, narrative and psychological at once. It is by the theme of the poem that their double nature is made clear."[13]

In the logic of Adam's existence, this doubleness is simultaneous, enough so to make it possible to construct an argument that in some existential sense the Fall has taken place as early as the first appearance of Adam and Eve.

The death that an epic poem centralizes is present in *Paradise Lost* as an actualized threat finally embodied, and the universality of the threat is written into the structure of the poem, through the comprehensive meaning of the "mortal taste" that "Brought Death into the World, and all our woe." The threat is always present because the poem is recapitulative in narrative structure: all is always present, past is always future. This past works almost any statement into a potential universal, a splendid instance being the first long sentence in the poem. The whole First Book—and so, by rhetorical as well as logical implication, the whole poem—is, to use a rhetorical term, an amplification of that first sentence, in the form of answering the question that follows it:

Who first seduc'd them to that fowl revolt?

This is the device of Homer, but intensified. All epic poets begin in *medias res,* as Horace formulates their practise. Milton did so with such intensity that his narrative line seems to get lost in the Vergilian amplifications, and his publisher requested him to summarize each book in the Arguments that now stand at the head of each.

The double time scheme of the poem keeps natural coordinated with supernatural, prelapsarian with postlapsarian. There is the poet writing in the present, digressively and encyclopedically, giving himself constant observations on the known fallen world.

In the poet's time Adam has already fallen. But in Adam's time, the time line doubled over and under the poet's—Adam moves from past into future. The presentness of the poem's opening invocation sets the "no middle flight" in which the two schemes are stated, rhythmically as well as rhetorically, to coalesce. In response to the demands of the doubling theme, and not out of any excessive self-reference, does Milton set amplified personal invocations at the points of major time shift for Adam—the beginnings of Books I, III, VII and IX.

In the doubling time of the poem everything is dramatic. We know Eden only after Satan approaches it, while Satan moves in it, while Raphael comes to ward him off, while Eve and Adam separate, and then Sin, and then unite, and then leave the Garden as it changes and the Angel approaches with the flaming sword. We know the creation of the Cosmos, and the Battle of the Angels, in the long after-dinner discourse of Raphael, which only politely pretends—in courtesy and charity for Adam's free will—to be a digression. Actually it functions dramatically as a cosmic dissuasion from the Fall. Later Michael's speech of the history of the world from Fall to Redemption serves dramatically to bolster Adam in his new condition.

Even after he had fixed on the Fall as his subject, Milton had trouble, as the drafts in the Trinity Manuscript show, in fixing on a narrative sequence for *Paradise Lost* that would adequately keep the simultaneity of his logic in command of the doubling time scheme. The order he finally evolved, taking the cosmic temporal sweep from Creation to Last Judgment, moves deliberately backwards in time before moving forward: first going immediately before the Fall, to the Devil's attack on Adam, A(I-IV); then dwelling on the presentness of the temptation, B(IV-V), then going back before the fall of the rebel angels to the War in Heaven, C(VI), followed by the Creation, D(VII) and an account of the prior order of the Cosmos, E(VIII). This "eternal" book, precedes the books of the Fall, F(IX-X); and the Expulsion, H(XII) is preceded by an account of subsequent history up to the Second Coming: G(XI-XII). This narrative order (indicated by the correct sequence of letters) as it jumbles the temporal order presents a "baroque" irregularity of pattern: E, C, D, A, B, F, H, G. The cosmological orders of E are prior, and in a sense atemporal. CD is out of order with AB, but D comes in temporal order after C as B does after A. G, however, does not come after F, but is interrupted by H; we have two groups of correct temporal sequences, and a third group of broken ones; and the order among the three groups is itself not sequential: [E]; 2(CD), 1(AB), 3(FHG), though there is no overlap between them as groups; that is, everything in group three follows everything in group two, which follows everything in group one. These complex symmetries of temporal simultaneity recall Milton's description of the Wheeles of the starrie Spheare: "mazes intricate,/Eccentric, intervolv'd, yet regular/Then most, when most irregular they seem." (V, 621-3). And there are comparable "digressive" movements of narrative within the individual books.

   Thus Adam, in the simultaneous logic of the poem, may find any aspect of his cosmos uppermost before his attention. The movement of simple events up to the Fall is slowed by a widened attention to the whole extent of Adam's freedom in obedience. As general Man, he faces by implication simultaneously all that Dante encounters

sequentially. Nor need he have had to die to be redeemed, had he
and Eve not changed their plastically yielding cosmos at the one
point they were not supposed to have it yield.

This simultaneity differs radically from the equally tense but sequential logic, of the metaphysical tradition, in which Milton began
by making some efforts that are notably clumsy and uncertain, in
sound and in sense:

> This rich Marble doth enterr
> The honour'd wife of *Winchester,*
> A Vicounts daughter, an Earls heir,
> Besides what her vertues fair
> Added to her noble birth,
> More then she could own from Earth.

The inept prosiness and platitude of this early attempt to write in
the vein of "obsequie," at which Donne was such a master, finds
here a rhythm uncertain to the point of brokenness, without even
the spontaneity of doggerel.

But after working up to the lushness of concrete, natural detail
in *Comus* and *Lycidas,* he was to learn to rib out his poems strongly
on a simultaneity of sense, perhaps from the Hebrew poetry that he
read and translated during his long near-silence. Hebrew metres are
based on parallelism of sense, a kind of logic foreign to Donne's, as
to anything else in English, Italian, and Classical poetry. This logic,
concentrated and simultaneous like that of the Prophets, rather than
successive, may have been the clue leading Milton to the quite new
achievements of the later sonnets. Their rhythm, like their statement, is so unitary, so simultaneous in effect, that they ride over
even the division of octave and sestet. These "Miltonic" sonnets, as
they are called, were invented by Milton to express something quite
new: a contribution of concentrated rhythm and sense to the poem
which the musical beauties of all his earlier work had lacked. The
sonnets are, however, spare as well as short. They go beyond, but
have not incorporated, the lushness of *Lycidas* and *Comus.*

We find the two, the strong ribs of simultaneous logic in the periods and accents of the sonnets, the concretizing lushness of the early poems, fused and transcended in *Paradise Lost*.

The simultaneities of the poem, cosmic in extent and plastic in their spiritual responsiveness, center on the aboriginal human pair, who need not die in the poem when they have brought Death into the world, and resume an epic stature so general that they need be called on to perform no epic acts. The central act of the Fall, through the central fiction of the poem and its architecture of sound and sense, reverberates into a definition of freedom through the radical compromise of freedom, reason through the perversion of reason, obedience through the total abrogation of obedience. The central act is so small as to be unfigural; it happens in a context so large as to be total.

Here, as in any epic poem, there is a strenuousness in the verse, as of the heavy echoes from the energy necessary to pull so much meaning together. And at the same time there is a calm to be heard at the center, a calm that Geoffrey Hartman[14] speaks of as occasioned by what he calls the "counterplot" of *Paradise Lost*. The calm, though, is chiefly tonal—another, ultimately rhythmic effect of the poet's triumph at stabilizing so great an order. Both strenuousness and calm are audible, too, in the half lines of *Beowulf* and the long Homeric hexameter; in the even, ranked movement of *Roland's* pentameters and in the weighted ordonnance of Vergil's refined cadences.

One may hear them in Dante, too: the poem orders an urgent energy into a calm. There calm predominates over strenuousness. But calm always lies somewhere at the heart of the epic poem, and its hero, in the most intimate voice of the verse, manages the strenuousness. Calm is heard in the *Cid's* language, seen in the Cid's bearing, from the very beginning. *Beowulf* closes calmly by saying that its hero, worthy of praise, was the mildest of kings. The last line of the *Iliad* calmly sums up the funeral lament for Hector, tamer of horses. In the *Odyssey* the resolution is a calm one, and the strenuous wanderings and difficulties of the hero are presented in the delicate irony of the verse, reminding us always that the direst of sufferings is transient, that the transient world itself is a lovely one of an enduring calm.

The people share in the hero's strenuous mastery of the unknown. They share in his final calm. The very rhymes, in the largely unrhymed *Samson,* insist on this point, which the chorus objectify by speaking of themselves in the third person:

> His servants he with new acquist
> Of true experience from this great event
> With peace and consolation hath dismist,
> And calm of mind all passion spent.   (1755-8)

If it is extravagant to call this "dramatic" poem epic, one may say with Staiger that "epic" is a mode for poetry that may be mixed with other modes.

Such mixtures are as rare as epic poems are themselves. Or were until Blake and Wordsworth expanded the function of lyric poetry. *The Prelude* works up historically to what *The Divine Comedy* gives us systematically, a totality of experience confronted through the cumulative inklings of a single consciousness. In *The Waste Land* fragments not of personal history but of a civilization's are ordered strenuously into a tonal reflection of total experience. These are "fragments shored," strenuously; yet the last word enjoins calm: *Shantih.* In the *Cantos* a number of problematically related personalities and masks converge, through their disjunctions, on an increasingly calm visionary world, lyric in its glimpses, its *Erinnerung,* to use Staiger's word, but epic in its tonal and experiential scope, what it objectifies, its *Vorstellung.*

The epic death grows slowly and abstractly in all these modern poems. The more purely epic Christ of *Paradise Regained* squarely confronts the lord of death under his Protean guises. Hence he

achieves a privacy that is complete, having perfected his knowledge
by perfecting his action. The strenuous poem, in the constantly
contained calm of its rhythm, ends calmly:

> hee unobserv'd
> Home to his Mothers house private return'd.
>
> (*P.R.* IV, 638-9)

Adam, less ideal, nevertheless lies closer to the human condition:
he is the human condition, Man. The total implications of his fall
are conveyed in a strenuous polyphony heard through the whole
poem, and so also in the syntactic suspensions and varied caesurae
of the last two lines' resolving calm:

> They hand in hand with wandring steps and slow,
> Through *Eden* took thir solitarie way.
>
> (*P.L.* XII, 648-9)

The Vergilian pathos is made to carry a biblical, and epic, breadth.
Milton even dares to wrench English towards Vergilian Latin at
the end of his penultimate line ("with wandring steps and slow").
The solitude is immeasurably sad, the more so that it is shared
("hand in hand"). The oxymoron of sharing something solitary
uses the refined style to touch lightly on what the calm rhythms
imply. If Paradise is lost, Eden may be named: the wholeness of
the human condition is imaginatively caught in every classic line
of this poem, and of its few peers that succeed in venturing beyond
a "middle flight."

Notes
Index

Notes

The lineation of all the longer poems discussed here is fairly standard. For the texts I have used the following editions: *Beowulf,* Klaeber, Boston, 1941; *La Chanson de Roland,* Bédier, Paris, 1927; *Poema de Mio Cid,* Menéndez Pidal, Madrid, 1929; *Homeri Opera,* Allen, Oxford, 1939; *Vergili Opera,* Hirtzel, Oxford, 1942; *Opere di Dante,* Moore and Toynbee, London, 1924; *The Student's Milton,* Patterson, New York, 1933.

The translations, unless otherwise indicated, are my own. Often, as I note, I alter a rendering someone else has made, usually in the direction of greater literalness. The few quotations from foreign languages that are not translated are left so because they stand to illustrate points almost completely dependent on the sound and sense of the original.

PREFACE

1. Staiger, Emil, *Grundbegriffe der Poetick,* Zürich, 1946.

INTRODUCTION

1. Poe, Edgar Allen, "The Poetic Principle," 1848; relevant section reprinted in Bate, Walter Jackson, *Criticism: the Major Texts,* New York, 1952, 352-356.

2. Arnold, Matthew, "The Study of Poetry," 1880; reprinted in Sutton, Walter, and Foster, Richard, *Modern Criticism,* New York, 1963, 94-107.

3. Parry, Milman, "Studies in the Epic Technique of Oral Verse Making," *Harvard Studies in Classical Philology*, XLI, 73-147 and XLIII, 1-50.

4. Lord, Albert Bates, and Parry, Milman, *Serbo-Croatian Heroic Songs*, Cambridge, 1953.

5. Schiller, J. C. F., "Über naive und sentimentalische Dichtung," 1795; in *Werke*, Berlin, 1924, XIV, 307-406.

6. Cassirer, Ernst, *The Philosophy of Symbolic Forms*, New Haven, 1953.

7. Bodkin, Maud, *Archetypal Patterns in Poetry*, Oxford, 1934, 96-150.

8. Miles, Josephine, *The Poem*, Englewood Cliffs, New Jersey, 1959.

CHAPTER ONE

1. Bronson, Bertrand, *Traditional Tunes of the Child Ballads*, Princeton, 1959.

2. Ibid.

3. Brooks, Cleanth, and Warren, Austin, *Understanding Poetry*, New York, 1952, 45-47.

4. Coleridge, S. T., *Biographia Literaria*, 1817, ed. Shawcross, Oxford, 1907, II, 16-17.

5. Ibid., II, 60-76; 115.

6. Sievers, Eduard, *Altgermanische Metrik*, Halle, 1893.

7. Pope, John C., *The Rhythm of Beowulf*, New Haven, 1942.

8. Klaeber, Friedrich, *Beowulf*, Boston, 1941, LXIX.

9. Moncrieff, Charles Scott, *Beowulf Translated*, London, 1921.

10. Hesiod, *Theogony*, 97-103.

11. Lévi-Strauss, Claude, *Anthropologie Structurale*, Paris, 1958, 227-255.

12. Banks, Theodore Howard, "Sir Gawain and the Green Knight," as reprinted in *The Norton Anthology of English Literature*, Abrams, Meyer Howard, et al.

13. Auerbach, Erich, *Mimesis*, New York, 1957, 98-105.

14. Op. cit., 17-98.

15. Moncrieff, Charles Scott, *The Song of Roland*, London, 1919.

16. Bédier, Joseph, *La Chanson de Roland*, Paris, 1927, II, *Commentaire*, p. 151.

17. Auerbach, 90.

18. Ibid., 97.

19. Bowra, Maurice, *Heroic Poetry*, London, 1952.

20. Salinas, Pedro, *Reality and the Poet in Spanish Poetry*, Baltimore, 1940, 3-29.

21. Ibid., 28.

CHAPTER TWO

1. Weil, Simone, *The Iliad or The Poem of Force*, Wallingford, Pennsylvania, n.d.

2. This, and other citations are taken (sometimes modified) from Lattimore, Richmond, *The Iliad*, Chicago, 1951.

3. *Briefwechsel Zwischen Schiller und Goethe*, Stuttgart, 1856, I, 295 (21 April, 1797).

4. Onians, Richard B., *The Origins of European Thought*, Cambridge, 1951.

5. Parry, Milman, "Studies in the Epic Technique of Oral Verse Making," *Harvard Studies in Classical Philology*, XLIII, 13.

6. Arnold, Matthew, "On Translating Homer," in *Essays Literary and Critical*, London, 1906, 210-276.

7. Holthusen, Hans E., *Ja und Nein*, Munich, 1954, 40.

8. Snell, Bruno, *Die Entdeckung des Geistes*, Hamburg, 1948.

9. Treu, Max, *Von Homer zur Lyrik*, Munich, 1955.

10. Snell, p. 29.

11. Adkins, Arthur W., *Merit and Responsibility*, Oxford, 1960.

12. Boisacq, Emile, *Dictionnaire étymologique de la Langue Grecque*, Heidelberg, 1916, sub voc.

13. Leaf, Walter, ed., *The Iliad*, London, 1888, II, on 19, 302.

14. Autenrieth, Georg G. P., *Homeric Dictionary*, tr. Keep, New York, 1895, sub voc.

15. Ebeling, Heinrich, *Lexicon Homericum*, Hildesheim, 1963, sub voc.

16. Cunliffe, Richard J., *A Lexicon of the Homeric Dialect*, Norman, Oklahoma, 1963.

17. Chantraine, Pierre, *Grammaire Homérique*, Paris, 1953, II, 180.

18. Staiger, Emil, *Grundbegriffe der Poetick*, Zürich, 1946, 90.

19. Parry, XLI.

20. Arnold, 214.

21. Koster, William John Wolff, *Traité de Métrique Grecque*, Leyden, 1962, 66-80.

22. Knight, William Francis Jackson, *Accentual Symmetry in Vergil,* Oxford, 1950.

23. Bowra, Cecil Morris, *Tradition and Design in the Iliad,* Oxford, 1930, 55-56.

24. Whitman, Cedric, *Homer and the Heroic Tradition,* Cambridge, 1958, 225-229.

25. McFarland, Thomas, "Lykaon and Achilles," *Yale Review,* New Haven, Winter, 1956, 191-213.

26. Whitman, 200.

CHAPTER THREE

1. Aristotle, *Poetics,* 1455b; 1459b.

2. Whitman, Cedric, *Homer and the Heroic Tradition,* Cambridge, 1958, 285-309.

3. Dimoff, George, "The Name of Odysseus," *Hudson Review,* New York, Spring, 1956, 52-70.

4. Aristotle, 1459b.

5. Stella, Luigia Achillea, *Il Poema d'Ulysse,* Florence, 1955, 302.

6. Treu, Max, *Von Homer Zur Lyrik,* 101-2.

7. Stella, 213.

8. Spengler, Oswald, *The Decline of the West,* New York, 1928, I, 186.

9. Auerbach, Erich, *Mimesis,* New York, 1957, 1-20.

CHAPTER FOUR

1. Staiger, Emil, *Grundbegriffe der Poetik,* Zürich, 1946.

2. Eliot, T. S., *Selected Essays,* New York, 1932, 199-240.

3. Brooks, Cleanth, *The Well-Wrought Urn,* London, 1949, 229-30.

4. Aristotle, *Poetics,* 1447b.

5. Havelock, Eric A., *Preface to Plato,* Cambridge, 1963.

6. Olson, Charles, "Review" (of Havelock), *Niagara Frontier Review,* Buffalo, Summer, 1964, 40-44.

7. Wimsatt, William Kurtz, *The Verbal Icon,* Lexington, 1954.

8. Davie, Donald, *Purity of Diction in English Verse,* London, 1952.

9. Ibid., 34-5; 43.

10. Wimsatt, 138.

11. Sewell, Elizabeth, *The Structure of Poetry,* London, 1951.

12. Wifstrand, Albert, *Von Kallimachos zu Nonnos*, Lund, 1933.

13. Davie, Donald, *Articulate Energy*, London, 1955.

14. Couat, Auguste, *Alexandrian Poetry*, tr. Loeb, London, 1931, 435-436.

15. One such discussion can be found in Longinus the Philosopher's scholia on Hephestion's Metrical Manual, in *Scriptores Metrici Graeci*, ed. Westphal, Leipzig, 1866, 81-94.

CHAPTER FIVE

1. Borchardt, Rudolf, *Reden*, Stuttgart, 1955, 264.

2. Sainte-Beuve, C. A., *Oeuvres*, Pléiade Edition, Paris, 1956, II, 550.

3. Apollonius, *Argonautica*, III, 744 ff.; *Aeneid*, IV, 522 ff.

4. Heinze, Richard, *Virgils Epische Technik*, Leipzig, 1928.

5. Ibid., 39.

6. Ibid., 115-116.

7. Haecker, Theodor, *Virgil, Father of the West*, tr. Wheen, New York, 1934, 92.

8. Pöschl, Viktor, *The Art of Vergil*, tr. Seligson, Ann Arbor, 1962, 141-142, and passim.

9. Knight, William Francis Jackson, *Accentual Symmetry in Vergil*, Oxford, 1950.

10. Ibid., 49.

11. Heinze, 285.

CHAPTER SIX

1. Curtius, Ernst Robert, *European Literature in the Latin Middle Ages*, New York, 1963, 222-225.

2. Richard of St. Victor, *Benjamin Minor*, in *Patrologia Latina*, ed. Migne, Paris, 1880, v. 196, 1-64.

3. Williams, Charles, *The Figure of Beatrice*, London, 1943.

4. Blackmur, Richard Palmer, *The Lion and the Honeycomb*, New York, 1955, 226-239.

5. Coleridge, S. T., "1818 Lecture on Dante," in Brandeis, Irma, *Discussions of the Divine Comedy*, Boston, 1961, 16-20, reprinted from Raysor, Thomas Middleton, *Coleridge's Miscellaneous Criticism*, Cambridge, 1936.

6. Auerbach, Erich, *Scenes from the Drama of European Literature,* New York, 1959, 11-78.

7. Singleton, Charles S., *Dante Studies I—Commedia: Elements of Structure,* Cambridge, 1954.

8. *Convivio,* II, 1.

9. Hugh of St. Victor, *Allegoriae in Vetus Testamentum,* III, 1, in Migne, op. cit., v. 175, 656 B.

10. Ibid., v. 196, 265-401.

11. As excerpted in Brandeis, 33-41.

12. Ibid., 49-51.

13. Blackmur, 230.

14. Brandeis, 52-55.

15. Eliot, T. S., *Selected Essays,* New York, 1932.

16. Prince, Frank Templeton, *The Italian Element in Milton's Verse,* Oxford, 1954.

17. Williams, 128.

18. Richard of St. Victor, *Benjamin Major,* IV, 23, in *Patrologia latina,* ed. Migne, Paris, 1880, v. 196, 163.

19. Curtius, 159-162.

CHAPTER SEVEN

1. Willey, Basil, *The Seventeenth Century Background,* New York, 1953.

2. Rajan, Balachandra, *Paradise Lost and the Seventeenth Century Reader,* London, 1947, 112-113.

3. Nelson, Lowry, "Gongora and Milton: Toward a Definition of the Baroque," *Comparative Literature,* 1954, 53-63.

4. Macaulay, T. B., *Essay on Milton,* 1825; reprinted in Thorpe, James, *Milton Criticism: Selections from Four Centuries,* New York, 1950.

5. Prince, Frank Templeton, *The Italian Element in Milton's Verse,* Oxford, 1954.

6. Eliot, T. S., *On Poetry and Poets,* London, 1957, 158.

7. Giedion, Siegfried, *Space, Time, and Architecture,* Cambridge, 1962.

8. Stein, Arnold, *Answerable Style,* Minneapolis, 1953.

9. Empson, William, *The Structure of Complex Words,* London, 1951, 101-104.

10. Brown, F., Driver, S., and Briggs, C., *A Hebrew and English Lexicon of the Old Testament*, Oxford, 1955, sub voc.

11. Empson, William, *Some Versions of Pastoral*, London, 1935, 154.

12. Williams, Charles, *Reason and Beauty in the Poetic Mind*, Oxford, 1933, 91-128.

13. Ibid., 96.

14. Hartman, Geoffrey, "Milton's Counterplot," *E.L.H.*, v. 25, 1958, 1-13.

Index